America's First Olympics

Sports and American Culture Series
Bruce Clayton, Editor

America's
First
Olympics

The St. Louis Games of 1904

George R. Matthews

University of Missouri Press
Columbia

Copyright © 2005 by
The Curators of the University of Missouri
University of Missouri Press, Columbia, Missouri 65211
Printed and bound in the United States of America
All rights reserved
First paperback printing, 2018

ISBN 978-0-8262-2181-0 (paperback : alk. paper)

Library of Congress Cataloging-in-Publication Data

Matthews, George R., 1950–
  America's first Olympics : the St. Louis games of 1904 /
George R. Matthews.
      p. cm.
Summary: "Explores the history of the 1904 Olympics,
held in St. Louis, Missouri, which featured first-time
African American Olympians, a controversial marathon,
and documentation by photojournalist Jessie Tarbox Beals.
Examines the controversy surrounding the transfer of the
games from Chicago to St. Louis"—Provided by publisher.
  Includes bibliographical references and index.
  ISBN 978-0-8262-1588-8 (hardcover : alk. paper)
  1.   Olympic Games (3rd : 1904 : Saint Louis, Mo.)—
History.   I. Title.
  GV7221904 .M38 2005
  796.48—dc22
                                                    2005006499

♾ ™ This paper meets the requirements of the
American National Standard for Permanence of Paper
for Printed Library Materials, Z39.48, 1984.

Typefaces: Minion and Bodoni Poster Compressed

For Blanche Shaffer

Whose Kind Heart and Gentle Soul Inspire All

With Gratitude and Love

Your George

Contents

Acknowledgments

It was a pleasure to conduct research in St. Louis, a pleasant city with many charms. The Missouri Historical Society Library, the premier repository for materials pertaining to the Louisiana Purchase Exposition and St. Louis Olympic games, is housed in a magnificent building. Forest Park, the site of the World's Fair and only a short distance from the library, is a botanical paradise and the home for the Missouri Historical Society Museum. Exhibits, a bookstore, and an exquisite restaurant with spectacular panorama views of Forest Park are provided in the museum including the restored Grand Basin with waterfalls cascading down from Art Hill. Washington University, adjacent to Forest Park, has preserved the stadium and gymnasium structures used for the St. Louis Olympics.

My appreciation is extended to the helpful staffs of the Missouri Historical Society Library and Museum. Special appreciation goes to Jean E. Meeh Gosebrink at the St. Louis Public Library, Special Collections for her professional and courteous manner in locating photographs and other materials. Jim Greensfelder, spokesman, and his three co-authors, Bob Christiansen, Jim Lally, and Max Storm gave permission to reproduce photographs from their book *1904 Olympic Games Official Medals and Badges.* Barney DePenaloza and family welcomed me to their home and provided a special photograph of great-grandfather Henri de Penaloza. The generosity and graciousness of Max Storm, past president of the 1904 World's Fair Society, is greatly appreciated.

A gifted writer, Sandra Marshall, provided the inspiration, encouragement, and constant support without which this book would not have been possible. Always gently conveyed, she also rendered invaluable constructive criticism. Words alone cannot express the depth of my gratitude.

America's First Olympics

Introduction

David Francis wanted the 1904 Olympic games. While governor of Missouri he had lost the 1893 World's Fair to Chicago, and it still rankled. But now St. Louis was to host the Louisiana Purchase Exposition and Francis, president of the exposition, was determined that his fair would be the largest, most spectacular festival the world had ever witnessed. Chicago newspapers announced in February 1901 that their city would make a bid for the Olympics at the May meeting of the International Olympic Committee (IOC) in Paris. A competing international event like that in any American city, but especially in the rival Midwest city of Chicago, would only detract from the St. Louis Exposition. Although not a sports fan, Francis was aware of the tremendous popularity of athletic competition in turn-of-the-century America, and was determined to make the Olympics an asset to the exposition, and not a coup for Chicago.

Francis, however, faced a small dilemma. There should really be no conflict, because the Louisiana Purchase Exposition was scheduled for 1903, and the Olympics for 1904. But Francis knew that two years' preparation for the fair was unrealistic. He fully intended to request a year's delay from the U.S. Congress, which had only that March granted official recognition and funding. But it would be politically embarrassing to ask for a delay just a month later, and an admission that Francis realized that two years' preparation was inadequate even as he made the proposal to Congress. Unable, for the present, to make any public moves, Francis was still certain that the exposition would be delayed until 1904. And so, he discreetly maneuvered to secure the Olympic games for his city.

In April 1901, one month before the IOC meeting, an envoy arrived unannounced at the Paris apartment of Baron Pierre de Coubertin, founder and president of the IOC. Count Henri de Penaloza, a thirty-one-year-old French national, had been living in St. Louis since 1897. His father-in-law, Louis Fusz, sat on the board of directors for the Louisiana Purchase Exposition. Fusz also lived in the same posh neighborhood and was a member of the same exclusive clubs as David Francis. Penaloza, a native speaker holding the title of Count (Coubertin was a snob about birth and titles), was the perfect emissary to bring a discreet proposition to the Baron's attention.

Penaloza explained that Francis wanted to host the Olympic games as part of the Louisiana Purchase Exposition in 1904, but that the delicate political situation prevented an official request from St. Louis until a delay for the exposition was formally granted. He assured Coubertin that a letter requesting the Olympics would be forthcoming, and trusted that Coubertin would use discretion. Diplomatically, Coubertin expressed his willingness to present the proposal to the IOC, and Penaloza, feeling an understanding had been reached, sailed for London. A few days later Coubertin received a cablegram from Penaloza, stating that although St. Louis could not, at the present, submit a written request for the Olympics, the city would be appreciative if the IOC waited until 1902 to name the American city that would host the 1904 Games.

True to the letter, if not the spirit, of the understanding, Coubertin told the May meeting of the IOC about Penaloza's visit, St. Louis's interest, and the request to delay an announcement. The information was relayed with such discretion that it was promptly ignored, and Chicago, always Coubertin's favorite, was chosen to host America's first Olympics.

A Tale of Two Cities

The St. Louis Olympic games of 1904 were originally scheduled to take place in Chicago. On May 21, 1901, the International Olympic Committee (IOC), meeting in Paris, unanimously voted to award the games of the third Olympiad to Chicago. More than a year and a half later, on February 10, 1903, the Baron Pierre de Coubertin, the man most responsible for the modern revival of the Olympic games and the president of the International Olympic Committee, announced from Paris that the Olympic games for 1904 had been transferred to St. Louis. Chicago and St. Louis, however, were not the only American cities that made attempts to host the 1904 Olympic games. Philadelphia, Buffalo, and New York were all possible candidates.

The first modern Olympic games, held in Athens, Greece, in 1896, were a huge success. At their conclusion, the Greek government proposed that Athens become the permanent home for the Olympics. Many, including the American athletes who participated in the Athens games, supported this proposal. While the ancient Olympic games inspired the

modern revival, Coubertin believed the modern Olympics should reflect the contemporary world (competition in modern, not ancient,
athletic events) and be international in scope. When the Olympic games
were revived in 1894, Coubertin had promoted the idea of rotating the
Olympic site every four years to ensure the internationalism of the
modern games. Success in Athens, as great as it was, did not persuade
Coubertin to alter this founding principle. In November 1896, Coubertin explained his rationale for rotating Olympic sites in an article
published in the United States.[1] He firmly stated that the Olympic
games for 1900 would be in Paris, and, in 1904, in New York, Berlin, or
Stockholm. At this point the specific site for the 1904 games had not
been determined, but they were not going to be in Greece.

The second Olympic games did take place in Paris in 1900, but were a
failure. At the end of the nineteenth century, only in England and
America did sports play a significant role in society. In France sport was
considered frivolous and a distraction from the more serious intellectual concerns such as art, literature, and politics. The French viewed
sports and games as English concepts and therefore non-French; French
chauvinism and the historical cultural antagonism between the two countries prevented adoption of these English cultural attributes.[2] Pierre de
Coubertin was the rare exception, and it is ironic that a French aristocrat was the person most responsible for the revival of the modern Olympic games.

Coubertin believed that the infant Olympic games would benefit from
association with an established international concept such as the World's
Fair movement, and wanted to weld the 1900 games to the Paris fair.
The World's Fair concept originated with national fairs in France at the
end of the eighteenth century, and in 1889, Paris, commemorating the
centennial of the French Revolution, hosted an extremely successful
World's Fair. The Eiffel Tower was constructed for this event. Coubertin
made elaborate and detailed plans for the 1900 Olympic games, but en-
countered instant and vigorous opposition when he presented his plans
to the officials of the Paris World's Fair. Alfred Picart, the director for
the Paris fair, believed sports to be utterly useless and absurd. Coubertin
tried to organize an Olympic program, but constant opposition and
hostility wore him down. Eventually, frustration led Coubertin to resign
from the Olympic Organizing Committee, leaving the organization of

the 1900 Olympic games in the hands of sport-antagonistic officials. The results were predictable. Construction of new athletic facilities was not even considered. Existing facilities were grossly inadequate. A clump of trees adorned the landing zone of the discus and hammer events, making the outcome of the throws an adventure. Organization of the sports events was chaotic and there was no comprehensive Olympic program. Instead, the sports were scattered throughout other classifications of the World's Fair, sometimes in ludicrous associations. For example, athletics (track and field) were part of Provident Societies (charities), rowing was under Life-Saving, and skating and fencing events were placed under Cutlery. As a final insult, the words "Olympic games" were never used in reference to any sports event! Coubertin, in regards to these games of 1900, stated, ". . . nothing Olympic about them. We have made a hash of our work."[3]

In May 1900, just before the opening of the Paris games, the International Olympic Committee met in Paris. On the agenda was a discussion of possible sites for the 1904 games. In 1894, London had been briefly considered as a site for the revival Olympics of 1896, but Athens was ultimately selected for that honor. London, however, was understood to have the inside track for the 1904 games, although there was no official agreement. During deliberations of the IOC in May 1900, William Milligan Sloane, the American member, suggested that the United States be considered for 1904. Philadelphia was the first American city to express an interest in hosting the Olympic games of that year. The University of Pennsylvania was the premier track and field power in the United States, winning nine of thirteen events at the American Intercollegiate Championships of 1899. Exalting in their success, Penn athletic officials planned a tour of Europe the following year, first competing against several universities in England, and then in France at the Olympic games. In May 1900, athletic administrators from the University of Pennsylvania contacted British Olympic athletic authorities about the possibility of "transferring" the Olympic games of 1904 from London to Philadelphia. Frank Ellis, a graduate of Penn and former chairman of the university's track and field committee, was selected to represent Penn in its efforts to host the 1904 games. His mission was to express Philadelphia's interest in hosting the third Olympiad to British Olympic officials, secure their consent and support, and then present the Philadelphia proposal to

Coubertin and the International Olympic Committee. British Olympic officials had indicated their receptiveness to the proposal from Philadelphia, so success in England was expected. Ellis and the Penn athletes sailed for Europe in early June. Ellis's efforts were indeed successful; on July 28, 1900, the *New York Times* and *Chicago Tribune* reported that the Olympic games were coming to America in 1904 and that Philadelphia would be the host city. Then, mysteriously, Philadelphia and Frank Ellis faded from the scene. There is an explanation. During the summer of 1900, while the Paris games were in progress, James E. Sullivan, assistant director of the American Olympic team in Paris and secretary-general of the Amateur Athletic Union in the United States, met in Paris with French track and field officials in an attempt to form an International Federation of Track and Field.[4] The American AAU was the dominant athletic organization in the United States and Sullivan was the power behind the AAU. Formed in 1888 to coordinate, direct, and control athletic competition among the numerous athletic clubs that had been formed in the major cities of America during the last third of the nineteenth century, the AAU had no rival for athletic supremacy in 1900 (the National Collegiate Athletic Association, NCAA, was not formed until 1906).

Sullivan did not share Coubertin's vision of the Olympic games as a grand international sports festival. He instead held a limited view of the Olympics as simply an international track and field competition. The formation of an international track and field organization was an attempt by Sullivan to wrest control of the Olympic games from Coubertin and the International Olympic Committee. James Sullivan was an aggressive and often bellicose American chauvinist who viewed track and field competition as a manifestation of a nation's strength and character. He was a blunt, combative, no-nonsense pragmatist obsessed with making the United States the world's greatest track and field power. He considered himself the ultimate authority on track and field and viewed Coubertin and the IOC with contempt. He later remarked, "Coubertin was a powerless, pathetic figure in charge of an inept committee."[5] Sullivan was convinced that the Olympic games required his leadership.

Sullivan had been chosen as the director of athletics for the Pan American Exposition to be held in Buffalo in 1901, and he wanted the Olympic games to be part of the athletic celebration in Buffalo.[6] Sullivan convinced two Americans to join and support his efforts: Casper Whitney, president and editor of *Outing Magazine* (one of the premier sports magazines of the day), and Philadelphian Frank Ellis. Sullivan persuaded Ellis to join his crusade to control the Olympics, supporting the new international track and field organization, the Buffalo Olympics of 1901, and abandoning efforts to promote the Olympic interest of Philadelphia. Ellis must have felt that patriotism and the Olympian ambitions of Sullivan required Philadelphia to surrender its Olympic quest.

On November 1, 1900, an article appeared in the *Boston Transcript* newspaper and the national *Public Opinion* magazine stating that an American committee composed of James E. Sullivan, Casper Whitney, and Frank Ellis had been successful in their efforts to have Buffalo host the Olympic games in 1901. Sullivan, having failed during the summer of 1900 in Paris to form an International Federation of Track and Field, still sought control of the Olympic games. Coubertin, aware of Sullivan's attempt to form a new international organization, recognized that effort as a threat to his own control of the Olympic movement.[7] Coubertin moved quickly to counter Sullivan's ambitions. In October 1900, Coubertin appointed two more Americans to join William Sloane on the International Olympic Committee: Theodore Stanton and Casper Whitney. Stanton was a complete novice to sport, a surprise choice in 1900, and his appointment to the IOC remains a mystery to this day. His tenure as a member of the IOC ended in 1904. The selection of Whitney, on the other hand, was pure genius on Coubertin's part. Whitney was not only one of the most prominent sports editors in America but also had been part of Sullivan's committee that challenged Coubertin and the IOC during the summer of 1900. Coubertin, in one masterful stroke, not only secured the loyalty and support of a prominent American journalist but also converted a member of Sullivan's own team to his cause.

The Pan-American Exposition was set to open in May 1901, in Buffalo, with James Sullivan as the director of athletics. In a direct assault on Coubertin and the International Olympic Committee, on November 1, 1900, Sullivan unilaterally announced that the Olympic games would be held in Buffalo in 1901. Coubertin, outraged, responded decisively. He confronted several individuals who had conspired with Sullivan, including some members of the International Olympic Committee, demanding loyalty. Count Brunetta d'Usseaux of Italy, Professor Bergh-Petre of Sweden, and G. de Saint-Clair and Pierre Roy of France quickly denied supporting Sullivan. Coubertin's aggressive action ended any possibility of defection and ended the bid of Buffalo to host the Olympic games in 1901. Still, Coubertin took no chances. On November 11, 1900, he announced publicly that the next Olympic games would be in 1904, and would be held in either New York or Chicago. Two days later, in an article in the *New York Sun,* the combative Sullivan, referring to Coubertin's resignation from the Paris Organizing Committee, responded to the Baron's public announcement, saying Coubertin had ". . . been stripped of his athletic powers by the French government and was no longer in control of international meetings."[8]

Sullivan was not concerned with Olympic principles and protocol, as evidenced by his attempt to subvert the quadrennial cycle of the Olympic games by conducting Olympic games only one year after the Paris Olympics of 1900. He viewed the Olympic games as an international track and field meet and as a venue for the United States to demonstrate athletic supremacy. But in January of 1901, Whitney, longtime friend of James Sullivan and recently appointed (October 1900) International Olympic Committee member, reminded Sullivan that his AAU was not only without international jurisdiction but also had no control of American college athletes.[9] Coubertin had gained an ally in Casper Whitney. Over the next several months, Sullivan reluctantly accepted the inevitable and acknowledged the authority of Coubertin and the International Olympic Committee.

New York, America's largest and best-known city at the end of the nineteenth century, was mentioned by Coubertin as early as 1896 as a possible site for the 1904 Olympic games. But New York made no effort to host the games. Coubertin named New York based on the city's international prestige and as a synonym for the United States. Again, in November of 1900, Coubertin publicly announced that the 1904 Olympics would be held in either New York or Chicago. The only specific reference to New York possibly hosting the Olympic games occurred in a letter written by William M. Sloane to Coubertin on December 12, 1900. Sloane says, "I am not sure, but I think it would be possible to unite our four oldest universities in a plan to hold games of 1904 in

New York."[10] Sloane is referring to Harvard, Yale, Princeton, and Penn. This plan also pointedly excludes James Sullivan and his Amateur Athletic Union. In the same letter, after mentioning the New York idea, Sloane states that he personally favors Chicago as the host city for 1904. There was never any organized effort by anyone to have New York host the 1904 Olympic games.

The precise origin of Chicago's attempt to serve as host for the 1904 Olympic games is unknown. It is likely that a group of Chicago movers and shakers, meeting at the Chicago Athletic Club, began discussing the possibility during the spring of 1900. The Chicago Athletic Club provided a gathering place for the wealthy and social elite of the city. By May, Chicago was very much aware of the Paris Olympic games. Albert G. Spalding, Chicago's favorite son, founder of the Spalding Sporting Goods empire, and co-founder of the Chicago Athletic Club, had been put in charge of the American athletes by the U.S. Commission to the Paris Exposition. The University of Chicago was represented on the American team by a group of track and field athletes coached by the legendary Amos Alonzo Stagg. The participation of these local athletes, Stagg, and Albert Spalding prompted the *Chicago Tribune* to offer extensive coverage of the games. A steady supply of stories wired from Paris by Chicago reporters told of the athletic successes of their local heroes. Illustrations accompanied many of the articles and kept Chicago readers informed on Olympic matters. This coverage undoubtedly created an interest in the Olympic movement among the socially elite and sports-minded citizens of the city, including Henry J. Furber, a prominent Chicago attorney and businessman and a member of the Chicago Athletic Club.[11] It is not unreasonable to imagine Furber and other members of the club reading accounts and discussing the Olympic exploits of Chicago and fellow American athletes in Paris and proposing that Chicago bring the 1904 Olympic games to their city.

Chicago's efforts to secure the Olympic games of 1904 began during the summer of 1900, probably in July or early August. Someone from the Chicago Athletic Club discussion group, probably Henry Furber, contacted Henri Merou, the consul-general of the French Consulate in Chicago. Consul Merou was cooperative and contacted Henri Breal, the secretary of the Franco-American Committee in Paris, asking if Breal would support the efforts of Chicago to host the next Olympic games.[12]

Henri Breal was aware of the Olympic movement since its inception in 1894. At the initial Olympic Congress of 1894, his father, Michael Breal, a close friend of Coubertin, had conceived the idea of the marathon run, an event unknown in either ancient or modern times, but based on the legendary run of the Greek messenger Pheidippides. Dispatched from the battle of Marathon (490 BCE) to Athens, Pheidippides ran the twenty-four miles to Athens, proclaimed the Greek victory over the Persians, then died from exertion.

The longest race in the ancient Olympic games was an event called the dolichos, which varied from between 20 and 24 stades, about 2 miles. The official marathon distance of 26 miles, 385 yards was established at the London Olympic games of 1908. Coubertin thought the marathon a bit extreme, but recognized the symbolism of such an event and agreed to include the marathon run in the Olympics to honor the glory and heritage of ancient Greece. Michael Breal, after conceiving the idea, also donated a silver cup, which was awarded to the winner of the first marathon race at Athens in 1896.

Henri Breal, the son, agreed to represent the interests of Chicago and to meet with Coubertin to discuss the idea of Chicago as the 1904 Olympic host city. On August 29, 1900, Breal wrote to Henry Furber stating that he had "set to work . . . concerning the Olympic games project," and that "in order for headway to be made plans must become more precise and the help of the University of Chicago enlisted." Almost two months passed without a response from Furber. On October 19, 1900, Breal sent a second letter to Furber warning, "the University of Pennsylvania has made precise and serious efforts through its athletic association to secure the honor of hosting the Games." Breal further stated that Chicago needed to take immediate action and send an official letter, which he would deliver to Coubertin, "enumerating the grounds, moral, political or financial (for this item should not be overlooked) which mitigates in favor of Chicago." This letter prompted Furber to take action. On October 30, 1900, Furber wrote to William Rainey Harper, president of the University of Chicago, "Now my dear Mr. Harper, in as much as Consul Merou of Chicago, at present in Paris, and Mr. Breal, as well as myself, have undertaken to create a movement in favor of Chicago, we must ask that, in justice to all concerned, a committee, such as we already have considered, be appointed in order that we may formulate some definite plan of action and be able to follow up our general declaration of intention."[13]

President Harper had been a participant in the original Olympic discussion group at the Chicago Athletic Club during the spring of 1900. Seven years earlier, President Harper had met Pierre de Coubertin when the Baron toured America and visited the World's Fair in Chicago in 1893. Coubertin was impressed by Chicago and found the fair to be "really grand and beautiful." Coubertin was also quite taken by the luxurious accommodations and ultra modern athletic facilities of the Chicago Athletic Club where he was a guest. Original plans for the 1900 Paris Olympic games included a replica of the athletic facilities of the Chicago Athletic Club, which Coubertin proclaimed the most modern in the world.[14]

After receiving the letter from Henry Furber requesting the formation of a committee, President Harper promptly contacted, on November 1, 1900, five members of the faculty at the University of Chicago, requesting that they serve on a committee to formulate plans and submit a proposal to Coubertin and the International Olympic Committee to host the Olympic games of 1904 in Chicago.[15] Coincidentally, this was the same day that James E. Sullivan announced that he would hold the next Olympic games in Buffalo in 1901. The individuals contacted were Professors Frank F. Abbott, Shailer Mathews, Amos Stagg, O. J. Thatcher, and George E. Vincent. The most important of these was Amos Alonzo Stagg, the famous football and track coach. Stagg, now a veteran of Olympic competition, had recently returned from coaching the University of Chicago athletes at the Olympic games held in Paris the previous summer. Stagg possessed the practical experience and athletic administrative expertise necessary to plan, organize, and conduct a successful Olympic games competition in Chicago.

Coubertin's 1893 trip to the United States was both successful and enjoyable. The city of Chicago, the World's Fair of 1893 hosted by Chicago, and the Chicago Athletic Club all produced fond memories. It is very probable that once Coubertin, through the efforts of Merou and Breal, became aware of the city's interest in hosting the 1904 Olympic games, Chicago became his personal choice. As evidence, on November 4, 1900, Coubertin wrote to Henri Breal requesting an official proposal from Chicago.[16] Coubertin stated that the host site for the 1904 Olympic games would be decided by the International Olympic Committee in the spring of 1901. "I shall be delighted if I am able to communicate a definite plan," he added, meaning a plan from Chicago. But November 1900 was also a troubling month for Coubertin. Frank Ellis of Philadelphia had consulted with British athletic officials and gained their consent for Philadelphia to host the 1904 Olympic games. James Sullivan and French athletic officials were conspiring to create an international organization to take control of the Olympics, and Sullivan intended to host an Olympic games in Buffalo in 1901. Coubertin needed an official proclamation from Chicago to settle the issue of the 1904 Olympic site. But even without official word from Chicago, Coubertin was willing to announce that only New York or Chicago would host the 1904 Olympic games, knowing full well there was no effort on the part of New York to serve as host. After Sullivan's newspaper tirade against Coubertin's announcement of November 11, 1900, Coubertin countered by stating that European sport authorities did not take Sullivan seriously and that after all, "James Sullivan is not the American member of the IOC."[17]

Meanwhile, progress was being made in Chicago. During the Coubertin-Sullivan brouhaha, Henry J. Furber, on November 12, 1900, invited Amos Alonzo Stagg to lunch at Furber's opulent office in Chicago's Stock Exchange Building, "to discuss certain features of these games . . . before consulting with the committee of the whole." William M. Sloane in a letter to Coubertin in December 1900, after mentioning a possible plan for New York to host the 1904 Olympic games, stated his preference for Chicago: ". . . I rather incline to having them in Chicago. They would be a much greater educational force there than anywhere else in the country and would draw a larger, more enthusiastic audience." Sloane's letter prompted Coubertin, in January 1901, to boldly announce in the *Revue Olympique,* the official publication of the International Olympic Committee, that "It seems now very probable that the next Olympian games will take place in America, and people agree generally that, at the meeting which will be held shortly, the members of the International Olympic Committee will have to decide in favor of the new world. A rivalry was thought to arise between New York and Chicago; but Chicago seems to have already taken the lead."[18] Coubertin's fond memories of Chicago, and Sloane's comment that the games would be a greater educational force in that city, closed the deal for

Coubertin. The Olympic games were little known in the United States and practically unheard of outside the northeast corridor of the country. If the midwestern city of Chicago would be the best venue for spreading the Olympic gospel throughout the United States, then Chicago was the choice of Coubertin.

A group of prominent businessmen and faculty members of the University of Chicago, organized by Henry Furber, convened for the first time at the Chicago Athletic Club on the evening of February 13, 1901. Henri Merou, the French consul, was in attendance, as was William Rainey Harper. A committee of five assumed the task of preparing a prospectus on the financial viability of hosting the Olympic games. The major concern was securing funding for construction of a new stadium. Furber was elected committee chairman, and Stagg added his athletic organizational and administrative expertise to the committee. A local reporter observed the evening's proceedings. The next day the front-page headline of the *Chicago Tribune* blared, "Chicago wants Olympic Games."[19]

Soon after, Coubertin received an interesting and, for him, certainly a most gratifying letter from none other than James Sullivan, American czar of amateur athletics. Sullivan had capitulated. Casper Whitney's remarks to Sullivan in January 1901, and Whitney's support of Coubertin and the International Olympic Committee, had done the job. On March 21, 1901, Sullivan wrote Coubertin, "My Dear Baron, there is a great deal of talk here about Chicago getting the Olympian Games. I hope they do. The papers say they are raising a lot of money out there, one paper placing it at $200,000. If that is so, it is simply marvelous. They could never get that much money in New York."[20]

A month later Sloane wrote Coubertin, "I have seen Sullivan and he is entirely happy. He wants the games at Chicago and he will work like a good fellow." Casper Whitney wrote Coubertin on April 30, 1901, stating that he had met with Sloane and Sullivan, and "all agreed that Chicago is the place for these games, and we are prepared to back you to the full extent of our power, provided of course Chicago is prepared to make necessary arrangements." Theodore Stanton, the third American member of the International Olympic Committee, had cabled Coubertin on March 15, stating he believed Chicago should host the Olympic Games of 1904, pointing out the magnificent job Chicago had done in hosting the World's Fair in 1893.[21] It was unanimous. Chicago had the support of all three American members of the IOC as well as Coubertin's archrival James Sullivan and the Amateur Athletic Union of the United States. The cities of Philadelphia, New York, and Buffalo were no longer contestants for the honor of hosting America's first Olympic games. Coubertin must have been pleased with his efforts and for the prospects of Chicago serving as host in 1904. Finally, all seemed to be going well for Pierre de Coubertin and the Olympic movement.

In Chicago, work had proceeded since the February 13 public announcement that the city wanted the games, and on May 1, 1901, Coubertin finally received an official request from the Chicago Olympic Games Committee. Chairman Furber conveyed to Coubertin the official bid document signed by thirteen prominent citizens of Chicago. This document stated that "efforts we have made to secure the funds which properly provide for the holding of said contests, had been such as to convince us all of the warm support and interest of our fellow citizens and of our ability to carry out the plans proposed." Shortly afterwards, Coubertin received a letter dated May 2, 1901, from Henry Furber expressing the hope that Chicago, "which has never failed of success, will have the opportunity of exerting its energies in promoting this great work which you have so well organized." Appended to Furber's letter was a note from William R. Harper indicating that the Chicago Olympic Games Committee had the full support and cooperation of the University of Chicago in regards to "matters pertaining to grounds, grandstands, and training quarters."[22]

The International Olympic Committee convened in Paris at *Le Club Automobile de France,* a private social club for gentlemen, on May 19, 1901. American members William Sloane and Casper Whitney did not feel the need to attend. Theodore Stanton, the lone American representative, presented the request of Chicago to host the Olympic games of 1904. The Frenchman Henri Breal, who had been a zealous supporter of Chicago from the beginning, enthusiastically aided him. The vote was unanimous. Chicago was awarded the Games of the Third Olympiad. Henry Furber and Chicago were immediately informed; Coubertin sent a concise but emphatic telegram, "Chicago wins." Henri Breal bested Coubertin's brevity by cabling, euphorically, the single word, "Oui."[23]

Henry Jewett Furber, Jr., Chicago attorney and businessman, was the person most responsible for initiating, organizing, and ultimately securing the Olympic games of 1904 for the city of Chicago. He met with the president of the United States, Theodore Roosevelt, was received by European aristocracy and heads of state, and maintained a regular correspondence with American and French officials of the Olympic movement, the most prominent being the Baron Pierre de Coubertin himself. Shortly after the announcement of the International Olympic Committee that Chicago had been selected to host the Olympic games, Harper offered his congratulations to Furber and acknowledged and praised Furber's leadership: "No one knows more than I do how much of this success is due to you, and I can assure you that we appreciate your efforts."[24]

Henry J. Furber, Jr., was born May 12, 1866, in Green Bay, Wisconsin. Shortly after his birth the family moved to Chicago. His father became a prominent lawyer and successful owner of Chicago real estate, quickly joining the city's social and financial elite. Henry, Jr., was as much an achiever as his father. He graduated from the old University of Chicago in 1886 and then earned his master's degree from Bowdoin College. The next five years were devoted to study in Germany, culminating with a doctorate in economics from the University of Halle in 1891. Upon returning to Chicago, Furber published articles in economic journals and became a member of the Chicago Literary Society. The career path of Henry, Jr., followed in his father's footsteps, as the son became an attorney and real estate investor. He cemented his social status with membership in the Columbia and Chicago Yacht Clubs and the Chicago Athletic Club. By 1900, at the age of thirty-four, Furber was a member of the social and financial elite of Chicago.[25]

Chicago was the Olympic City, but events were occurring that would ultimately transfer the Olympic crown from Chicago to St. Louis. The city of St. Louis planned to honor the one hundredth anniversary of the 1803 purchase of the Louisiana Territory from France. A World's Fair with the official title Louisiana Purchase Exposition was deemed the most appropriate means to celebrate the centennial anniversary of the nation's largest land acquisition. Planning began in 1889 after the governor of Missouri, David R. Francis, failed in his attempts to secure for St. Louis the World's Fair slated for 1892, celebrating the four hundredth anniversary of the discovery of America by Columbus. Chicago had won that honor. Governor Francis immediately conceived the Louisiana Purchase Exposition and began working to make it become a reality. The exposition was planned for 1903, the centennial of the Louisiana Purchase, but as in Chicago, it became apparent that a year delay would benefit the success of the enterprise. As early as January 1901, officials of the St. Louis Exposition began to plan for a delay until 1904.[26]

Count Henri de Penaloza, a thirty-one-year-old French national who had lived in St. Louis since 1897, was the son-in-law of Louis Fusz, a prominent St. Louis businessman. Fusz, who emigrated from France in 1852, was a member of the board of directors for the Louisiana Purchase Exposition and a business colleague of the exposition's president, David Francis. Fusz and Francis were both members of the prestigious and exclusive St. Louis Merchants Exchange and lived in the same upscale neighborhood on the city's West Side. In April 1901, only one month before the IOC meeting, a courier, unannounced, arrived at the Paris home of Baron de Coubertin. Dispatched by Francis, Penaloza, native speaker, social peer, and contemporary (seven years junior) of Coubertin, was an excellent choice to serve as emissary to the Olympic president. After cordial introductions, Penaloza boldly conveyed the desire of David Francis to host the 1904 Olympic games as part of the Louisiana Purchase Exposition. Coubertin listened patiently as Penaloza explained the delicate political situation that prevented an official request from St. Louis until a delay for the exposition was formally granted, but stated that Coubertin would nevertheless receive a letter from St. Louis in the very near future requesting the Olympics. Ever the diplomat, Coubertin politely expressed his willingness to present such a request to the IOC. Leaving Paris, Penaloza traveled to London. A few days later Coubertin received a cablegram from Penaloza stating St. Louis officials could not at this time submit a letter, but did request that the IOC wait until the following year to name the American city to host the 1904 Olympics. Francis fully intended to request a year delay from the U.S. Congress, which had only that March granted the exposition official recognition and funding. But it would be politically embarrassing to ask for a delay just a month later. Unable, for the present, to make any public moves, Francis was still certain that the exposition would be delayed until 1904. And so, he discreetly maneuvered to secure the Olympic games for his city. True to his word, Coubertin informed the IOC of Penaloza's visit and subsequent delay request, which was promptly ignored. Later that summer Coubertin mentioned Penaloza's visit in an article in the *Revue Olympique*, the official publication of the IOC.[27]

St. Louis officials, while discreet, could not keep their Olympic aspirations secret for long. Prominent sports leaders, Casper Whitney for one, became aware of the Olympic ambitions of St. Louis and immediately recognized the potential conflict with the Olympic plans of Chicago. On April 30, 1901, Whitney, editor of the sports magazine *Outing* and a member of the International Olympic Committee, wrote two letters. The first, to Coubertin in Paris, expressed support for Chicago to be the Olympic venue. The second warned University of Chicago President Harper that St. Louis had made a bid for the 1904 Games. "In their application they profess to have unlimited financial backing and propose most elaborate and costly preparation. Mr. de Coubertin, President of the International Committee, and Prof. Sloane, Mr. Sullivan and I have just had a talk on the subject. We are agreed that Chicago is the place for these games . . . I am writing you for some definite guarantee as to what Chicago will really do."[28]

David Francis had done all he could without an official postponement of the exposition. The minutes of the International Olympic Committee meeting of May 21, 1901, state that three cities, Chicago, Buffalo, and St. Louis, were candidates for hosting the Games of 1904. Buffalo was not a serious contender and was only mentioned because of the shenanigans of James Sullivan. The efforts of St. Louis and Henri Penaloza were revealed to the IOC by Coubertin, but without an official representative present to convey its interests, St. Louis was dismissed from consideration. The IOC was not receptive to delaying its vote until 1902. Chicago was the only city to send a representative to present its interests. The committee's choice was an easy one.

Chicago prepared to celebrate. The *New York Times* reported the organizational plans, the Chicago citizens' elation at the prospect of hosting the Olympics, and the imminent celebration. "Great gratification was expressed today over the award of the Olympian Games of 1904 to Chicago. The local committee which has had in charge the work of securing the games will at once form a permanent organization. . . . the original plans would be carried out. These involve the erection of a stadium in Lake Park, and the preparation of athletic grounds in other parts of the city for the convenience of the athletes. A monster celebration will be held tomorrow night by the students of Chicago University [*sic*] in honor of the assignment of the Games to Chicago."[29]

Coubertin received newspaper accounts of the Chicago celebrations from Furber and promptly published an article in the *Revue Olympique* describing the enthusiastic and jubilant events.[30] Coubertin told of the wild and frenzied affair that occurred on Marshall Field at the University of Chicago campus. A crowd of more than six thousand gathered around a huge bonfire to welcome representatives of several local Chicago organizations; listen to congratulatory speeches, including one from Henry Furber; and propose toasts and salutes to their Olympic city. Chicago was excited.

After the initial rush of euphoria and jubilation, Chicago began preparations to host the international sports festival. Furber had been largely responsible for securing the Olympic games; now he assumed responsibility for organizing them. The Olympics were scheduled for September 1904. Three years and three months provided ample time for the Chicago Olympic Organizing Committee. While there was much to do, there was plenty of time to proceed deliberately. Five immediate areas needed to be addressed: funding, facilities, athlete eligibility, international participation, and the involvement of the president of the United States. Furber and the Organizing Committee proceeded to develop a plan of action and, over the course of the next twelve months, began to implement their plan.

Corporate bequests, state and local government contributions, and appropriations from Congress would provide the funds to finance the cost of hosting the Olympic games. While the University of Chicago had agreed to provide facilities for the games as a condition for Chicago being awarded the Olympics, it was understood that a new stadium was needed. Chicago Alderman W. H. Thompson prepared a construction plan for review by the License Committee of the City Council. By January 1902, architectural designs planned for a structure to accommodate seventy-five thousand spectators, with six main entrances, 108 exits, and, most sensational of all, a retractable canvas roof for use during inclement weather.[31]

While Chicago prepared diligently and deliberately, Coubertin, in characteristic fashion, acted immediately. Seven days after the International Olympic Committee awarded the Games to Chicago, on May 28, 1901,

Coubertin wrote to President William McKinley requesting that he serve as honorary president of the Chicago Olympic games of 1904. McKinley never responded. On September 5, 1901, McKinley arrived at the Pan-American Exposition in Buffalo and gave a short public address. The next day he stood in a receiving line in front of the Temple of Music Exhibition as citizens filed by for a chance to shake the hand of the president. Shortly after 4 p.m., Leon F. Czolgosz, a twenty-eight-year-old unemployed wire worker, made his way toward the president. His right hand was wrapped in a bandage and concealed a .32 pistol. As McKinley extended his hand toward him, Czolgosz fired two shots at point-blank range. The president doubled over and fell backwards into the arms of a Secret Service agent. As he lay there, he turned to his secretary and said, "My wife, be careful . . . how you tell her—oh, be careful." Doctors performed two operations at a hospital on the exposition grounds. McKinley was then taken to the home of the exposition president, John G. Milburn, for postoperative recovery. At first the president seemed to be improving. On September 11 his condition had improved to the point that he felt well enough to request a cigar and solid food. The food was given, the cigar was not. But the next day he suffered a relapse from which he never recovered. In the early morning hours of September 14, 1901, William McKinley died of gangrene. Later that day Vice President Theodore Roosevelt was sworn in as the twenty-sixth president of the United States. The assassin, Czolgosz, a self-avowed anarchist, admitted guilt and was tried on September 23, 1901. After a trial of nine hours, it took the jury only thirty-four minutes to return a verdict of guilty. The judge pronounced the sentence of death by electrocution. Czolgosz proclaimed, "I killed the president because he was the enemy of the people—the good working people. I am not sorry for my crime."[32] After the electrocution, sulfuric acid was poured over the assassin's body to accelerate decomposition.

The new president was an avid outdoorsman and an enthusiastic supporter of athletic competition. Sickly as a child, Roosevelt had turned to sports, primarily gymnastics, weight training, and boxing, to remake his frail body. The Olympic games could not have had a more sympathetic patron. After only two months in office, Roosevelt received a letter from Pierre de Coubertin. The Baron asked Roosevelt to accept the honorary presidency of the Chicago Olympic games, implying deceptively that McKinley had agreed to do so before his death. Roosevelt rebuffed the Baron, responding three weeks after receiving the invitation, "My Dear Sir . . . It is a matter of very real regret to me that I do not feel at liberty to accept your very kind request that I become honorary president of the Chicago Olympic Games. Unfortunately, after consultation with members of the cabinet, I feel it would not do for me to give the unavoidable impression of governmental connection with the Games."[33]

Coubertin was not deterred. On December 22, 1901, he sent another letter to Roosevelt explaining precedents set in 1896 and 1900, which would allow the president to reconsider.[34] Governmental connection with the Olympic games was exactly what Coubertin wanted. But Roosevelt, without a request from American Olympic officials, was unwilling to become an associate of the Olympics.

By May of 1902, however, Roosevelt had been persuaded, after meeting with Henry Furber, that his involvement was not only appropriate but also absolutely essential to the success of America's first Olympics. Furber was planning a tour of Europe to promote international participation in the Chicago games. He realized that his intention to meet with European heads of state would be immeasurably enhanced if he possessed letters of introduction from the president of the United States. To this end, Furber contacted the White House requesting an audience with Roosevelt. His request was granted and in early May of 1902, Furber and Benjamin Rosenthal, a committee colleague, traveled to Washington for a meeting with Roosevelt. The president agreed to write letters of introduction and discussed other related matters, including possible appropriations from Congress to assist in the financing of the games and the role of the president in serving the Olympic cause. Upon his return to Chicago, Furber wrote Roosevelt to express "personal gratitude" for the warm reception accorded them by the president during their recent Washington trip. Roosevelt responded to Furber with offers of support and encouragement for their Olympic endeavors. Roosevelt wrote, "I earnestly wish you success in your undertaking . . . I shall do all in my power to contribute to their success, and it will give me great pleasure to open them."[35]

Henry Furber had secured the patronage of the president of the United States, who offered to officially declare the Chicago Olympic games open. Furber notified Pierre de Coubertin of these positive developments and warned him that Roosevelt's comments had been made in private and should not be made public. On May 31, 1902, Furber wrote Coubertin, "I think it preferable that no mention be made of President Roosevelt's assurances."[36]

In St. Louis, while Henry Furber was meeting with Roosevelt in Washington, the Executive Committee of the Louisiana Purchase Exposition officially requested a one-year delay for the opening of the exposition until April 30, 1904. The public announcement for the postponement appeared in Chicago newspapers on May 2, 1902. Chicago Olympic officials, including Henry Furber, were not initially concerned. They had known as early as the spring of 1901, even before Chicago was awarded the games on May 21, that the St. Louis Exposition would probably not take place until 1904.[37]

The success of his trip to the White House propelled Henry Furber toward his next great objective. Letters of introduction in hand, Furber, along with John B. Payne and Laverne W. Noyes of the Chicago Olympic Committee, boarded the Hamburg-American ocean liner *Graf Waldersee* and set sail on July 1, 1902, for Europe. The primary purpose was to generate support for the Chicago Olympics among European leaders in order to ensure an international field of athletes for the Games. This European support had an additional purpose, "so that expressions can be used as leverage on Congress for mustering American support," according to Furber.[38] What he meant, of course, was congressional appropriations to help with the financing of Olympic expenses.

For the next four months Furber and colleagues toured the palaces and government offices of Europe, visiting France, Germany, England, Belgium, and Switzerland. The American press, particularly the *New York Times*, published extensive accounts of the meetings, dinners, and gala receptions accorded the Chicagoans. On June 28 the U.S. Congress approved a one-year postponement of the St. Louis Exposition and, on the very day that Furber departed for Europe, President Roosevelt officially proclaimed that the Louisiana Purchase Exposition would open in 1904.

Meanwhile, organizational planning continued in Chicago. On July 13 the *New York Times* reported the formation of the Final Committee on Athletics for the games. The headlines read, "Men Chosen to Govern

Olympian Games in 1904," "Sporting Experts Selected," "Big Carnival in Chicago Will Be Run by Men Familiar with Branch of Sport They Will Arrange For." The *Times* explained, "to this committee will be delegated the final work in preparing and arranging the details of the Olympian games of 1904, an event which is sure to be handed down to posterity."[39] Albert Goodwill Spalding, former professional baseball player, founder and president of the Spalding sporting goods empire, and one of Chicago's most prominent citizens, was selected to chair the Final Committee on Athletics.

Spalding, born a short distance from Chicago, spent his entire adulthood, until 1900, in the city, first as the star pitcher on the Chicago White Stockings professional baseball team, then as co-founder of the National League in 1876, owner of the White Sox team, and finally as sporting goods mogul. He had been one of the founders of the Chicago Athletic Club and the director of the American team to the Paris Olympics of 1900. But Spalding, acceding to the wishes of his wife, had moved to California in 1900 and was not involved in Chicago's initial efforts to host the 1904 Olympic games. The summer of 1902 was the beginning of Albert Spalding's association with the Olympics of 1904. He stated the goal of the Final Committee on Athletics for the *New York Times*: "It is our intention to have the Olympian games of 1904 an Olympiad that Americans can feel proud of and one that will long be remembered in the history of sport in the civilized world."[40]

Spalding and the Final Committee planned to have extensive gymnastic events on the Olympic program. Gymnastics, at the turn of the century, was the core element in the American system of physical culture, which evolved into the modern discipline of physical education. The experts chosen for the gymnastics subcommittee included legendary leaders in physical education: William G. Anderson (1860–1947), director of physical education at Yale University and founder of the American Alliance of Health, Physical Education, Recreation, and Dance; Dudley A. Sargent (1849–1924), Harvard professor and pioneer in strength testing; Luther Gulick (1865–1918), director of physical education for New York City Schools and founder of the Public School Athletic League; and R. Tait McKenzie (1867–1938), noted sport sculptor and director of physical education at the University of Pennsylvania.

St. Louis was not idle. While Henry Furber and his committee were in

Europe, and Albert Spalding was organizing the Final Committee on Athletics in Chicago, David Francis and Frederick J. V. Skiff, director of exhibits for the exposition, decided that all amateur sports competitions held in conjunction with the fair would be part of the Department of Physical Culture, and would be conducted under the jurisdiction of the Amateur Athletic Union of the United States. A decision was also made to request that the AAU's 1904 National Track and Field Championships be included as part of the program. On July 23, President Francis sent Jerome Karst and Henri Garneau, both officials of the Western Association of the Amateur Athletic Union, to the New York headquarters of the AAU to officially request that the National Championships be held in St. Louis in 1904.[41]

At the end of August, Henry Furber was in England as the guest of Scottish-born businessman, philanthropist, and sportsman Sir Thomas Lipton, whose face, topped with a yachting cap, still adorns packages of tea. Lipton invited Furber on a cruise in the North Sea on his yacht *Erin*, and just prior to departure Furber learned of the attempt by St. Louis to secure the AAU Championships. This information set off alarm bells for Furber. He realized, for the first time, that there was a serious clash of interests between St. Louis and Chicago set to occur in 1904, and that the matter required his immediate attention. From his quarters aboard the millionaire's yacht, Furber wrote to William Harper, "I have just been informed that the St. Louis Exposition is trying to secure the AAU championship contests in 1904. As the AAU virtually controls athletics in the United States, this would seriously injure the Olympian Games."[42]

Furber had gone to Paris on August 1 intending to meet with Coubertin, but the Baron was out of town. After waiting in vain almost three weeks, Furber left Paris on August 17 and continued his tour of the continent. Furber left a note for Coubertin: "I have not despaired at the chance to see you before I myself leave for New York" and suggested they meet in September. The two men finally met the weekend of September 20–21 at the estate of Coubertin's mother-in-law in the province of Alsace. Furber, having just learned of the athletic plans of St. Louis, was nervous about Chicago's midwestern rival, but financial concerns also troubled him. Government funding and contributions from Chicago interests had not yet materialized. Burdened with these concerns, Furber failed to make a favorable impression. The Baron, sensing these concerns, began to lose confidence in Furber's ability to successfully organize the Chicago interests. Coubertin shared his impressions of Henry Furber and his concerns with Chicago in a letter written to fellow IOC member and close friend Godefroy Blonay of Switzerland. After referring to Furber as "the honorable president of the Chicago committee," Coubertin wrote, "Furber is a very interesting individual, extremely shrewd and egotistical. He is intelligent, but much of a bluffer, just like a Chicagoan. I handled him to the best of my ability." Then Coubertin revealed his reservations and proposed a most dramatic course of action. "I am thinking about expressing my views, in spite of the horror of a move." Coubertin was most concerned that seventeen months after being awarded the Olympics, Henry Furber and the Chicago Organizing Committee lacked the necessary financial resources to guarantee the success of the games. Events continued to move swiftly. Furber and Coubertin had met in September. During the first week of October 1902, Albert Spalding received a telephone call from Frederick Skiff, director of exhibits for the St. Louis Exposition.[43] Skiff was from Chicago and personally acquainted with Spalding. At Chicago's World's Fair of 1893 Skiff had served as the director of the Mines Department. In 1894 he became the curator of Chicago's Field Columbian Museum and was one of six administrators Francis recruited from Chicago with 1893 World's Fair experience. Skiff secured a leave of absence in 1902 to accept the position of director of exhibits in St. Louis and after the exposition returned to his curator post in Chicago.

Skiff and Spalding talked of the scheduling conflict between the Olympic games in Chicago and the AAU championships that St. Louis intended to host in 1904. While it is not known for certain, in light of events only three weeks later, it is plausible that during the conversation with Spalding, Skiff requested that the Olympic games of 1904 be transferred to St. Louis. Spalding responded to Skiff in a letter from New York dated October 9, 1902:

> Dear Mr. Skiff:
>
> Following up our telephonic conversation of last week, I have given that matter considerable thought since then, have made myself pretty well acquainted with the athletic situation in Chicago relative to the Olympian

Games of 1904, have had a conference with some of the prominent athletic men of New York, and with the slight knowledge I have of the athletic situation in St. Louis for 1904, I have come to the conclusion that it would be well, in the interest of all concerned, to have an *early* conference between the representative of the St. Louis committee, a representative of the Olympian Games, some of the athletic officials of national importance and myself. Unless some action looking towards harmony is taken soon, I fear athletic politics will become a factor in the situation which I think an early conference and exchange of ideas might avoid. It is my personal opinion that the interests of both St. Louis and Chicago athletic games for 1904 will be better served by some harmonious action and relationship than to have reverse conditions.

I am informed that Mr. Furber, president of the International Olympian Games Committee, will be in New York (on his way from Europe), about the 15th inst. And I expect to meet him here soon after his arrival. It is impossible for me to discuss this by letter, therefore, following up our telephonic conversation of last week, I am prompted to suggest that a representative of the St. Louis athletic department come on to New York prepared for a conference with Mr. Furber of the Olympian Games Committee, some of the athletic officials and myself. If this suggestion meets with your approval and you will so advise me by return mail, I will suggest the same thing to Mr. Furber upon his arrival, and if agreeable to him, as I am quite sure it will be, I will wire you asking that a representative of St. Louis Athletic department come to New York as soon after receipt of the telegram as possible. For reasons that I can not very well explain by letter, I deem it very much better that this conference take place in New York rather than either St. Louis or Chicago. Whoever comes on representing the St. Louis interest, I rather hope the representation can be limited to one or two men, and I hope they can come with sufficient power to close any arrangement or understanding that may be decided upon at the conference.

I think it important that this matter be treated entirely in confidence and avoid publicity. My personal acquaintance with you prompts me in expressing a hope that you may be the one selected by the St. Louis athletic department to represent them, and if you can arrange to come I feel quite sure a plan can be outlined that will make the two enterprises work in harmony.

Kindly let me hear from you by return mail that I may know your wishes and that I may take the matter up understandingly with Mr. Furber upon his arrival.[44]

Furber arrived in New York on October 21, 1902, from his promo-

tional tour of Europe. He had barely stepped ashore when Albert
Spalding met him. Spalding informed Furber of the communications
between himself and Frederick Skiff. Furber may have been anxious
about conferring with St. Louis officials, but he agreed to do so. He may
have thought that a scheduling compromise could be reached that would
allow American athletes to compete in American championships in
St. Louis as well as the separate Olympic games in Chicago. Such thoughts
were dismissed once Furber met with Skiff and Alfred Shapleigh, chairman of the Physical Culture Committee. The three men met in New
York on October 27. The St. Louis representatives immediately made it
clear that Olympian games in Chicago would be in competition with
their enterprise and would detract from its ultimate success. They were
not willing to consider two athletic festivals in the two respective cities.
The only solution satisfactory to the interests of St. Louis was to transfer the Olympic games to that city as part of the Louisiana Purchase
Exposition. Furber listened to the demands of Skiff and Shapleigh, politely stated that a transfer of the games was a matter for the
International Olympic Committee, and that he would discuss the request with the Chicago Olympic Committee upon his return to Chicago.[45] Furber, stunned, needed time to think.

Furber returned to Chicago about a week after his conference with
the two St. Louis officials. A message was waiting for him from David
Francis. Francis requested that a conference be arranged in Chicago between St. Louis officials and the Chicago Olympic Committee board of
directors. Furber immediately arranged an evening banquet for
November 10. During the course of the evening, Frederick Skiff addressed the assemblage describing the plans for the St. Louis World's
Fair. While explaining the various departments of the exposition, Skiff
alluded to athletic features: "Physical culture in an immense hippo-
drome, in which the athletes of the world will exhibit their prowess, skill
and endurance, and contest for unusual prizes. In this particular feature
of the Exposition St. Louis feels confident of securing the co-operation
of Chicago in a movement to transfer the Olympic games, heretofore
announced to be held there, to St. Louis."[46]

It was official, and now, for the first time, public. St. Louis wanted the
Olympic games of 1904 in their city. Furber finally wrote to Coubertin
and provided him the following account of the meeting:

Upon my arrival in New York a month ago, I was informed that the Exposition officials wished to confer with me at once in view of the conflict of dates arising through the postponement of the St. Louis Fair. I consented, and in response to a telegram a delegation came on to New York. They informed me politely but clearly, that the Olympian Games of 1904 threatened the success of their World's Fair and that if we insisted on carrying out our program they would develop their athletic department so as to eclipse our games . . . dwelling upon the impossibility to concede to us the slightest point, they concluded by requesting a transfer of the Games from Chicago to St. Louis. I informed them that this was a matter in which only the International Olympic Committee had power; but that when I reached Chicago our Board of Directors would discuss the matter.[47]

David Francis and Frederick Skiff had devoted their careers to business, politics, and public administration. Neither man had experience with athletics, but both recognized America's recent explosion of interest in sports and realized that a World's Fair without a significant emphasis on sports competition would be incomplete. Skiff had conceived the idea of including, for the first time at any World's Fair, a department of physical culture, and Francis had heartily concurred. While the Olympic games were an unknown concept to Francis and Skiff, both understood that an international sports festival in another city posed a threat to the attention and prestige of the exposition's own athletic efforts. On the other hand, having the Olympic games in St. Louis as part of the program of events of the Department of Physical Culture only added luster and a sense of completeness to an extensive athletic program which was to occur throughout the seven-month period (April 30–December 1, 1904) of the exposition. While the top officials of the Paris World's Fair had been openly hostile to the Olympic games of 1900, in 1904 the president and director of exhibits were not only enthusiastic partisans but also adamant in their desire to incorporate the Olympics as a distinctive feature of the St. Louis Fair.[48]

At the conclusion of festivities, as Henry Furber was leaving the banquet hall, a reporter from the *Chicago Chronicle* approached him. Asked to comment on the status of the Olympic games, Furber stated, "There are three positions open to us. One is to have the games as scheduled in 1904. Another is to transfer the games to St. Louis. The third is to postpone the games until 1905." When pressed by the reporter to elaborate on the three scenarios, Furber said that it would not be possible to conduct the games in 1904 as scheduled, "that would be discourteous to St. Louis." As far as transferring the games to St. Louis, Furber would only say, "The directors will have to answer that question." Furber himself favored postponing the games for one year. Chicago newspaper headlines the next day proclaimed, "May Yield the Games to St. Louis Exposition," "May Lose Big Games," and "May Lose Olympian Games." The possible transfer of the games to St. Louis generated immense publicity for the Olympics. Americans were not only told about the possible transfer but also received an education on Olympic history and philosophy. Newspapers large and small, in major metropolitan centers and in small towns across America, told the Olympic story. A better public relations campaign to promote interest, understanding, and enthusiasm for the Olympic games movement could not have been devised.[49]

The reaction in Chicago was predictable and immediate. The students, faculty, administrators, and alumni of the University of Chicago were particularly vocal. The university community had enthusiastically supported hosting the Olympic games from the beginning and were unwilling to give them up. The student newspaper, the *Daily Maroon,* reported the possible loss of the Olympic games on November 12. Three weeks later the Student Council organized a mass assembly to express its opposition to transferring the Olympics to St. Louis. Coubertin later referred to this gathering as *"un colossal meeting d'etudiants."*[50] While Coubertin exaggerated, there was no doubt that the students voiced a strong sentiment in favor of Chicago keeping the games. The official resolution adopted by the Student Council urged the International Olympic Committee to hold the games in Chicago in 1905, and, if a postponement was not agreeable, to honor the original decision and hold the games in Chicago in 1904. However, the faculty and administration of the University of Chicago recognized that Chicago could not host the Olympics during the World's Fair in St. Louis. Professor Max Ingres, an original member of the Chicago Olympian Games Bid Committee, succinctly made the case against St. Louis, but then conceded reality and expressed the hope that the Olympics could be postponed until 1905. His remarks appeared in the December 12, 1902, issue of the *Daily Maroon.* "We have gone to much labor in making plans for the games. St. Louis cannot make a success of the games, as there is a danger of their being overshadowed by the exposition. St. Louis is not the center of the United States, its water is bad, hotel accommodations insufficient, its athletic field is nearly two miles from the exposition grounds. The only way out . . . is for a postponement to 1905."[51]

Furber wrote two letters to Coubertin on November 26, 1902. The first was an official correspondence as president of the Organizing Committee in which Furber explained the serious predicament of Chicago in regards to competition with St. Louis as the Olympic venue for 1904.

> Dear Sir—It becomes the duty of the Directors of this association to acquaint you with certain very serious embarrassments arising from a conflict in dates occasioned by the postponement of the Louisiana Purchase Exposition until 1904, . . . The officials of the Exposition have informed us that the Olympian Games . . . will be a menace to their enterprise, and have invited a transfer of our contests from Chicago to St. Louis . . . We have no reason to believe that St. Louis would consent to aid our contests by abandoning her own, especially as in her eyes the Olympian Games in Chicago constitute a menace, which she must, if possible discourage. Lest we seem to overestimate the difficulties of our position, we would suggest that the Louisiana Purchase Exposition has $15,000,000 in its treasury; is officially recognized by the government of the United States, and acts with its sanction and assent . . . we feel that rival contests in St. Louis and Chicago would be disastrous, and that Chicago should be willing to make any sacrifice to sustain the dignity of your honorable committee. Should you, therefore, in view of the attitude and invitation of St. Louis desire to transfer to that city the Olympian Games of 1904, Chicago would, in the best interests of the sports, cheerfully relinquish them. Lest, however, this suggestion should seem to qualify our appreciation of the great honor you have conferred upon us, and the deep desire of Chicago to carry out our program as prepared, we would earnestly recommend . . . that you postpone the celebration of the games until 1905, and hold them in this city, in that year. This, sir, is no precipitate advice. We have . . . deliberated, pondered, and consulted with leading citizens and representatives of every influential class. We understand most fully that a basic feature of the games is that they should be quadrennial and that an essential principal might be impaired by a delay. But after all, would not the success which would attend postponement, for which there certainly are precedents in ancient times, justify the step? Circumstances have arisen unexpected by both your committee and ourselves. We are in the presence of *vis major*. Should we then not strive to secure the largest possible results, by accommodating ourselves to the conditions which present themselves, even though a principle may be strained to some extent? The World's Fair at St. Louis is a national enterprise; and the honor of our government is in a sense involved in its success. To embarrass it

in any way would invite the disapproval of our people; whereas, a postponement of the games in a spirit of broadminded magnanimity would appeal to
our entire nation; and convert our present difficulties into a new and effica-
cious source of strength.[52]

Furber supplemented his official letter with a personal communication to Coubertin, as he said, "as friend to friend, placing you in possession of further facts which may assist your judgment in disposing of the
questions raised by our complications with St. Louis."[53] In this personal
letter, Furber used more direct language to make the same points he
made with his official correspondence.

> Now, my dear Baron, the difficulties which confront us are very serious. If we
> try to carry out our program in 1904, St. Louis will jeopardize our enterprise.
> She will prevent us from securing appropriations; will hamper us abroad, and
> will injure us in a thousand different ways. I will frankly say, although we
> never would desert you, that in the interest of the Games it would be better to
> accept the invitation of St. Louis and transfer the Games to that city, than to
> attempt to conduct them at Chicago in the face of the difficulties with which
> St. Louis would oppose us.[54]

Competition with St. Louis in 1904 was not an option for Henry
Furber. Practicality, patriotism, and political reality demanded recognition of the preeminence of the American centennial celebration of the
Louisiana Purchase as a great national event. The Olympic games could
be held in Chicago, just not in 1904. Furber went on to recommend a
solution to Coubertin.

> . . . my dear friend, I do not believe that this would be the wisest course
> (transferring the games to St. Louis). In my official letter I have suggested a
> postponement to 1905. If this plan should meet with your approval, I see the
> greatest possible success for us. We can conciliate St. Louis by vacating the
> field in 1904; and can secure from the states comprised in the Louisiana
> Purchase their assistance in securing appropriations and other governmental
> aid. Our yachting and naval display will bring us the support and patronage
> of our lake region. The western states can be won through the National
> Livestock Association by the equestrian and cavalry features of our program.
> To New England we appeal because of the scientific ends it is our purpose to
> subserve; and we are now in a position where by yielding the field to St. Louis

in 1904, we can enlist the goodwill of the Southern states as well; and gain in 1905 the undivided support of our entire country.[55]

Furber felt postponement was the logical reaction to St. Louis demands. Not only would postponement allow Chicago to honor the agreement with the International Olympic Committee to host the third Olympiad, but the strident attitude of St. Louis could be circumvented as well. Furber expressed his true feelings toward St. Louis in his letter to Coubertin.

> . . . I should regret to see St. Louis chosen. Besides my interest in Chicago and the Games themselves, I feel that St. Louis, although she has not been unfair in any way, has not been as considerate as she might have been. When she encroached upon our year, she should have abandoned sport. Instead of this she is by the adoption of a policy that surely is not generous, trying to seize upon our Games, for which your Committee once decided St. Louis was not the proper place . . . At least her attitude is flattering to our Games.[56]

Adherence to the founding principle of the quadrennial sequence of the games was the only reason not to postpone until 1905. Furber recognized that Coubertin would be reluctant to assume responsibility for deviating from the Olympic code. He suggested a way for the Baron to ease his conscience, explaining that by deferring to a presidential request, Coubertin would appear gracious and honorable.

> Should you now be inclined to favor a postponement; St. Louis will join Chicago in asking Mr. Roosevelt, President of the United States, to make the request of your Committee. Your dignity will thereby be sustained; and you will appear in a light before the entire world of granting a favor to a mighty nation, whose gratitude I am sure you would never undervalue.[57]

Finally, Furber specifically addressed the quadrennial cycle. The temporary sacrifice of an Olympic principle for the near term would be compensated for by the greater long-term benefits to Olympic prestige.

> I know that the quadrennial principle will be disturbed by such a course (postponement). But should not this be made to bend a little in view of the great objects to be gained? Ten years hence the success for which Chicago is now working, will mean more to you than the fact of having rigidly con-

formed to an unyielding principle, whose best protection in the future will be the prestige you gain through the Chicago Games.[58]

Furber's six-page letter, in a final attempt to persuade Coubertin of the wisdom of a postponement, offered one final comment, and concluded with a plea to common sense and an appeal to his vanity.

> A final point. We need not fear that St. Louis will anticipate our program, should we postpone until 1905. Her classification and her general scheme is radically different from ours; and she will do nothing that can harm us, unless we become her competitor in 1904.
>
> Such, Baron, are the complications which confront us; and I think I have made clear to you my views. We are in a position where we must use the highest of all human qualities, plain and honest common sense; and I assure you it is an inexpressible satisfaction that in a moment of such grave responsibility, we can turn to you whose confidence in our devotion we feel to be no less great, than is our reliance on your friendship and your wisdom.
>
> Awaiting an early cable message, in which we hope for at least an intimation of your personal views, even if you are not in a position so speedily to inform us as to the sentiment of your Committee. . .[59]

It was all up to the president of the International Olympic Committee, Pierre de Coubertin. In December 1902, pressures intensified from both Chicago and St. Louis partisans. Henri Merou, head of the French Consulate in Chicago and one of the original (since 1900) allies recruited to assist in promoting Chicago, publicly announced his opposition to a transfer to St. Louis. In a December 1 article in the *Chicago Record-Herald* Merou outlined four major reasons against St. Louis:

1. Limited sports facilities;
2. Games would be obscured by larger St. Louis Fair;
3. Languid climate in St. Louis during the summer months would have a negative impact on athletic performance, and might even discourage European athletes used to cooler weather from attending; and
4. Chicago had made a commitment to the International Olympic Committee and this should be honored.[60]

The next day Merou sent word to Coubertin that both he and President Harper of the University of Chicago strongly opposed a transfer to

St. Louis. Chicago should host the games as planned and ignore the demands of St. Louis. Further, Merou stated that Harper felt Furber was a weak leader and would be replaced. There is evidence to support this contention. In a letter dated November 5, 1902, Professor George E. Vincent, dean of the junior colleges at the University of Chicago and a member of the Chicago Organizing Committee, wrote to President Harper, "I have just received the letter from Mr. Furber, dated August 30. I have delayed in this matter of the committee because I got the impression from you that a re-organization was impending and that Mr. Furber was going to be relegated to the rear. If I am wrong in this impression please let me know at once, and I will go ahead promptly." Although Furber retained his position as president of the committee, there was considerable opposition within the Chicago Olympic community to his willingness to concede to St. Louis, if a postponement was not possible.[61]

There may have been mixed feelings in Chicago, but in St. Louis there was harmonious unity. St. Louis officials wanted the Olympic games transferred to their city, and they were determined to get them. At about the same time that Merou was contacting Coubertin, David Francis cabled Coubertin explaining the need for the games to be transferred to St. Louis. Francis also contacted Michael Lagrave, the French commissioner of commerce and the appointed commissioner general of the French exhibit planned for the St. Louis Exposition, requesting that he use his influence to convince Coubertin to approve the transfer. Lagrave obliged Francis. Coubertin was besieged from three camps at once: transfer the games to St. Louis, leave them in Chicago, and postpone them for a year. Furber must have thought that Coubertin would realize the advantages of a postponement, for on December 3, Coubertin received a cable from Furber requesting that if a postponement was decided upon, Coubertin should keep his decision private. This would allow Furber to relinquish 1904 to St. Louis in return for St. Louis pledges of support in 1905.[62] Coubertin anguished over his options, and kept silent.

Coubertin's silence prodded Furber to try another tactic. Victor Lawson owned and published two newspapers in Chicago, the *Daily News* and *Record-Herald*. Furber requested that Lawson instruct his Paris correspondent to contact Coubertin for information. A Paris Bureau reporter, Lamar Middleton, obeying instructions from Chicago, sent a message to Coubertin, "I understand that no action has been taken on a proposed transfer . . . and that you have decided to leave the matter in President Roosevelt's hands." The Baron was prompt with his reply to Middleton. The day after Middleton's inquiry, December 10, Coubertin responded, "The IOC will allow a transfer, but will never permit the suggested postponement. I have written to President Roosevelt to that effect . . . and I have nothing more to say on the subject." On December 15, Coubertin, without deciding the transfer question, informed Henry Furber that a postponement was not possible. Furber was disappointed that he had been unsuccessful in his efforts to convince the Baron to alter the quadrennial sequence of the Olympic games. On December 31, Furber wrote to Coubertin, expressing his disappointment: "Your letter of the 15th inst. has been received, and while regretting that you do not feel able to advise a postponement of the Games, I readily understand the embarrassment which that might place you under. We sincerely regret that circumstances have arisen so to disarrange our plans, but I do not know that I can add anything to my letters of the 26th ult."[63] Frustrated, Furber accepted reality: Chicago would not host the Olympic games in 1904 or 1905.

Meanwhile, back in Paris, newspaperman Lamar Middleton continued to press Coubertin for information. On December 20 Middleton sent another letter of inquiry to Coubertin: "I trust I have not annoyed you too much relative to the ultimate decision, from whatever source it comes, regarding the Olympian games. Since it is unavoidable that the Chicago press should occupy itself with the matter, and since untrue reports have been circulated there of late, Mr. Lawson . . . is desirous of printing the truth of the question as it now stands, and as, of course, you would like to have it stated."[64] Later, in the same letter, Middleton asked Coubertin to respond to four specific questions:

1. Will the International Committee eventually have a meeting and decide definitely as to the proposed change of the games from Chicago to St. Louis?
2. Before making this decision is the committee awaiting a response from President Roosevelt as to his opinions in the matter?
3. Will his reply be known in the United States possibly before it is received by you here in Paris?
4. What is the real opinion of the President of the International Committee regarding the proposed change?[65]

In St. Louis, speculation that President Roosevelt would ultimately decide the matter of the transfer gave cause for anticipatory success. Not only had the government of the United States appropriated funds for the St. Louis Exposition, but also the president's enthusiastic support of the Louisiana Purchase Exposition was well known. There was no doubt in the minds of St. Louis residents that Theodore Roosevelt would decide in their favor. The *St. Louis Republic* reported, "Roosevelt's part in the negotiations is explained by his great interests when the Olympic Games were assigned to Chicago and because of his position as the head of a government which is a heavy financial partner in the Exposition. The next advice on the subject, it is expected by the management, will come from Washington."[66] Roosevelt, ever the astute politician, realized his involvement was unnecessary. St. Louis officials, David Francis and Frederick Skiff, were forceful and determined negotiators. When Pierre de Coubertin refused to consider a postponement of the Olympics, and with the mixed feelings in Chicago, a transfer of the games to St. Louis seemed inevitable to many. Roosevelt never became involved in the dilemma.

In Paris, Coubertin had not responded to reporter Middleton's latest inquiries. Persistent, Middleton paid a visit to Coubertin at his home on the morning of December 22. After a brief conversation with the Baron, Middleton cabled Chicago, "The Baron is unwilling to admit that the entire matter has been left to President Roosevelt, though that is a well founded impression in Paris." The temerity of Middleton caused Coubertin to issue a brief and terse statement: "Because of the absence of many members' responses of the international committee we are awaiting several replies before making our final decision regarding the Olympian Games." Coubertin had written to members of the International Olympic Committee on December 21 outlining the transfer dilemma and presenting a positive case for both transferring to St. Louis and keeping the games in Chicago. He pointed out that only "by a weak majority" did the Chicago Committee favor a transfer and that most citizens of Chicago and the "totality of the student body" of the University of Chicago wanted the Olympic games to remain in their city. Coubertin concluded his letter to IOC members with, "Given the exclusive national character of the difference of opinion between the two cities and the necessity to promptly arrive at a resolution of this difference, I believe it is appropriate to rely on the judgement of President Roosevelt who wishes to demonstrate constant interest and who is very competent in all sport questions. I would be grateful to receive your opinion on this matter."[67]

Pierre de Coubertin deserves a great deal of respect and admiration for his primary role as founder and promoter of the modern Olympic games, but on the issue of the transfer of the 1904 Olympic games he must be held accountable for his deceptive behavior and statements. Coubertin had not written to President Roosevelt regarding the transfer dilemma, as he stated to journalist Lamar Middleton. Roosevelt was not involved in the decision-making process as Coubertin implied in his letter to members of the International Olympic Committee, and twenty-nine years after the fact, Coubertin wrote in his memoirs, "I wrote unofficially to ask President Roosevelt to decide the matter. As I had expected, he opted in favor of the transfer."[68] There is absolutely no historical evidence to corroborate these statements.

After Coubertin made his statement that the transfer question would be settled after he received responses from members of the Olympic Committee, Lamar Middleton sent word to Chicago that he had contacted twenty-one members of Coubertin's committee and all were opposed to transferring the games to St. Louis. The Baron later claimed in his memoirs that he received, ". . . mainly favorable messages from my colleagues (14 in favor, 2 against, 5 abstentions)." While Middleton's survey of the views of members of the committee cannot be substantiated, there are seven surviving responses to Coubertin's letter. All seven defer to "letting Roosevelt decide," but otherwise oppose the transfer to St. Louis.[69]

For Coubertin, a postponement of the games was out of the question, leaving the games in Chicago was undesirable, and a transfer to St. Louis was distasteful. As the Baron pondered the dilemma, a compromise solution came to mind. Chicago and St. Louis were in close proximity to one another in the midwestern area of the United States. Perhaps the Olympic games could be part of the St. Louis Exposition, but take place in Chicago, "a sort of athletic annex to the St. Louis Exposition."[70] The thought died a quick death. Just as well; St. Louis would never have agreed to such a proposal.

Henry Furber, dismayed with Coubertin's refusal to consider a postponement, cabled Coubertin one more time, on Christmas Eve, 1902, asking for instructions.[71] Furber wanted a resolution of the matter. Members of the Chicago Olympic Organizing Committee, especially Furber, had expended much time and energy preparing for the day when the Olympic games would come to Chicago. The city was in a state of suspension. Only a year and a half remained before the Olympics were to take place; a decision had to be made, and the sooner the better. Coubertin did not reply to Furber's cable. January came and went, and still Coubertin dallied. After the short-lived "athletic annex" idea, Coubertin pondered his options. Chicago's resolve for the games, once a postponement was rejected, was seriously in question, as was the financial capability of Chicago to assure success. Still, Coubertin had fond memories of his visit to the Windy City. St. Louis, on the other hand, conjured only negative impressions. During his trip to America in 1893 Coubertin had visited several American cities. Chicago, San Francisco, and New Orleans all received high praise from Coubertin. He was not so favorably disposed toward St. Louis. Commenting upon his impressions of the city, the disappointed romantic wrote, "I harbored great resentment against the town for the disillusionment caused by my first sight of the junction of the Missouri and Mississippi Rivers. After reading Fenimore Cooper, what had I not been led to expect of the setting where those two great rivers with their strange resounding names actually met! But there was no beauty, nor originality. I had a sort of presentiment that the Olympiad would match the mediocrity of the town."[72]

Coubertin continued to deliberate. Slowly, pragmatism began to sway the Baron toward St. Louis. As the Olympic host city for 1904, St. Louis offered several positive assets. The officials of the Exposition were eager to host the Olympic games, were financially secure, promised new athletic facilities, and had already developed the organizational structure to administer the games. The Louisiana Purchase Exposition was to be an international extravaganza, hosting an international sports festival. The American public and the president of the United States enthusiastically supported the efforts of St. Louis, and the best athletes from around the world would participate in the St. Louis Olympics. Coubertin had only to dismiss his initial unfavorable impressions of St. Louis from a visit made nine years before, and to address the four major objections that opponents of a transfer had raised. St. Louis officials had the financial resources and promised that state-of-the-art sport facilities would be provided for Olympic competition. While the Paris World's Fair had suffocated the Olympics of 1900, St. Louis officials sought to highlight the Olympics of 1904. The summer weather in St. Louis, while humid, would be the same for all competitors, and would not lower performance levels. The argument that Chicago and the International Olympic Committee had made commitments to one another that should be honored failed to recognize that circumstances had changed, and commitments made sixteen months before needed to be reevaluated.

Finally, Furber received a curt two-word cablegram from Coubertin on February 10, 1903: "Transfer accepted." Furber was equally strident and direct with his reply two days later: "Instructions just received will transfer accordingly."[73] The dreams of Henry Furber were at an end. Two and a half years of effort, including a four-month Olympic promotional tour of Europe by Furber and two committee members, facility planning, expenditure of funds, extensive committee organization involving numerous prominent citizens of Chicago, and even the publication of an Olympic pamphlet, all were set aside by the succinct message from the president of the International Olympic Committee.

Protocol demanded communication in greater detail be made with the entire Chicago Organizing Committee. Coubertin met his obligation the day after sending his brief note to Furber. On February 11, 1903, Coubertin sent the following message to the Chicago Committee.

> Gentlemen:
> The telegram which I sent yesterday I wish to complement by a few words in that you may understand how we had to wait for the answers from members of our committee before we could say what the decision of the committee was about the proposed transfer of the games of 1904 from Chicago to St. Louis. I am directed by the committee to say that while regretting that such a transfer should have been necessary as we are bound by the fundamental laws of our constitution not to allow any change in dates of the Olympiads we consider that there was no room for another solution and we do not wish to place your committee in a position of acknowledged antagonism with the authority of the Louisiana Purchase Exposition. Thanking you, gentlemen, for the efforts you were ready to make in order to celebrate the opening of the third Olympiad of the modern period in a way worthy of your great city as well as of our institution.[74]

America's awareness of the Olympic games had been confined to a narrow corridor of the northeastern United States in 1896, and had only expanded to the Midwest with the Paris games of 1900. The awarding of the Olympics to Chicago in 1901 had increased interest in the games still further, but the newspaper reporting of the transfer controversy between Chicago and St. Louis raised awareness of the Olympics to new heights. From late October 1902, when news of the contest between Chicago and St. Louis for the games first surfaced, until the official proclamation transferring the Olympics to St. Louis was made by Coubertin on February 10, 1903, the American public, from coast to coast, was fed a steady diet of Olympic news.[75] The transfer controversy whetted the appetite of the American public for Olympic news, but newspapers did not restrict their information to the competition between the two cities. The history of the modern games and their link to the heritage of classical Greece was also told. Americans were informed of the prestige and honor conveyed to their country as host to the 1904 Olympic games. Photographs of Pierre de Coubertin were published. Americans were receiving a first-rate education on Olympic matters. Newspaper coverage of the Olympics would be continuous. After the transfer question had been settled, newspapers turned their attention to St. Louis Olympic plans and speculation as to who would be selected as the director to lead America's efforts to host the 1904 Olympics and, finally, the events of the Louisiana Purchase Exposition and the Olympic games themselves were reported to an American public eager to consume Olympic news.

The Ghost of Plato

The Alpheus River flows beside a broad meadow just outside the small village of Olympia in the southwest region of modern Greece. Here the ancient Olympic games took place to honor Zeus, the supreme god of the ancient deities. Coroebus, a resident of Elis, the Greek province in which Olympia lies, was crowned with a wreath of wild olive for his victory in the stade footrace (approximately 220 yards) in the year 776 BCE.[1] There are no records of earlier Olympic champions, but archaeologists have dated the Temple of Hera on the grounds of ancient Olympia as having been constructed several centuries before Coroebus. The mist of legend and myth shrouds the deeds of the earliest Olympic athletes.

The ancient Olympic games were a staple of Greek society, and in 146 BCE, when Rome conquered Greece, the games continued under Roman rule. It was not until 394 CE, more than five hundred years later, after Christianity was officially sanctioned as the state religion of the Roman world, that the pagan Olympic games were terminated. The Christian emperor of Rome, Theodosius, issued the proclamation prohibiting the

Greek Olympic games after more than a thousand years of existence spanning the two classical civilizations.

The Olympic and Greek spirit lay dormant for centuries. Greece slept as Roman power slowly eroded, split into east and west, and the eastern empire evolved into the Byzantine Empire. Greece remained in the shadows of the dominant Byzantine culture for the next thousand years, only to be submerged once again when the Ottoman Turks conquered Byzantium and Greece in 1453. The world had forgotten Greece and the Olympic games.

During the middle of the eighteenth century the world witnessed a revival of interest in ancient civilizations. The discovery of the ancient Roman cities Pompeii and Herculaneum, buried intact under the volcanic ash of Mount Vesuvius in 79 CE, unearthed relics of art and architecture and inspired scholars to study the ancients. The new science of archaeology provided a scientific approach to the study of antiquities. Johann J. Winckelmann, the father of classical archaeology, published histories of Roman and Greek art, contributing to the intellectual movement known as neoclassicism. The more specific Greek revival originated with two Englishmen, James Stuart (1713–1788) and Nicholas Revett (1720–1804). They traveled to Greece to record measurements and produce drawings of classical Greek buildings, the Parthenon and Erechtheum in particular, and published *Antiquities of Athens* (London, 1762).[2] Their work and publication provided the impetus for the *gusto Greco*, an enthusiasm for all things Greek. In literature this enthusiasm for Greece became a theme of the Romantic poets, best exemplified by the English poets: John Keats (1795–1821), Percy Shelley (1792–1822), and George Gordon, Lord Byron (1788–1824). Keats published the poems "Hymn to Apollo" (1815), "Ode to Apollo" (1815), and "Ode on a Grecian Urn" (1818). Shelley composed "On the Manners of the Ancient Greeks" (1818), and his poem "Hellas" (1822) was inspired by the political movement for Greek independence. But Lord Byron's infatuation with Greece was without bounds. He traveled extensively between 1809 and 1811, including several sojourns to Greece, composed the poem "Maid of Athens," swam the Hellespont, and became obsessed with political independence for Greece from the Ottoman Turk empire. His obsession exceeded the realms of Romantic literature and travel in January of 1824 when Byron returned to Greece, formed a military unit called Byron's Brigade, and made plans to conduct a military campaign to free Greece from the despotic rule of the Turks. He did not live to achieve military glory. In April 1824, only four months after landing in Greece, Byron contracted a fever and died before ever engaging the enemy in battle.[3]

Greek independence, achieved largely with the assistance of England, France, and Russia, was realized in 1829 with the signing of the Treaty of Adrianople, ending two thousand years of subservience. French archaeological teams conducted the first excavations at Olympia in the same year. Classical Greece and the site of the ancient Olympic games were exposed to the modern world. During the War of Independence (1821–1829) a young Greek poet of the Romantic school, Panagiotis Soutsos (1806–1868), became a passionate patriot for the cause of freedom. Born in Constantinople but moving to the new Greek capital city of Nafplion in 1833, he began publishing a newspaper called *Helios,* the Greek word for sun. The modern Greeks were a poor and disorganized country in 1829. The first years of independence were chaotic due to external pressure and internal strife. The first president of modern Greece was elected in 1827 and assassinated in 1831. The allies, England, France, and Russia, decided political stability required the establishment of a monarchy and installed a German prince as King Otto II in 1833.[4] The arrival of Otto in Greece precipitated the move of Soutsos to Nafplion.

Soutsos immediately began publishing his newspaper promoting the cause of Greek unity and culture. He was not so much interested in having Greece join the circle of contemporary nations of nineteenth-century Europe, but instead sought to restore the glory of ancient Greece as a foundation upon which to build modern Greek pride and patriotism. An awareness and appreciation for the ancient culture, including art, sculpture, architecture, poetry, history, and sport, was essential in the mind of Soutsos if modern Greece was to succeed as an independent nation. Soutsos fervently admired his ancient ancestors and the civilization they had created. He often wandered about the ancient ruins of his homeland imagining conversations with the spirits of ancient Greek heroes. Just such an encounter manifested itself during a dream when the ghost of Plato appeared to Soutsos and provided the inspiration to compose the poem "Dialogue of the Dead" (1833). It is primarily a patriotic poem celebrating the recent independence of Greece from Turkish rule, but Plato is not impressed with the new Greece. Political independence did not restore the glory of the ancient culture. During the dialogue Plato asks the question, "Your great festivals, your great theaters, the marble statues, where are they?" Finally Plato asks, "Where are your Olympic Games?"[5] It is a rhetorical question, but it is the genesis of the rebirth of the Olympic idea. A second poem by Soutsos, "Ruins of Sparta," was published later in the same year. In this poem the ghost of Leonidas, the greatest military hero of classical Greece, appears among the ruins of his homeland and speaks to modern Greece.

> You have matched us ancients in bravery of battle.
> Now match the old times in education and culture too.
> Bring back to your land the days of Miltiades and Themistocles.
> Bring back the glorious days of Pericles for this rebirth . . .
> And let the only contests that you have be those national games,
> the Olympics, to which the olive branch once summoned the sons of
>   Greece in ancient times.[6]

Panagiotis Soutsos, the twenty-seven-year-old newspaper publisher, Romantic poet, and Greek patriot, had resurrected the Olympic spirit from the ancient ruins of Olympia. The year 1833 marks the beginning of the idea for an Olympic revival, but the idea is only an admonition from the two poetic ghosts of Plato and Leonidas. Soutsos, however, did not allow the Olympic idea to remain merely a poetic suggestion. Two years later, in 1835, Soutsos gave substance to the Olympic idea in the form of a proposal sent to the minister of the interior, Iannis Kolletis. Soutsos proposed that March 25, Greek Independence Day, be made a national holiday and that the Olympic games be part of the annual national celebration. Specifically, the proposal established a four-year rotational format for the games among the cities of Athens, Tripolis, Mesolongion, and the island of Hydra. This was a reflection of the ancient quadrennial cycle of Olympian, Pythian, Isthmian, and Nemean games. The four new stadiums and hippodromes were to be six hundred and twelve hundred feet in length, respectively, as were the ancient facilities. Each Olympic site was to have a throne for the modern king to view the athletic competition and special seating for judges and government officials. Marble pillars were to be constructed with the names of the heroes of the recent War of Independence inscribed upon them. A portico at each site would provide for works of art to be displayed and a theater to host drama contests. Each political subdivision of Greece would send, besides athletes and other competitors, two choirs, one of twenty-four men and one of twenty-four women, to provide musical performances. Cash prizes of varying amounts were to be awarded to the victors in the various competitive categories of philosophy, literature, painting, sculpture, and athletics. Soutsos reserved the highest monetary award of ten thousand drachmas for philosophy, while the winners of the foot races would receive the lowest award of two thousand drachmas. The Olympic festival, commencing on Independence Day, March 25, was to last for more than a week. Soutsos later remarked on his Olympic intentions, "I had in mind, besides these athletic games, the exhibition of agricultural goods and tools, along with industrial products, and to award prizes for poetry and the writing of history."[7]

The minister of the interior, Kolletis, approved the Soutsos proposals and officially recommended them to King Otto. A year later, in 1836, Kolletis was replaced as minister. The new minister of the interior, Rhodartos, approved March 25 as a national holiday, but ignored the Olympic revival part of the Soutsos proposal. Soutsos was not alone among Greeks desiring to reestablish the Olympic games, however. In 1838 the citizens of Letrini, a small town near ancient Olympia in the district of Elis, voted to adopt a resolution to revive the Olympics, "those noble games which were held every four years in ancient Elis." The document, signed by the village secretary, states that the games were to be called the Letrinian Games and celebrated on the national holiday of March 25 each year, "wishing to recall those noble times and wanting to make glorious the current celebration of the rebirth of Greece." These were noble intentions, but there is no evidence that the grand plans of the Letrinians were ever put into practice. However, the Olympic idea survived. One of the committee members of Letrini, Pavlos Giannopoulos, later became the vice president of the 1875 Athens Olympic Organizing Committee.[8]

Soutsos renewed his Olympian efforts in 1842 with another plea to revive the ancient games. In that year he composed another lyric poem, this time featuring Georgios Karaiskakis, a modern Greek hero of the recent revolution. His plea occurs not in the poem itself, but in the dedication to King Otto preceding the poem.

And so I appropriately dedicate this poem to you, my king! A poem that celebrates the Greek struggle, since you have revealed by royal decree that every year on the 25th of March there will take place a universal festival to memorialize the resurrection of the Greek nation. And may it be at this annual assembly . . . there may be held the ancient games of Olympia! And in this gathering of an inspired race may there be crowned the new Pindars, the new Herodotuses of Greece![9]

Three years later, Soutsos, before a crowd of fifteen thousand at the tomb of Karaiskakis in Athens, delivered a speech, again calling for an Olympic revival. Still later, in 1851, Soutsos once more reiterated his call for re-creating the Olympic games of antiquity. "England has made its influence known on two hemispheres through its industrial expositions. Greece happens to have no power for that competition. But if Greece would re-establish the Olympic Games, . . . on every 25 March . . . then the peoples of the world would respect Greece."[10]

After independence Greece was a poor nation struggling to provide political and economic stability for her citizens. While King Otto was at least receptive to the Olympic idea, there were many government officials who felt Greece could not afford to spend time and money on what was perceived as a romantic and impractical proposal to resurrect an event from classical times. Eighteen years had elapsed since Plato's apparition had inspired Panagiotis Soutsos to poetically challenge modern Greece to revive the ancient Olympics, and still the games remained only a dream in the mind of the dedicated poet. Throughout the years, all the eloquence of Soutsos had failed to produce any tangible results.

Early in 1856 King Otto received a letter from one Evangelis Zappas, a wealthy Greek businessman living in Bucharest, Romania. Born in northwestern Greece in 1800, Zappas began a military career as a mercenary soldier in the Ottoman Turk army of Ali Pasha, later joining his countrymen in the Greek War of Independence. During the conflict Zappas became the aide-de-camp and close personal friend of the renowned Markos Botsaris. In 1831 Zappas migrated to Romania and made a fortune in land and agriculture. Investing in the Greek shipping industry brought more riches, and by the 1850s he had become one of the wealthiest men in eastern Europe. Zappas sent his letter to the king through regular diplomatic channels. The Greek ambassador to Romania,

S. Skoufos, read the letter's contents and forwarded it from Bucharest to Athens. In his letter Zappas magnanimously offered to fund the entire cost of permanently reviving the ancient Olympic games, including cash prizes for the victors. The Zappas proposal, minus the funding offer, sounded familiar, and indeed, was strikingly similar to the earlier proposals of Soutsos. In fact, Zappas was inspired by Soutsos. Zappas, like Soutsos, revered the classical traditions and ancient heroes of Greece and, after reading the poems of Soutsos, decided to take action. Zappas proposed that the Olympic games be held the very next year, 1857. Since the letter of proposal was from Romania, King Otto gave the letter to his foreign minister, Alexandros Rangavis, for review and action. Rangavis, Soutsos's cousin, was also a poet and a classics professor, but he did not share his cousin's Romantic view of classical Greece. Rangavis did not believe that athletics were a worthwhile activity in the modern world, but were a regression to the primitive times of antiquity. Several months went by without a reply from Rangavis. Ambassador Skoufos, acting on behalf of Zappas, sent a follow-up letter on June 6, 1856, to Rangavis requesting a response and proposing the first revival of the Olympic games take place the following March 25, and reiterated that all expenses, including the construction of a new Olympic building for Greek art and industry exhibits, and a museum for antiquities, would be paid by Zappas. Rangavis replied promptly, bestowing military honors on Zappas for his part in the War of Independence and thanking him for his splendid idea, but stated "that times have changed since antiquity. Today nations do not become distinguished, as then, by having the best athletes and runners, but the champions in industry, handiwork, and agriculture."[11] Rangavis concluded his letter by suggesting that Zappas abandon athletics and concentrate on founding "industrial Olympic games."

Zappas's reply was courteous, but steadfast. After expressing his admiration for Rangavis and agreeing that industrial exhibits be part of the program, Zappas insisted that athletics be the prominent feature of the revived Greek Olympic games and that Panagiotis Soutsos and his brother, Alexandros, be appointed members of the Olympic Organizing Committee. He also included a personal check for a large sum of money (two thousand Austrian florins) made out to Rangavis to pay for the first of the modestly called "Olympiads of Zappas."[12]

Rangavis remained reluctant to accept athletics and informed Zappas that his date of March 25, 1857, for the first revival was impossible. Zappas accepted a postponement to 1858 and then still another delay until 1859. Zappas was not silent during this period, conducting a methodical correspondence urging the Olympic revival with Greek government officials including Rangavis. After giving money for an industrial building, Zappas proposed that the ancient stadium in Athens be restored for athletic competition. He asked Rangavis to obtain the services of the best architects to develop plans and to send the cost estimates to him. Rangavis, in an attempt to dissuade Zappas from his Olympic plans, sent an exorbitant cost estimate (1.2 million drachmas) to Zappas. To his surprise and chagrin, Zappas "accepted this expense if it were necessary."[13]

The generosity and persistence of Zappas finally produced Olympic results. On August 19, 1858, a royal proclamation was issued establishing the Greek Olympic games. The decree stated that "National Contests" would be held every four years in Athens and be called "Olympics." The first Olympiad was scheduled for the four Sundays in October 1859. Both Zappas and, previously, Soutsos had proposed an annual Olympics to be part of the great national holiday celebration of independence on March 25. The quadrennial sequence mirrors the ancient Olympics, but four Sundays in October was a novel deviation from the Zappas and Soutsos proposals, and the origin of the idea is unknown. The first Sunday was reserved for the opening religious service, to be followed by academic competition in lectures and books. The second Sunday was devoted to contests in animal husbandry, including horse racing. Agricultural contests were scheduled for the morning of the third Sunday, with the athletic events taking place in the afternoon. The proclamation read, ". . . in the afternoon, solemn, public athletic games in the stadium, which will be fittingly prepared for the event. There will be money prizes ranging from 50 to 100 drachmas, and olive crowns." The restored ancient stadium was to be the site of the athletic contests, as requested by Zappas. The last Sunday of the Olympics scheduled the awarding of prizes in the industrial competitions and concluded with the performance of a new Greek drama specially prepared for the occasion. The proclamation further specified that in addition to prizes of cash and olive crowns, medals (gold, silver, and bronze) were to be awarded the victors. The medals were to bear the bust of King Otto on the obverse with the legend, "Founder of the Olympics." The reverse was to read, "First (or Second, or Third) Place Olympic Crown, Evangelis Zappas, Sponsor of the Games."[14]

Soutsos, twenty-five years after he conceived the idea, published the full text of the royal proclamation establishing the Greek Olympic games and acknowledged the man responsible for converting his dream into reality. "All the newspapers of Greece have praised Zappas with one voice . . . because of his lavish philanthropy." Previously, Soutsos had written that once the Olympics were established the name of Zappas should be ranked among the ancient heroes of Greece, "beside the names of the Herakleses and the Theseuses, the founders of the (ancient) Olympics and Panathenaics."[15]

News of the Olympic revival and proclamation spread throughout Europe during the autumn of 1858, reaching England on October 6. On that date an article appeared in a Shropshire newspaper, *Eddowes's Shrewsbury Journal.* It was a brief but ultimately portentous announcement for the Olympic movement:

> A correspondent writing from Athens under the date September 4 says, "the Queen Regent has just signed a royal decree for the re-establishment of the Olympic Games, after being discontinued for nearly 1,550 years. They are to be held in Athens, in the ancient Stadium, which is still in a very perfect state of preservation . . . and are to take place in October, every fourth year, commencing in 1859. The Games are to include horseraces, wrestling, throwing quoits and other athletic sports."[16]

The design of the medals and the role of Zappas in the Olympic revival were also included in the article.

In the small town of Much Wenlock, Shropshire, in northwest England, the town's leading citizen, Dr. William Penny Brookes (1809–1895), read the Olympic announcement with avid interest. His medical career allowed Dr. Brookes to care for the health needs of his fellow citizens and neighbors, but as a young doctor, in 1840 he organized the Much Wenlock Agricultural Reading Society (WARS) to encourage local farmers and the working class to learn to read and improve their minds. He provided books and a public reading room for this purpose. Ten years later, Brookes, a member of the English Romantic movement and a scholar of antiquity with a special interest in the ancient Olympic games, expanded the reading society to include physical exercise and athletic contests to improve the physical development of the working classes.[17] This emphasis on the working classes had a later impact on the development of the concept of amateurism, a term not yet in existence. Admiring the ancient Greek Olympics, Brookes attached the term "Olympian" to his new enterprise. The purpose of the Wenlock Olympics was clearly stated in the minutes of the founding meeting of February 25, 1850:

> . . . desirable that a class should be established . . . for the moral, physical, and intellectual improvement of the inhabitants of the town . . . of Wenlock and especially of the working classes, by encouragement of out-door recreation, and by the award of prizes annually at public meetings for skill in athletic exercises and proficiency in intellectual and industrial attainments. That this section of the Wenlock Agricultural Reading Society be called *The Olympian Class.*[18]

The first Wenlock Olympic games took place October 22–23, 1850. Opening and closing ceremonies were part of these initial Olympics. There was a parade of athletes and organizing committee members to the athletic field, led by the "Wenlock band and six flags," prior to the commencement of athletic competition. The athletic program included nine events. Three were strictly English activities; cricket, football (soccer), and quoits (similar to horseshoes with round disks with a hole in the center). The other nine events were track and field sports imitating the ancient Olympics (modern track and field in 1850 was only in the embryonic stage of development). There was a high jump, long jump, and three footraces for three age divisions (adult, under fourteen, and under seven). The one final event was a fifty-yard hopping-on-one-leg race. After the competition on the final day, the band and "two young victors in the footrace, borne on the shoulders of two tall men, and their brows encircled with their laurel crowns"[19] led everyone, including spectators, in a parade from the athletic field back to town.

The Wenlock games were initiated as annual athletic contests for the sole benefit of the local citizens of Much Wenlock. While Brookes did not intend to revive the ancient Olympic games, his contribution to the Olympic idea is significant. Brookes was the first to form an organization, inspired by the Olympics of antiquity, to conduct athletic contests using the term "Olympics," and establishing much of the pageantry later adopted for the modern Olympic games. The Wenlock Olympics provided the model and the foundation for the later Olympic movement. During the course of his long life, Brookes worked tirelessly to expand and promote the Olympic idea, dying at the age of eighty-six in 1895, the year before the first modern Olympic games in Athens.

The Wenlock Olympics were eight years old when Brookes read the article announcing the Zappas revival of the ancient Games in Greece. Brookes cut out the newspaper article, pasted it in his scrapbook, and immediately became involved in the Greek Olympic efforts. He wrote to the British ambassador in Athens, Sir Thomas Wyse, informing him of his own Olympic games and his interests in the Greek Olympics. Wyse wrote back asking Brookes what events should be included on the Athens program. On December 23, 1858, Brookes sent a list of the athletic events of the 1858 Wenlock Olympic games to Wyse, suggesting the Greeks adopt his program of events. Wyse thanked Brookes for his suggestions in a letter of February 10, 1859, but explained that while the Greek Olympics were going to have athletic competitions, agricultural and industrial contests were to highlight the games. The extensive athletic program suggested by Brookes was too ambitious. Brookes, ever the optimist, continued to assume that his program of events would be implemented. He even sent prize money (ten pounds sterling) to be awarded the victor in an event he had just initiated in the 1858 Wenlock Olympics called "tilting at the ring." This event, borrowed from the medieval jousting tournament, required a mounted horseman with lance to charge at a small metal ring suspended from a frame. The objective was to insert the lance through the ring, removing it from the frame while keeping the ring on the lance. This event became the featured attraction of subsequent Wenlock Olympic games and in later years was considered by Brookes to be their trademark. From October 1858 to September 1859, Brookes, using appropriate diplomatic channels, persistently wrote to Ambassador Wyse offering recommendations for the Greek Olympics, all without a single request for such assistance from the Greeks. The Greek committee did accept the ten pounds sterling forwarded by Ambassador Wyse, but never implemented the tilting at the ring event, instead awarding the prize money to the victor of the distance race (just under a mile).[20] While the influence of Brookes on the Greek Olympics of 1859 was minimal, the importance of his attempted involvement is vitally significant to the modern Olympic movement. The Greek Olympic games not only had a profound impact on the development and expansion of the Wenlock Olympics in England but also introduced the concept of internationalism to Brookes, which he bequeathed to the future Olympic movement.

The Greek Olympic games of 1859 were only moderately successful. King Otto and Queen Amalia attended the opening ceremonies held on October 18. Panagiotis Soutsos, his Olympic dream finally realized, published an account of the day's events, paying tribute once again to the man responsible for the Olympic revival. "Glory and honor to Evangelis Zappas, designer of grand plans. He waited and waited, and finally he brought to reality my idea, which was called 'poetic.' . . . Here is a man who brought to fruition what the whole nation ought to have done." Competition began the following week. Chariot races were held as in classical times, with authentic results—four of the six chariots crashed. Ambassador Wyse, informing Brookes in England, reported that Christos Vassiliou of Bulgaria survived the ordeal and was crowned the victor. The athletic events consisted of footraces at three distances, three jumping events, two types of discus throws, two javelin throws, and a pole climb. Prize money of fifty or one hundred drachmas was awarded the winner of each event. The royal proclamation had stipulated that the ancient stadium in Athens be restored and serve as the site for these events. Zappas had provided the funds (1.2 million drachmas) for the restoration, but the foreign minister, Rangavis, still antagonistic to athletics, refused to even purchase the property on which the stadium remained. He claimed the private owner required too much money. Instead, Rangavis used the Zappas funds to excavate the famous theater of Dionysus at the base of the Acropolis. Deprived of the ancient stadium, the athletic events were held on November 15, 1859, at a city square on the northwest edge of Athens. Then called Plateia Loudovikou, today the square is known as Koumoundourou. The king and queen were in attendance to witness the competition among athletes from all over the Greek-speaking world. Athletes came from as far away as Turkey, Crete, Cyprus, and Albania. The weather, cold and windy, was not the best, but a large crowd encircled the square to watch the athletic contests. Unfortunately, only a few spectators had a good view of the events due to the level spectator area. Negative reviews by the local press were reported of this first of the Zappas Olympics. They complained about the ineptness of the organizing committee and the failure to restore the ancient stadium as the site for the athletic contests, which would have provided for many more spectators. While the press generally considered them a failure, the greater significance of the Greek Olympics of 1859 lies not in their fulfillment of a poet's dream, but in the influence they, and the subsequent Zappas Greek Olympics of 1870 and 1875, had on Brookes in England.[21] These games profoundly altered the Olympic view and provided the inspiration for Brookes to conceive the international Olympic movement that in time gave birth to the modern Olympic games.

Even before the Athens games commenced in November, Brookes, inspired by news of the revival, greatly expanded his own Olympic games in July 1859. He increased the number of athletic events and imitated the Greek games by adding the javelin throw. Prizes were awarded for the best essay on physical education, and, recalling Pindar, poet of the ancient Olympics, Brookes established a prize for the best poem on the Wenlock Olympics. The pageantry and ceremonies were greatly expanded as reflected by an article entitled "the Wenlock Olympic Games" in the *Shrewsbury Chronicle:* "Gay banners, beautiful flowers, festoons, colours, and every imaginable token of festivity was there to greet us." Brookes closed his Olympic festival with these words: "Such meetings as these bring out free minds, free opinions, free enterprises, free competition for every man in every grade of life. These Olympic Games bring together different classes, and make them sociable and neighbourly."[22] Here is the genesis of the later Olympic creed of promoting mutual respect, understanding, and international goodwill among the different races and nations of the world.

In 1860 Brookes, still inspired by the previous November Greek Olympics, sought to enlarge the scope of his Olympics from the local to regional level. On May 3, the Wenlock Olympic Committee officially approved Brookes's proposal, "Resolved that it was desirable that annual Meetings for Olympian Games for the whole county, to be called 'The Shropshire Olympian Games,' should be held in rotation in the following Boroughs and other large towns: Shrewsbury, Ludlow, Oswestry, Bridgenorth, Wenlock, Wellington."[23]

The first Shropshire Olympics were held in conjunction with the eleventh annual Wenlock Olympian games in 1860. The revival of the Greek Olympics had a dramatic impact on Brookes, which was reflected in the program and pageantry of these expanded regional Olympics in England. Greek mottoes were displayed on many of the banners during the parades, and the Wenlock Olympic medal featured Nike, the Greek goddess of victory, surrounded by a quotation by Pindar, the Greek poet of the ancient Olympics.[24]

The beginnings of an international Olympic movement occurred on May 2, 1861, when Theocharis, president of the Greek Olympic Committee, wrote to Brookes expressing the mutual influence and cooperation of the English and Greek movements upon one another.

> [The Greek Olympic committee] is happy to have found in the same nation which has so many claims to our profound gratitude, a sister institution of the same name, so nobly announced by the benevolent cooperation which it [the Wenlock committee] has lent its [the Greek committee's] work from the start, and the generous expressions for Greece which it [the Wenlock committee] has incorporated in its own program.
>
> The Olympic Committee of Athens, being very grateful for all its acts of good will, sends its most cordial greetings to its esteemed sister committee, and expresses its wishes for the progress of the Wenlock Olympics and the achievement of the civilizing aims which unite [our two committees] in the same course.[25]

Two Englishmen, Charles Melly and John Hulley, formed the Liverpool Athletic Club in 1862. They espoused the philosophy of muscular Christianity, which was the belief that the development of the body enhances intellectual and spiritual growth. They adopted the Latin phrase *mens sana in corpore sano* (a sound mind in a sound body) and stated that the club's purpose was "the encouragement of Physical Education." Hulley was a close friend of Brookes, and, undoubtedly influenced by the Wenlock Olympics, the two founders decided that the Liverpool Athletic Club would also sponsor Olympic games. The athletic events included footraces and hurdles at various distances, high jump, triple jump, discus throw, pole vault, fencing, wrestling, and gymnastics. Contrary to the Wenlock Olympics, which were for the benefit of the working classes, the Liverpool Olympics were exclusively reserved for the "gentlemen Amateurs" of England. The working classes, considered professionals, were excluded from competition.[26]

The first Liverpool Olympics were conducted on June 14, 1862. In autumn of the same year Brookes staged the third Shropshire Olympics in conjunction with the thirteenth Wenlock Olympian games. During the course of his annual Olympic speech, Brookes, supporting the mission of the Liverpool Olympics, stressed the importance of physical education in the defense of the nation:

> Why not direct our attention to the physical improvement of those who are to constitute the living defenders of our freedom? I feel sure that the introduction of a system of gymnastic training into our national schools . . . would be a national good, would be the means of raising up . . . a race of healthy, active, vigorous youths, a noble, manly race, whose reputation for pluck, bodily power, and endurance, would inspire far more terror on the battlefield than the arms they bore."[27]

The movement to incorporate compulsory physical education in English schools played an important role in the history of the Olympic games. It was this concept of improving the national character through physical fitness that brought the Frenchman, Pierre de Coubertin, to England, where he met Brookes and was exposed to the Olympic movement.

The Liverpool Olympics of 1863 were the first to attempt to become international. Newspaper announcements proclaimed that "Gentleman Amateurs of all nations" were invited to compete in Liverpool on June 14.[28] It was a grand idea, but outside of England there were no "Gentleman Amateurs," so only Englishmen competed. A year later the Liverpool Olympics gave occasion for the *Liverpool Mercury* to praise the Olympic tradition.

> We hope that these attempts to revive the games of the Olympiad will not alarm the fearful and timid. . . . Ancient Greece . . . owed nearly all her wondrous skill in the art of life to her grand combined physical and mental education. . . . How striking does this revival of the Olympic Games illustrate the proverb "There is nothing new under the sun." . . . Now, after a lapse of two thousand years, we find the men of Liverpool entering the lists and competing in the very same games, which, in her prosperity, attracted the chivalry and the beauty of Greece and made the stadium ring with shouts of exultant joy.

It was a gratifying reflection . . . to consider that these men had come together—many of them long distances—not in the sordid hope of winning so much money, but, as in old Grecian times, simply for the honour which rewards success. . . . Indeed, the most ardent admirer of muscular development could have wished for no more earnest and unanimous public testimony to the worth of the cause. It was a scene to recall the romantic days of ancient chivalry."[29]

The Olympic revival movement achieved a milestone with the formation of the National Olympian Association (England) in November 1865. A modern sports facility, the Liverpool Gymnasium, was constructed under the watchful eyes of Hulley and Melly. Prominent guests were invited for the opening celebration. Brookes and E. G. Ravenstein, president of the German Gymnastic Society in London, were among those in attendance. During the course of conversation, Hulley, Brookes, and Ravenstein decided a national organization was needed to stage a national Olympic games, promote the national Olympic movement, and coordinate the various Olympic societies that had recently organized in England: Lancaster, Cheshire, and Somerset as examples. Their efforts resulted in the Articles of Foundation, which provided a framework for the later International Olympic Charter. In part the articles read:

Resolved. That a National Olympian Association be established for the encouragement and reward of skill and strength in manly exercises, by the award of Medals and other Prizes, money excepted at general meetings of the Association, to be held annually and in rotation in or near one of the principal cities or towns of Great Britain. That Professional athletes shall be excluded from competition.

That this Association shall form a centre of union for the different Olympian, Athletic, Gymnastic, Boating, Swimming, Cricket, and other similar Societies, enabling them . . . to assist one another; and affording to the most expert of their athletes an opportunity of contending and distinguishing themselves in a National arena.

That the competition of this Association shall be international, and open to all comers.

That the first Annual Meeting will be held next July (1866), in London.

That the Badge of the Association be a wreathe of oak, and its Motto *Civium vires civitatis vis* (the strength of the nation lies in the strength of its citizens).[30]

There are several notable points that have significance for the later international Olympic movement. The motto indicates that a nation's military security lies in the physical conditioning of its youth. Professional athletes, while not defined, are barred from competition. The national games are to be rotated among the principal cities of England. Medals and prizes, excluding money, are to be awarded the victors, and the competition is to be international.

Brookes, named president of the Olympic Organizing Committee for the London Olympic games, immediately began preparations for the following summer. Competition was scheduled for a three-day period, July 31 to August 2, 1866. The program of events, swimming, track and field, gymnastics, wrestling, boxing, and fencing, was quite comprehensive and bore a striking similarity to subsequent early Coubertin Olympics. The gymnastics and track and field competitions were held at the original Crystal Palace, the home of the very first World's Fair of 1851. The Crystal Palace, the engineering marvel of the day, built of iron girders and glass panels, was prefabricated and movable. It was the world's first indoor sports facility. Originally erected at Hyde Park for the great exhibition of 1851, the structure was dismantled and reassembled (1852–1854) at Sydenham Hill, Norwood district, the site of the 1866 Olympics.[31]

There were two more interesting features of these London Olympics. One of the world's most legendary athletes and the most famous cricket player of all time, W. G. Grace of Bristol, was first an Olympic champion. Grace remains the most esteemed athlete in the annals of British sport history. His reputation in Britain is even greater than that of Babe Ruth in America. On August 1, 1866, the eighteen-year-old Grace entered the 440-yard hurdles event. An eyewitness account described the race: "Grace took the lead from the start, followed by Collins and Emery . . . and Grace, making the pace a cracker, led by 20 yards at half the distance, and eventually won with ease by 20 yards." The other noteworthy feature of these Olympics was the first case of an athlete being disqualified for not being an amateur. Like the later celebrated Jim Thorpe incident of 1912, the victor in the one- and two-mile races, C. Nurse, was declared a professional and stripped of his titles.[32] Information explaining why Nurse was considered a professional, and why a protest was lodged and by whom, has not survived.

Newspaper accounts provided an assessment of the London Olympics and the role of Brookes. "The festival at the Crystal Palace appears to have been a genuine success," and "The presentation of the prizes was preceded by an address from Mr. W. P. Brookes . . . who may be termed 'the father of the Olympian movement.'"[33] Pierre de Coubertin later intentionally ignored the monumental contributions of Brookes to the eventual establishment of the modern Olympic games. Only recently have scholars begun to recognize the pivotal significance of Brookes's efforts. The honored title "father of the Olympian movement" is truly justified. By 1866 Brookes had been working for sixteen years to advance the Olympic idea. He would continue his Olympic efforts for the next twenty-nine, until his death.

The speech of Brookes on August 3, 1866, afforded him a national forum to present his contention that the physical training of a nation's youth was critical to the national defense. He made his plea that physical education should be mandatory in the English school system. As an example to prove his point, Brookes compared the success of physical training in the schools and military preparedness in Germany with the failure of the French to include physical exercise in their schools and the subsequent high rate of military conscripts rejected as physically unfit. Brookes viewed the Olympic games as a manifestation of the value accorded physical training. The published version of this speech years later profoundly influenced Pierre de Coubertin, the founder, but not the father, of the modern Olympic games. In 1867 Brookes received an additional tribute from the Wenlock Olympic Society, a silver medal and the recognition that he was the man "who, if not absolute originator of these manly sports, is, at all events the reviver of them in modern days, and the leading pioneer of the athletic movement."[34]

Two events of Olympic importance occurred in 1867. The first truly international competition took place at the Liverpool Olympics when athletes from Paris and Marseilles participated. The first modern Olympic oath was administered at the Wenlock Olympics of that year. In order to participate, athletes had to swear, "I will never compete for money, nor with Professionals, nor ever make Athletic Exercises or Contests a means of livelihood."[35] Brookes introduced the amateur oath to the National Olympics in 1868. Again, the athletes swore they had never competed for money, but the phrase declaring abstention from ever competing professionally was dropped. The concept of amateurism was more than concerns over receiving money for competing. Amateurism was really conceived as an attempt to restrict the mingling of the social classes. Amateurism sought to insulate the aristocratic "gentleman" from the working classes.

A rival Olympic organization had immediately arisen in response to the National Olympic Association of Brookes: the Amateur Athletic Club, which later became the British Amateur Athletic Association. This group added the "mechanics clause" to the definition of amateur. Anyone "who is by trade or employment, a mechanic, artisan, or labourer" was excluded from amateur status.[36] Brookes never added the class exclusion to his definition of amateurism, and it was this difference that caused conflict for the Olympic movement in England, with the Amateur Athletic Club prohibiting athletes from competing in the National Olympics. While their initial boycott efforts in 1866 were unsuccessful, by 1868 the power of the AAC was such that their opposition to the National Olympics had a crippling effect. After 1868 only the Wenlock Olympic games continued in England.

The Greek Olympic proclamation of 1858, as in antiquity, called for the quadrennial celebration of the games, but after the initial Olympics of 1859 internal political turmoil prevented such a cycle. By October of 1862 the citizens of Greece had forced King Otto to abandon his throne and the country. The Greek people almost unanimously voted for Prince Alfred, the second son of Britain's Queen Victoria, to be the next King of Greece. Alfred had attended the 1859 Olympics and given the prize to the victor of the chariot race. But Alfred, obeying his mother's wishes, declined the honor. In 1863 another prince, George of Denmark, was offered the Greek throne and accepted, becoming King George I of Greece. The new monarch had an interest in the Olympic games, and despite the political uncertainty in Greece, the government announced in 1869 that Olympiad II would be celebrated the next year.

Evangelis Zappas died in 1865, leaving his entire fortune to the Greek government to fund the continuation of the Olympics. In his will, Zappas again specified that the ancient stadium in Athens be excavated and restored to accommodate the Olympic contests. His will contained some other rather unique features. He wanted his body buried at a church in Romania, but after four years, exhumed and decapitated. The body was then to be reburied at his childhood school in his native village in Greek Albania. His head was to be interred at the new Olympic building in Athens with a plaque, inscribed in ancient Greek, reading, "Here Lies the Head of Evangelis Zappas."[37] Ultimately, on October 20, 1888, during the dedication of the Zappeion Olympic building in Athens, his head was enshrined with the requested inscription and remains there to this day.

The Olympic Committee spent only a small portion of the Zappas funds for the stadium excavation by the German archaeologist E. Ziller in 1869, and less on restoration. Instead of the marble seating Zappas desired, spectators at the 1870 Olympics endured wooden bleachers; nevertheless, the design of the ancient stadium provided a fine view of the events. The Olympic athletic competition, as requested by Zappas, was held in the ancient stadium.[38]

The games were, by any standards, a huge success. The Organizing Committee issued a call for athletes three months prior to the games, and as in ancient times they had to report six weeks prior to competition for training. The athletes swore to the Olympic oath: "I promise that I will compete honorably within the rules and regulations, and not cheat my fellow competitor." As in 1859, athletes came from all areas of the Greek-speaking world. The games opened with an Olympic hymn on November 15. King George, honoring the ancient custom, placed an olive wreath on the head of each Olympic victor. The crowds were large and enthusiastic, with more than thirty thousand spectators jamming the renovated stadium. As the games came to a close an appreciative audience accompanied the departure of their king and queen from the stadium with applause. Newspaper accounts proclaimed the games a success: ". . . Complete order reigned. Everyone enjoyed the height of satisfaction, and there was universal gratitude to the organizing committee," and "Let the founder of the Olympics E. Zappas take comfort, if those in the other world have any perception, as he sees that his hopes were not deceived. [The 1870 Olympic Games] enjoyed, as is well known, unbelievable success."[39]

While the games themselves were a success, the English concept of amateurism spread to Greece. The first public expressions of this class-oriented amateurism occurred shortly after the 1870 Olympics. Philip Ioannou, a Greek professor, classical scholar, social elitist, and a judge at the 1870 games, stated that the event was a failure because "some work-ing men had competed" who were "scarcely pried away from their wage earner jobs."[40] Ioannou and others quickly organized to exclude the working class from future Olympic competition.

By 1875 the class amateurism philosophy dominated the Greek Olym-pic Committee. Athletic participation in the third Olympiad excluded the working class. The games were a disaster. Spectators laughed more often than applauded the athletic efforts of the upper-class competitors. Even the participants made light of their lack of physical skills. The local newspaper account of the 1875 Olympics summed up the dismal nature of the games:

> Everything assumed the color of comedy. . . . The crowd seized every oppor-tunity for merriment. . . . Neither the judges nor the competitors took any in-terest in the form of the proceedings. Products of another society, another kind of civic life, the athletic games of the Ancients, when revived today, be-come nothing but a direct mockery of antiquity."[41]

The decade of the 1870s was a difficult time for the infant Olympic movement. Despite the successful Greek Olympiad of 1870, the emer-gence of class amateurism and anti-athletic fervor temporarily stalled the Olympic idea. In England, Brookes, compelled to suspend the an-nual National Olympics, attempted National games only twice more, in 1874 and 1877. Neither attempt could be considered successful. Even the local Wenlock Olympics, still conducted every year, experienced dif-ficult times with financial troubles and fewer athletes competing. In an effort to lend prestige and credibility to the National Olympics, Brookes came up with the idea of associating prominent politicians and person-alities with the games. In 1874 Brookes convinced the Earl of Bradford to serve as the figurehead president of the National Olympic Committee. Thomas Hughes, author of *Tom Brown's School Days,* was coerced to be a member of the National Olympic Games Council.[42] Brookes tried again to advance the National Olympics in 1877 by associating the games with modern Greece. He requested King George to honor the British Olympics by donating a prize for the winner of the pentathlon, just as Brookes had given a prize for the 1859 Greek Olympics. The king agreed and sent a silver cup with a Greek inscription that read:

George I, King of the Hellenes,
for the man who won the Pentathlon
at the Modern Olympics of the British
at Shrewsbury in August, 1877[43]

Brookes responded in his speech by thanking the Greek monarch: "To the monarch who now reigns over the Hellenic Kingdom, and who takes a lively interest in our modern Olympian Games, we feel deeply grateful for the honour he has conferred on the National Olympian Association and the town of Shrewsbury by the gift of a prize for the pentathlon."[44] But Brookes's efforts could not salvage the National Olympics. By 1880 the English Olympics were in serious trouble and the Greek Olympics, after the fiasco of 1875, were never held again. Only the greatly diminished Wenlock Olympics limped along.

Instead of giving up, in the fall of 1880 Brookes took a bold initiative. He wrote to the Greek minister in London, John Gennadius, proposing that an international Olympic games be held in Athens. Gennadius regretfully responded, ". . . the most excellent proposal you now make to us, we regret deeply that in the present and troubled state and critical circumstances of the kingdom it would not be possible to carry out in a befitting manner the theme of your proposal." Despite the negative response, Brookes persevered. A Greek-language newspaper in Trieste, *Kleio,* reported on June 25, 1881, ". . . Brookes, this ardent philhellene, is now at work so that an International Olympic Festival may be held soon in Athens." The *Shrewsbury Chronicle* of September 29, 1882, stated that Brookes "had been trying to establish an International Olympian Association at Athens, and hoped in a few years to see his efforts become successful."[45] Over the next thirteen years Brookes repeatedly contacted Gennadius, proposing that the Greek nation hold an international Olympic festival in Athens, and always he received the same cordial but negative response.

Brookes tried one more time to conduct a National Olympics, in 1883, and again the games were a failure. This was the last National Olympics in England, but Brookes would not admit defeat. During the course of the 1883 games the *Shrewsbury Chronicle* reported Brookes's remarks concerning his Olympic efforts: "I often think of a remark of O'Connell's that 'There are but two classes in the world; one to hammer, and the other to be hammered at.' So I shall hammer on in the belief that others will succeed me who will strike with more effect, and what is right in itself . . . will ultimately prevail."[46]

Brookes, seventy-four years of age in 1883, recognized that a new crusader would have to carry the Olympic idea forward. Somewhat surprisingly, he did not have any disciples in England, and the continuing political chaos in Greece always diverted attention from Olympism. The new crusader arose from an unlikely location. Opposed to the Olympic idea at first, he later claimed full credit and denied any efforts before his own to revive the Olympic games.

One day early in 1889 Brookes, now eighty, came across an interesting notice in the newspaper. A young aristocratic Frenchman, the Baron Pierre de Coubertin (1863–1937), had placed a notice in several English newspapers explaining his interest in British sports and physical education and requesting that any Englishmen who had similar interests contact him. Brookes, always prompt, acted immediately. He mailed a full packet of his writings on the subject to Coubertin, including the two most important, a copy of his speech delivered at the conclusion of the first British National Olympics in London, 1866, titled "Address on Physical Education," and a recent letter to the National Physical Recreation Society titled "National Disaster, the Penalty for National Degeneracy."[47]

France had suffered a devastating defeat in the Franco-Prussian War of 1870. Coubertin, only seven years old, grew up in a climate of national humiliation. Soon, Coubertin, like all patriotic Frenchmen, burned with a desire to redeem his country's prestige. Reaching adulthood, the young aristocrat pondered his career options. Military service and a career in law were both briefly considered, but Coubertin ultimately settled upon the idea of educational reform. As a member of an upper-class aristocratic family, Coubertin was not expected to be a wage earner. The Baron began by examining the cause of the national humiliation of 1870, and concluded the answer lay in the educational systems of France and Germany. The obvious difference between French and German education was the emphasis on physical training, or, in the case of France, the lack thereof. The German system of gymnastic training prepared the youth of Germany for the physical demands of war. In contrast, French education focused almost exclusively on traditional academic preparation, ignoring physical training. Coubertin quickly concluded that the French educational system had to be reformed to include physical training, but he did not advocate that France adopt the German system. As a teenager, Coubertin had read Tom Hughes's *Tom Brown's School Days*, a novel about the experiences of a student at the Rugby School during Thomas Arnold's time as headmaster. Significant to Coubertin was the English devotion to sports and games as part of the educational experience. He became convinced that English methods should serve as a model for the reorganization of French schools. Coubertin first visited England in 1883. He returned in 1886, touring many schools and universities, including Rugby. Upon his return to France, he was more convinced than ever of the value and need for France to adopt the English sports and educational model.

In 1888 Coubertin founded the Comite pour la Propagation des Exercises Physiques for the express purpose of introducing English sports into French schools. In response, a rival organization, the Ligue Nationale de l'Education Physique led by Paschal Grousset, immediately arose to oppose English influence in French schools. Grousset and the Ligue became active at all levels of education and worked to establish physical education in the French schools, but with an independent Gallic tradition. Since there was no sports tradition in France, Grousset proposed the establishment of an annual French national athletic festival modeled after the ancient Olympic games. The idea was to create an athletic institution that would reflect contemporary French culture as the ancient Olympics had reflected the culture of Greece. Coubertin immediately reacted by condemning rather than embracing the idea. The man destined to be the founder of the modern international Olympic games belittled the notion of Olympic games in France. "Grousset's Ligue makes a great fuss . . . it has reminiscences of the Olympic Games and visions of ceremonies at the foot of Eiffel Tower, where the Head of State will crown the young athletes with laurel. . . . This is all a lot; it is even too much."[48] Both Grousset and Coubertin, in 1888, were unaware of Brookes and the English Olympic tradition. This all changed for Coubertin the next year, and within four years the Baron had assumed the mantle of Olympic apostle.

Brookes advocated compulsory physical education in English schools. He acknowledged the value of English sports to the nation, but concluded the national defense was at risk unless all English youth received physical training as part of their education. Brookes frequently compared the French and German educational systems to demonstrate the need for compulsory physical training in English schools. In his 1866 Olympic speech, "Address on Physical Education," Brookes traced the development of physical exercise in Germany.

> Towards the close of the last century a German, named Gutsmuth introduced into his own country a system of gymnastic exercises . . . After him Frederick Jahn introduced gymnastic schools into Prussia, But these were at last suppressed. . . . But when debility and disease, mental as well as bodily, began to increase, the ban against physical education was relaxed . . . and from that period until the present, physical exercises . . . have been encouraged and supported throughout . . . Prussia.

In the same speech, Brookes spoke of the French.

> . . . if we turn to our neighbors the French for information on this subject, we find that out of 1,000 youths registered in 1863, as the contingent to be furnished by certain cantons for the conscription, 731 were rejected . . . as physically unfit to bear arms, a degeneracy which a writer in the *Siecle* attributed to two causes, viz., excessive labour in the manufacturing districts, and the want of physical training in the public schools.[49]

Coubertin eagerly read the materials sent to him by Brookes. In June, France hosted the World's Fair in Paris. Coubertin used the occasion to organize an International Congress on Physical Exercise. In his speech before the congress Coubertin quoted Brookes at length advocating the necessity of physical education for the youth of France. Coubertin informed Brookes of his speech to the International Congress and on November 1, 1889, the *Shrewsbury Chronicle* reported, "It is a pleasure to us to note, from the proceedings of the above Congress, that the efforts of our Countryman, Dr. Brookes . . . were alluded to by Monsieur Pierre de Coubertin at the close of his eloquent . . . speech by a quotation from Dr. Brookes's address at the National Olympian Festival . . . in August 1866." In the first issue of *Revue Athletique* (January 1890), a publication founded by Coubertin, Brookes's contributions are acknowledged by the Baron: "I have received some interesting documents from Mr. W. P. Brookes, who is following with lively sympathy, from his home in Much Wenlock (England) the movement for a physical renaissance in France."[50]

In July, Brookes finally succeeded in having the National Physical Recreation Society pass a resolution supporting compulsory physical education in the national schools of England. He sent a copy of the resolution to Coubertin and extended an invitation to the Baron to visit him in Much Wenlock. Coubertin replied on August 9, 1890, accepting the invitation.

> I was very much interested in reading the resolution adopted at the meeting held in London on the 27th of July and I wish you every success in your attempt to bring forth a general reform in your National Schools. . . .
>
> I quite agree with you that bodily training in National Schools is of very great importance to the whole nation; but it is of no less importance that boys fifteen and young men should be fond of athletic games and sports and enjoy out of doors life and every manly form of recreation. Such was not the case with us and I shall do my best to make Athletics popular amongst my countrymen, for I firmly believe that the wonderful "Expansion of England" and the "Grandeur of the British people" are the consequences of athletic education and that you are indebted for it to cricket, football and rowing.
>
> I will be delighted to talk the subject over with you when we meet in October. I must go to Birmingham and Rugby and intend starting toward the 20th of October; if it is convenient to you I can proceed directly to Much Wenlock.[51]

As planned, Coubertin arrived in Much Wenlock by train in October 1890. Brookes made extensive preparations for the young Frenchman's visit. The regular Wenlock Olympics had been held in May, but Brookes decided to stage a special edition to honor his guest, and, in the words of Brookes, "to enlighten Baron Pierre de Coubertin, a French Gentleman, who desires to introduce athletics more largely among his own countrymen." Coubertin witnessed a full rendition of the Wenlock Olympic games, athletic contests, and, most significantly, all the associated pageantry. This included an opening parade of competitors and villagers, from the town to Linden Field, led by a herald on horseback. A large banner, reading "Welcome to Baron Pierre de Coubertin and Prosperity to France," greeted Coubertin at the entrance to the athletic field. Other banners, inscribed in ancient Greek, quoted the ancient authors.[52]

Upon their arrival at Linden Field, Brookes informed Coubertin, "The members of the Wenlock Olympian Society have a custom which they have great pleasure in carrying out, viz., that of paying honour to distinguished personages by dedicating beautiful trees as memorials to them. We are happy in having an opportunity of performing this ceremony in remembrance of your visit to Wenlock and Linden Field." Coubertin's tree still lives, older than the Olympic games he founded. Coubertin had come to Wenlock to talk of the physical education movement in the schools. He had not expected an introduction to the Olympic movement. The eighty-year-old Brookes viewed the twenty-seven-year-old Coubertin as a possible successor who would carry on the Olympic movement. During Coubertin's visit Brookes shared the whole history of the Olympic movement. He told him of the founding of the Wenlock Olympian Society in 1850 and the yearly games held ever since. Coubertin learned of the Greek National Olympics, of Zappas, and of the National Olympics in Britain. He was informed of the correspondence between Brookes and Greek officials and the exchange of gifts during specific Olympiads. Finally, and most significantly, Brookes shared his ultimate dream, to initiate an international Olympic games with the first Olympiad to be held in Athens.[53]

Despite Brookes's enthusiastic torrent of information, Coubertin was slow to warm to the idea. Indeed, soon after returning to Paris Coubertin wrote an article praising Brookes's work in physical education, but remained unconvinced of the merits of Olympism, stating that in modern times there was "no longer any need to invoke memories of Greece and to seek encouragement in the past."[54]

Brookes continued to write to Coubertin and, in 1891, invited him to Wenlock for the regular Spring Olympics. Coubertin, citing athletic meetings in Paris that needed his presence, declined, but sent a medal to be awarded as a prize. During the next year a regular stream of letters arrived in Paris from Brookes. Coubertin, in July 1892, finally sent a reply, apologizing, "You must forgive me if I have not answered your last letters for I am now swallowed up by the work I have to do." The work that had swallowed up Coubertin concerned his activities in the French Union of Athletic Sports Clubs (USFSA), the French equivalent of the American Amateur Athletic Union and the British Amateur Athletic Association. Work on the Olympic revival did not consume him. Coubertin had been the principal founder of the USFSA in 1890, and, in

1892, he planned a sports conference to commemorate the founding. In his letter of apology he informed Brookes of the upcoming conference: "We shall have an eight day festival in Paris from Nov. 20 to Nov. 27 to commemorate the founding of the Union five years ago." Coubertin claimed the founding of the USFSA began with an organization three years previous to the actual founding of the USFSA, thereby committing his first documented act of self-aggrandizement. Coubertin's letter is significant for what he does not mention to Brookes. He makes no mention of any plans to publicly call for the establishment of an international Olympics at the November festival. Ironically, on September 10 an article appeared in the *Wellington Journal* summarizing the history of Brookes's efforts in reviving the Olympic games and paraphrasing part of his recent speech delivered to six thousand people: "If he lived long enough, Dr. Brookes hoped to go and witness an international festival at Athens, or upon the old spot where the Olympic games were started."[55]

On the evening of November 25, in the middle of the commemorative festival, Coubertin arose as the last speaker of the night and presented the case for international sport competitions as a means of promoting peace among nations. He closed his speech with an impassioned plea that his listeners join with him "to pursue and realize . . . this grandiose and beneficent project; namely, the re-establishment of the Olympic Games."[56]

On at least two previous occasions (1888 and 1890) Coubertin had publicly opposed an Olympic revival. In late July 1892, Coubertin apparently had no plans to revive the Olympic games, or presumably he would have so informed Brookes in his letter. During a four-month period in 1892 Coubertin seemingly underwent a conversion from Olympic antagonist to apostle. What caused Coubertin to change his mind? Certainly Brookes had been an influence, but Coubertin never acknowledged his priority or influence. In 1908 Coubertin wrote that he, himself, was the sole originator of the Olympic revival idea and that his inspiration, since adolescence, had been ancient Greece:

> When and how this need associated itself in my mind with the idea of reestablishing the Olympic Games I couldn't say . . . I was familiar with the term. Nothing in ancient history had made me more of a dreamer than Olympia.

> This city of dream . . . raised its colonnades and porticos unceasingly before
> my adolescent mind. Long before I thought of drawing from its ruins a prin-
> ciple of revival, I would rebuild it in my mind, to make the shape of its sil-
> houette live again. Germany had exhumed its remains. Why should France
> not succeed in renewing its splendors? From there it was not far to the less
> dazzling but more practical and more fruitful project of reviving the Games.[57]

Coubertin completely ignored the previous Herculean efforts of
Brookes and neglected to mention his own visit to Wenlock in 1890. Even
more disturbing, Coubertin directly contradicts earlier statements when
he claims inspiration from Olympia: "There was no longer any need to
invoke memories of Greece and to seek encouragement in the past."[58]
Coubertin's regrettable deception did a great injustice to Brookes,
Evangelis Zappas, Panagiotis Soutsos, and other Olympic pioneers. He
also soiled, unnecessarily, his own reputation. Pierre de Coubertin, while
not the father, was certainly the founder of the modern Olympic games,
and his contributions to their establishment is without question. He
made the Olympic dream a reality. What a shame he did not acknowledge
his predecessors and even document his own conversion to the movement. His reputation would have been enhanced, not blemished.

The response to Coubertin's Olympic plea in 1892 was one of indif-
ference. But Coubertin was now committed to an Olympic revival and
pressed forward to make it happen. The concept of amateurism, always
difficult to define, was a topic of much concern in the sporting world by
1893. Adolphe de Palissaux, a member of Coubertin's USFSA, proposed
that an international congress be convened to resolve questions concerning amateurism.[59] Coubertin immediately seized the opportunity
and, in August 1893, scheduled an international congress on amateurism to be held in June 1894. Coubertin hoped to use the congress as
a venue for promoting the Olympic revival. Almost immediately, in the
fall of 1893, Coubertin traveled to the United States to seek support for
his idea.

He had made a previous visit to the United States in 1889 as an official representative of the French government, commissioned by the
French minister of public instruction to investigate the organization of
schools and universities in Canada and the United States. Coubertin was
not an advocate for Olympic revival in 1889, having just the year before
criticized his countryman, Grousset, for suggesting the idea. His interest

was with the role of physical education and sports in the schools. Among the universities Coubertin visited were Harvard, Amherst, Montreal, Cornell, Chicago, Virginia, Johns Hopkins, and Princeton. At Princeton he made the acquaintance of William Milligan Sloane, a history professor who had become interested in intercollegiate sports in the early 1880s, had chaired the Athletic Advisory Committee at Princeton in 1884, and in 1889 was still a member of that committee. In November Coubertin had been invited to attend a conference on physical training in Boston. He heard a lively debate discussing the merits of the German, Swedish, and English systems of physical training and various proposals for which system should be adopted in the United States. On the last day of the conference Coubertin was asked to speak. He made it quite clear which system he favored.

> I was asked the other day what, in my opinion, American education was like. I answered that in some respects it looked like a battle-field where English and German ideas were fighting. While I fully acknowledge that from the physical point of view nothing can be said against the German system, I believe, on the other hand, that from the moral and social point of view no system, if so it can be called, stands higher than the English athletic sport system as understood and explained by the greatest of modern teachers, Thomas Arnold of Rugby. His principles are the ones on which was founded last year the French Educational Reform Association. I wish I could give you a detailed account of the work our Association is engaged in carrying out; it is no less than a general reform of secondary education.[60]

Coubertin's 1893 tour of America included a visit to the World's Fair in Chicago and an introduction to President William R. Harper of the University of Chicago, who showed an interest in Coubertin's plans. At Princeton, Coubertin spent three weeks renewing his association and sharing his ideas with Sloane, forming a friendship that would continue throughout their lives. Sloane became the most enthusiastic and vocal supporter of the Olympic games in America. On November 18, 1893, Sloane wrote to the board of governors of the Amateur Athletic Union of the United States, ". . . you must see your way clear to sending representatives to the [1894 Paris] congress . . . It is very important that America should be well represented in such a moment."[61] The AAU apparently was not interested and ignored Sloane's plea. Sloane then assembled representatives of Harvard, Yale, Princeton, and Columbia to hear Coubertin present his Olympic proposal. Response was polite, but indifferent. Coubertin felt that the ongoing war between the universities and the AAU for control of amateur sports in the United States so engaged the respective parties that they were incapable of focusing on any progressive idea which would distract their attention from their struggles. Asked by Coubertin to serve as the American representative to the Paris Congress in June 1894, Sloane consented and began his lifelong membership as a member of the Olympic governing body.

Shortly after his return to France, Coubertin began preparing for the conference at which the Olympic games would be born. In January he mailed conference information to numerous individuals and sports clubs throughout Europe, America, and the British colonies. Mr. Charles Herbert, secretary of the British Amateur Athletic Association, representing England and the English colonies; William Sloane, representing America; and Coubertin, representing France and the rest of Europe, were listed as the organizers of the conference that the Baron first called an International Congress of Amateurs. The agenda included eight items: the first seven dealt with the issue of amateurism, but the eighth and last read, "The possibility of re-establishing the Olympic Games. Under what conditions would it be feasible?" By early spring there was still very little interest expressed in Coubertin's congress, but by April Coubertin began assembling an impressive list of dignitaries associated with it. He convinced Baron A. C. de Courcel, a former senator and French ambassador to Germany, to serve as president of the congress, and eventually secured the consent of more than fifty prominent men representing the nobility of Europe to be honorary members. Four impressive titles headed the list: "the King of Belgium, the Prince of Wales, the Crown Prince of Sweden and Norway, and the Crown Prince of Greece."[62] The last, Constantine of Greece, was an avid supporter of the Olympic games and proved instrumental in the eventual success of the first modern international Olympic games held in Athens. Indeed, without the efforts of Constantine, Olympic games would not have taken place in Athens in 1896.

After the Racing Club of Paris agreed to host the grand congressional banquet on June 21, 1894, Coubertin sent out his invitations. He asked that attendees submit their opinions on the revival of the Olympic games in general, and amateurism in particular. He also dropped the phrase "of Amateurs" from the title, calling the meeting simply the "International Athletic Congress." The first seven items on the agenda remained the same, but Coubertin expanded item eight to three separate points under a separate heading:

Olympic Games

VIII—The possibility of re-establishing them.—Advantages from the athletic, moral and international points of view.
IX—Conditions to be imposed on competitors.—Sports represented.—Material organization and frequency of the revived Olympic Games.
X—Nomination of an International Committee responsible for preparing their re-establishment.[63]

Brookes finally received word from Coubertin of the upcoming congress and an invitation to attend in May, only a month before the meeting. Brookes promptly replied on May 22, writing:

Dear Baron Coubertin,

   I have called a meeting of the Members of the Wenlock Olympian Society to be held on Thursday next, May 26, to consider the various propositions contained in the circulars you sent me, many of which they will be satisfied to leave to the decision of the Congress. In one, however, you will, I feel assured, have their cordial concurrence, viz., the establishment of an international Olympian Association and the arrangement that such gatherings be held in rotation in or near the Capitals of all nations joining in the Movement. This has long been a cherished idea of mine so far as making Greece the centre, but the plan of your Congress, embracing as it does all nations, is a really superb one, and deserving of the liberal support of all nations.[64]

Brookes, citing his advanced age (eighty-five) and poor health, declined Coubertin's invitation to attend, saying, "I wish I were younger."[65]

In early June, shortly before the scheduled opening of the congress on June 16, Coubertin changed the name for the final time: Paris International Congress for the Re-establishment of the Olympic Games. Coubertin had never been much interested in amateurism, but realized that most men in sporting circles were. Coubertin used amateurism as a ploy to achieve his ambition of reviving the Olympic games. In his memoirs he later wrote, "Amateurism. That! Always that. . . . Today I can risk the confession; I was never much concerned about the question of amateurism. It had served me as a screen to convene the Congress to Re-establish the Olympic Games. Seeing the importance which others lent it in the sporting world, I would show the expected zeal without real conviction."[66]

Pierre de Coubertin, unsuccessful in 1892, learned from his failure and left nothing to chance in 1894. The proceedings of the congress were carefully scripted to ensure the success of his objectives, and he was not above using political intrigue to secure the support of Europe's nobility. Coubertin asked Charles Waldstein, head of the American School of Classical Studies in Athens, to intercede on his behalf and request the support of the royal family of Greece. Coubertin had met Waldstein in Cambridge during one of his visits to England in 1886. In early April the royal family paid a visit to Waldstein's excavation site at ancient Argos in southern Greece. During the course of their visit Waldstein informed Prince Constantine of Coubertin's plans to establish international Olympic games. Constantine, already an avid supporter of Greek Olympic games, having proposed a Greek Olympiad for 1892 which fell victim to Greek political and economic turmoil, enthusiastically agreed to serve as an honorary member for Coubertin's Olympic Congress and, based on subsequent events, in all probability offered Athens as the site for the initial Olympic games in 1896.[67] Coubertin, if not before, now decided that Athens should host the inaugural Olympics. This decision required a Greek representative to attend the Olympic Congress; enter Demetrios Vikelas, the man destined to be the first president of the International Olympic Committee.

Vikelas, a resident of Paris since 1877, had made his fortune as a businessman, primarily marketing grain. Once financially secure, he abandoned his business interests and devoted himself to his real love, literature. Vikelas had never met Coubertin nor been involved with athletics in any capacity, but he was Greek, and he was already in Paris.

. . . the mailman brought me a package, from which I withdrew a certificate that made me a member of the Panhellenic Gymnastic society. I knew absolutely nothing about this Society—and had not asked for membership, nor did I have any qualifications. The next morning the mailman, coming again, resolved my perplexity. He brought me a huge envelope, containing a letter from the Society, asking me to represent it at the International Athletic Congress. It was an official document, accompanied by letters from friends of mine, members of the Society, requesting that I say "Yes"—and specifically by telegram, since the Congress was to begin in a few days. My first impulse was to say no. I did not even know that an International Athletic Congress was soon to meet in Paris. What did I have to do with athletics?[68]

The Panhellenic Gymnastic Society had been organized in 1891 in Athens largely as a result of the royal decree of June 22, 1890, signed by Prince Constantine, declaring that the government would resume Greek Olympics in 1892. Constantine was, himself, the honorary president in 1894. Vikelas did not say no, attended the Olympic Congress, and within three weeks was president of the International Olympic Committee.[69]

On June 19 the members of the Olympic Congress took up the question of where the first international Olympic games would be held. Most of the representatives expressed support for London.[70] Coubertin insisted on Athens. When agreement could not be reached, Coubertin had the question tabled until the final session, set for June 23. The minutes of the June 19 meeting state:

> The opinion . . . is that the first games could take place at London in 1896, the second at Paris in 1900. . . . As to the site of the first games, de Coubertin sees some difficulties in . . . choosing London. . . . He proposes to take . . . Athens. M. Duval objects that Athens is a bit outside the center of Europe, especially for the first meeting of the games. He proposes—and Viscount de La Rochefoucauld seconds his motion—to choose London. M. Coubertin moves that the question be tabled until the arrival of Mr. Herbert, delegate of the British AAA . . .[71]

Encountering opposition, Coubertin sent a telegram to King George in Athens that very same day. The contents of that telegram have been lost, but King George replied on June 21:

> With deep feeling toward Baron de Coubertin's courteous petition, I send him and the members of the Congress, with my sincere thanks, my best wishes for the revival of the Olympic Games. George.[72]

The timing of the telegram from King George, June 21, two days before the congress even voted to revive the games, indicates that Coubertin and the royal family had at least an understanding that Greece was willing to host the first international Olympics. Such an agreement would explain why Coubertin, a staunch Anglophile, would oppose London as the initial site. It would also resolve the mysterious nomination of Vikelas, an Olympic novice, to attend the congress and his subsequent acclamation, at the urging of Coubertin, as president of the Olympic committee.

June 23, 1894, witnessed the realization of Coubertin's quest. The International Olympic Congress voted to revive the Olympic games and was persuaded by Coubertin that Athens should have the honor of host city for 1896. Time was of the essence. Only two years remained for Coubertin and Vikelas to make the preparations necessary for a successful Olympic revival. The mission for Vikelas, as president of the Olympic committee, was to go to Athens and meet with politicians and the Greek Olympic Committee to begin negotiations. Coubertin planned to join Vikelas shortly.

It was the end of September before Vikelas arrived in Athens. Neither the king nor Prince Constantine was in Athens at the time. Vikelas was able to meet with Charilaos Trikoupis, the prime minister. Trikoupis, citing mostly economic concerns, voiced his opposition to having Greece host an international Olympics. Before Coubertin could join him, Vikelas received a telegram that his wife was very ill in Paris. He left Greece immediately. He met briefly with Coubertin in Paris, apprising him of the strong opposition in Greece led by the prime minister. Coubertin set out for Athens. Immediately upon his arrival on November 8, he was presented with a letter from Trikoupis stating that he was wasting his time, that the Greek Olympic Committee had met after the departure of Vikelas and voted not to host the Olympic games. On November 10 Prime Minister Trikoupis paid a visit to Coubertin at the Hotel Grande Bretagne and expressed his firm opposition, stating that he would personally ensure that Athens would not host the Olympics.[73] Coubertin was not dissuaded, and over the next several days met twice with Prince Constantine, who had returned to Athens. Constantine was supportive and gave much-needed encouragement to Coubertin, and, on November 16, upon invitation, Coubertin addressed a meeting of the Parnassus Literary Society presenting the essence of the Olympic idea and appealing to Greek patriotism.

. . . Gentlemen, did your fathers carefully weigh their chances of victory before rising up against the Turks? If they had, you here would not be free men this very moment. Those are considerations one simply does not examine; they are unworthy of you!

   When we had begun to play football matches against the English, we expected to lose. But the seventh time we played them, we beat them. . . . Dishonor here would not consist of being beaten; it would consist of not contending.[74]

The last sentence, slightly altered later by Coubertin, became the Olympic creed, "The important thing in the Olympic Games is not winning but taking part." Coubertin was working hard to unite Greek public opinion in his support.

Coubertin's speech and the support of Prince Constantine produced results. Shortly after his Parnassus speech Coubertin again met with Trikoupis, and while the prime minister still refused to endorse the Olympics, he did agree to a pledge of neutrality on the subject. Coubertin next wrote a letter to the editor of the Greek newspaper *Asty* announcing the meeting soon to be held to form an Olympic organizing committee, and to offer a challenge to the Greeks. "In our country we have a proverb that says the word *impossible* is not French; someone told me this morning that it was Greek. I do not believe anything of the kind." On November 24 Coubertin conducted a meeting attended by some members of the Zappas Greek Olympic Committee and some individuals Coubertin had recently met in Athens. At the meeting Coubertin announced that Prince Constantine had agreed to serve as president of the 1896 Olympic Organizing Committee and stunned the thirty-two men present by declaring that they constituted the committee's membership. Coubertin pressed his initiative and had the committee elect several vice-presidents and secretaries. Coubertin then met with Constantine, conveyed the results of the committee formation, and, considering his work complete, prepared to leave Athens.[75]

On November 28 Coubertin arrived in the port city of Patras to connect with a ferry to Italy and was welcomed by members of the Panachaean Athletic Society, a Greek athletic club. The next morning a personal guide took Coubertin to the ancient site at Olympia. Coubertin walked for the first time among the ruins of ancient Olympia, which he later claimed inspired his revival of the games. Coubertin would return to Olympia again, and for the last time, in 1927. Only twice in his lifetime, both brief visits, did Coubertin walk upon the sacred grounds of the ancient Olympiads, yet he left instructions that upon his death his heart was to be removed from his body and entombed separately at ancient Olympia. The heart of Pierre de Coubertin was placed in a marble pillar and for many years stood at the entrance of the ancient site. The pillar was later moved to the grounds of the International Olympic Academy a short distance away, where it remains to this day.[76]

The Olympic Committee organized by Coubertin met soon after his departure from Athens and, led by members politically allied with the anti-Olympic prime minister, decided that Greece would not host an international Olympics and disbanded. On December 6 Prince Constantine, Olympic president, received an official report from the committee stating their belief that it was impossible and undesirable for the Olympic games to be held in Greece. The report also contained the formal resignation of all committee members. Constantine accepted the report and said he would consider it at his leisure. The prince, a political foe of Trikoupis, was determined that Athens would host the first international Olympic games.[77]

The Olympic question was debated in the Greek parliament, largely along political lines: royal family supporters were pro-Olympics, while the prime minister's allies were anti-Olympics. The debate did not change any minds in the Parliament, but it did stir the pride and passions of the Greek people. Letters to the editor appeared in the Athenian press expressing disappointment with the opposition to the Olympics, support for the Olympic efforts of Constantine, and appeals to Greek patriotism to generate public support.[78]

Demetrios Vikelas, having buried his wife, returned to Athens on Christmas day 1894. The next day he held a press conference to promote the Olympic revival in Athens. He met again with Trikoupis, without success, and then in consultation with Prince Constantine began working to form a new Olympic organizing committee. This was accomplished by January 10, 1895. Vikelas wrote Coubertin, "The committee is already formed. I consider that part of my mission achieved. As for the money, it will be found. People are not going to let the Crown prince expose himself to a checkmate." The new committee consisted of an administrative council of twelve; the former mayor of Athens, Ti-moleon Philemon, served as secretary-general and Constantine remained as president. The Greek populace rallied to the cause. Private donations began to arrive, filling Olympic coffers. Coubertin, now home in France, seemed to disappear. Throughout his efforts to restart the committee Vikelas wrote him frequently, asking for guidance and advice with no reply. Finally, on January 17, 1895, the thirty-two-year-old Coubertin responded to Vikelas, explaining he had been distracted from Olympic matters due to his own planning for his forthcoming marriage.[79]

After a rousing patriotic speech made by Vikelas before members of the trade unions on January 16, almost the entire populace of Athens enthusiastically supported hosting the Olympic games. The political divide between the royal family and Prime Minister Trikoupis widened and, after public sentiment overwhelmingly coalesced in support of the Olympics, on January 22, 1895, Trikoupis submitted his resignation to King George.[80] The new Olympic organizing committee met for the first time on January 25 and from this point on worked diligently and effectively to ensure that the first international Olympic games would meet with success.

In mid-December Brookes wrote to Coubertin expressing his support for the Athenian Olympic venture.

> I am looking forward . . . to the receipt of the next *Bulletin* respecting the International Olympian Association and the arrangements for the first festival at Athens. The Greek government should, I think, gladly acquiesce in the honour France wishes to confer upon Greece by holding the first festival at Athens, which will be a mark of the respect and good feeling towards Greece of all the nations which have joined the movement.[81]

Brookes gave full credit to Coubertin for his efforts "to organize a splendid international institution," and then expressed his desire to be ". . . 20 years younger, i.e. only 65 instead of 85; how pleased and proud I should have felt to have been one of your Lieutenants. I hope, however, that I shall live long enough to rejoice in the success of your patriotic and philanthropic undertaking."[82] Brookes died on December 10, 1895, at age eighty-six, almost exactly one year after his last letter to Coubertin and only four months before the first modern Olympic games. For founding the Wenlock Olympic games (which continue to this day), and for his support of Greek Olympics since their inception in 1859, his own call for an international Olympic movement in 1880, and his education of Pierre de Coubertin, Dr. William Penny Brookes truly deserves the designation, Father of the Modern Olympic Games.

Baron Pierre de Coubertin, father of the modern Olympic games. His memoirs, published in 1931, presented a false image of the St. Louis Olympics. From James E. Sullivan, *Spalding's Official Athletic Almanac for 1905: Special Olympic Number, Containing the Official Report of the Olympic Games of 1904.*

Count Henri de Penaloza, the emissary sent by David Francis to Coubertin to present the unofficial St. Louis request to host the 1904 Olympics. Photo courtesy of the DePenaloza family.

President Theodore Roosevelt, honorary president of the St. Louis Olympics. From James E. Sullivan, *Spalding's Official Athletic Almanac for 1905: Special Olympic Number, Containing the Official Report of the Olympic Games of 1904.*

Alice Roosevelt, daughter of the president. She made two visits to the World's Fair and presented medals to American athletes at the Amateur Athletic Union Track and Field Championships. Photo courtesy of the Library of Congress.

David Francis, president of Louisiana Purchase Exposition and St. Louis Olympic games. From James E. Sullivan, *Spalding's Official Athletic Almanac for 1905: Special Olympic Number, Containing the Official Report of the Olympic Games of 1904.*

Frederick J. V. Skiff, director of exhibits, Louisiana Purchase Exposition. From James E. Sullivan, *Spalding's Official Athletic Almanac for 1905: Special Olympic Number, Containing the Official Report of the Olympic Games of 1904.*

James E. Sullivan, chief of the Physical Culture Department and director of the St. Louis Olympics. From James E. Sullivan, *Spalding's Official Athletic Almanac for 1905: Special Olympic Number, Containing the Official Report of the Olympic Games of 1904.*

The featured article of the October 1904 *World's Fair Bulletin,* the official publication of the Louisiana Purchase Exposition. Courtesy of the St. Louis Public Library, Special Collections.

Cover of April 1904 *World's Fair Bulletin,* announcing the Olympic games and featuring the honorary president of the Olympics, Theodore Roosevelt. Courtesy of the St. Louis Public Library, Special Collections.

Headlines in the February 12, 1903, *New York Times* announce that the International Olympic Committee has officially transferred the 1904 Olympic games from Chicago to St. Louis.

The honor of your presence is requested at the third celebration of the revival of the

Olympic Games,

at the Stadium, Louisiana Purchase Exposition,

Saint Louis, Missouri,

August twenty-ninth to September third, Nineteen hundred and four.

J. E. Sullivan,
Chief, Department Physical Culture.

David R. Francis,   A. L. Shapleigh,   F. J. B. Skiff,
President.   Chairman, Physical Culture Committee.   Director of Exhibits.

The official Olympic games invitation (track and field) sent out by James Sullivan, chief of the Department of Physical Culture and director of Olympic games. From Jim Greensfelder et al., *1904 Olympic Games Official Medals and Badges.*

A stadium crowd awaits the beginning of Olympic games competition. From Mark Bennitt, ed., *History of the Louisiana Purchase Exposition.*

Participation medal given to every athlete that competed in any athletic event. From Jim Greensfelder et al., *1904 Olympic Games Official Medals and Badges.*

Medal design cast in gold, silver, and bronze for three top finishers in each event. The name of the event was inscribed on reverse. From Jim Greensfelder et al., *1904 Olympic Games Official Medals and Badges.*

All athletic medals bore inscription, "Olympic Games." From Jim
Greensfelder et al., *1904 Olympic Games Official Medals and
Badges.*

James Sullivan, number 35, dominates this group of Olympic officials. From Mark Bennitt, ed., *History of the Louisiana Purchase Exposition.*

Transfer Accepted

St. Louis, with a population of 575,000, was the fourth-largest city in the United States in 1904 behind New York, Chicago, and Philadelphia. The site had been founded as a fur trading post in 1763 by Pierre Liguest Laclede, a French trapper and trader, who named the post St. Louis in honor of Louis IX, the Crusader King of France. Louis IX ruled France from 1214 to 1270 and was canonized in 1297. In 1803 the United States negotiated the purchase of the Louisiana Territory from France and St. Louis became an American settlement. St. Louis served as the capital of Louisiana Territory (1805–1812) and the Territory of Missouri (1812–1820). As part of the Missouri Compromise in 1820, Missouri, as a slave state, and Maine, as a free state, were admitted to the Union. St. Louis relinquished the capital to Jefferson City, but remained the premier city of Missouri. St. Louis was incorporated as a town in 1821 and as a city in 1823. Located at the junction of the Missouri and Mississippi Rivers, St. Louis was the natural point of departure for the American West. Lewis and Clark departed from St. Louis up the Missouri River in 1804 on their epic voyage of discovery. American fur

traders based their operations from St. Louis, and with the advent of the
steamboat and river commerce the city became a prosperous transportation center.

The city's nickname, the Mound City, is derived from the original in-
habitants of the St. Louis area. The Hopewell Indians occupied the area
for about a thousand years (500 BC–400 AD) and constructed earthen
mounds as temples and burial sites. The most famous are located at
Cahokia Mounds State Park in Illinois just across the river from St.
Louis. The most prominent landmark in St. Louis today is the Gateway
Arch, a 630-foot high stainless steel monument symbolizing the city's
heritage as the gateway to the great American frontier.

The French explorer LaSalle, in the name of Louis XIV, claimed all
the land drained by the Mississippi River and its tributaries to the west
for the French Empire in 1663 and proclaimed such lands be called
Louisiana. A century later in 1763, after the defeat of France in the
Seven Years' War, Spain received title to Louisiana. In 1800 in a secret
treaty, Spain, threatened by the military ambitions of Napoleon Bona-
parte, ceded Louisiana back to France. Three years later, preparing for
war in Europe, Napoleon realized he could not defend French posses-
sions in America from the greater naval power of the British. At the
same time Americans desired to secure rights of commerce on the Mississippi River. President Thomas Jefferson instructed the American
minister to France, Robert Livingston, to discuss possible options with
the French court. Livingston, in a meeting with the prime minister of
France, Talleyrand, and Napoleon, was stunned when Napoleon suddenly asked how much the Jefferson administration would pay for all
the territory of Louisiana. James Monroe, the minister to England,
joined Livingston in Paris for the negotiations and eventually reached
an agreement with the French for the United States to purchase the entire territory, more than 828,000 square miles, for $15 million, about
three cents an acre. On October 20, 1803, the U.S. Congress ratified the
treaty transferring possession of the Louisiana Territory, and two months
later, on December 20, U.S. troops marched into New Orleans pro-
claiming American sovereignty. The vast lands of Louisiana doubled the
size of the country and eventually became the states of Arkansas, Missouri, Iowa, Minnesota, North and South Dakota, Nebraska, Oklahoma,
Kansas, Louisiana, almost all of Montana, a large portion of Wyoming,

and about a quarter of Colorado. The area was larger than Great Britain, France, Germany, Spain, Portugal, and Italy combined.

In 1890 the Governor of Missouri, David R. Francis, headed a delegation to Washington, D.C., for the purpose of securing the World's Fair for the city of St. Louis to commemorate the four hundredth anniversary of the Columbus discovery of America. The governor and his fellow delegates were unsuccessful. On April 28, 1890, President Benjamin Harrison signed a bill awarding the World's Columbian Exposition to Chicago. Francis, dismayed but not deterred, announced that St. Louis would undertake efforts to host a World's Fair to celebrate the centennial anniversary (1903) of the Louisiana Purchase.

By the end of the nineteenth century the world fair movement had achieved international prominence and prestige. Hosting a World's Fair symbolized a high level of urban achievement and was a matter of civic pride for any city fortunate enough to host an international festival. The concept originated in France with a national fair in 1797. The purpose of the first national fair was to promote French commerce by displaying the products and crafts of the country. In the 1820s national exhibits were held in England. In addition to commercial products, the English showcased the latest scientific and mechanical devices. The very first international World's Fair occurred at the Crystal Palace in London in 1851. The official proclamation succinctly stated its purpose as "to forward the progress of industrial civilization."[1] International fairs quickly evolved into venues for comparing national lifestyles and promoting national achievements. Nationalism was a constant theme at international festivals. The French built the Eiffel Tower in 1889 for the World's Fair of that year to commemorate the centennial of the French Revolution.

In the United States, Horace Greeley organized a national fair in New York in 1853 and at the last minute, in an attempt to emulate the British Crystal Palace Fair two years earlier, sent invitations to various nations of the world, but it remained largely an American event. The first real World's Fair in America occurred at Philadelphia in 1876 to celebrate the centennial of American independence. President Ulysses S. Grant opened the fair on May 10, 1876. Thirty-seven nations participated. The next American World's Fair was the Chicago exposition in 1893. Inventor George Ferris displayed a new mechanical marvel at Chicago, the Ferris Wheel. At the Congress of Historians an unknown scholar,

Frederick Jackson Turner, presented his paper, *The Significance of the Frontier in American History.* Eighty-six nations came to Chicago.

After failing to secure the 1893 World's Fair, David Francis continued his crusade and in January of 1896, speaking at a meeting of the Business Men's League of St. Louis, stated:

> I do not think it is any too early to begin laying plans for a great celebration. The Louisiana Purchase was the most important feature of the history of this state. An international exposition would be just the thing for a celebration. Congress should be asked to make an appropriation for a government exhibit as was done at the World's Fair (1893), and to assist us by official recognition. St. Louis is the most appropriate city for such a celebration as it is the gateway from the East to all the territory embodied in the original purchase. I think we could make an exposition on as large a scale as the World's Fair (1893), and have exhibits from all the countries on the globe.[2]

St. Louis newspapers took up the idea and began discussing the possibility of a centennial celebration of the Louisiana Purchase and in January of 1898 the Missouri Historical Society appointed a special committee of the society to investigate and recommend the most appropriate means of celebration. The special committee, agreeing with David Francis, proposed a World's Fair for St. Louis. A month later a bill was introduced in the Missouri House of Representatives for an international exposition at St. Louis for 1903. Three years later, on March 3, 1901, the U.S. Congress passed the Louisiana Purchase Exposition bill. In May 1901, David Francis was formally elected president of the Louisiana Purchase Exposition Company, the same month that the International Olympic Committee awarded the 1904 Olympic games to Chicago. A year later, on June 28, 1902, Congress voted to delay the World's Fair for one year to 1904. President Roosevelt issued the fair delay message on July 1, 1902. Seven months later on February 10, 1903, Coubertin transferred the Olympic games from Chicago to St. Louis.

The same day (February 10, 1903) that Henry Furber in Chicago was notified "Transfer accepted," Coubertin composed a letter to Francis:

> I have the pleasure of stating that the International Olympian Committee has consented to the proposed transfer of the Games of 1904 from Chicago to St. Louis. . . . The members of the International Committee, whose names I

enclose, being away and there being no possibility of calling a meeting before the Spring it took some time to write to them and collect their answers. I feel glad that we can help in some way to the success of your great and noble enterprise and you may be assured that all the National European Committees as well as the members of our International Committee will do their best to co-operate with you in that direction.[3]

Coubertin implied that the members of the IOC were supportive of moving the Olympics to St. Louis, but in fact all were opposed. Coubertin alone made the decision but was obviously unwilling to acknowledge this fact. The other notable features of Coubertin's letter to Francis are his request for Olympic program information as soon as possible, his request for the application of the term "Olympic games" as part of the World's Fair, and his recommendation for organizational responsibility for the Olympic games. Coubertin's letter continues:

It becomes necessary however, that the program, dates and duration of the games be known in Europe as soon as possible. The end of September remains undoubtedly the best season from the European point of view, the young men who will take part in the games being, as a rule, prevented from leaving their offices or work before the second part of August. As to the technical part of the program, it needs to be made public not less than a whole year before the games begin. I mean the details about the events, conditions, entries, status and amateurs, etc.

We took it for granted of course that the whole celebration of the games while officially connected with the Exposition would continue to bear the heading of Olympian Games of 1904 or the Olympian Games of Saint Louis. We would be very glad to hear that Mr. Spalding and the Amateur Athletic Union of the United States will remain in charge of part of the games or be asked to draw up the program.

Any information which you will be able to send promptly as to the organization of the games will be of great interest and very useful to us.[4]

St. Louis may not have impressed Coubertin during his visit in 1893, but once he made the decision to transfer the 1904 Olympics Coubertin initially was determined to ensure their success.

Michel Lagrave, the French commissioner to the St. Louis Exposition, sent a letter from Paris to Francis on February 17, 1903. Lagrave confirmed the Olympic transfer to St. Louis and then conveyed two requests of Coubertin.

My dear President:

    I am glad to let you know that the International Committee of Olympian Games has definitely sanctioned the removal of the Games to St. Louis: and from now they bear the name of the St. Louis Olympian Games.

    The Committee has asked only that this title . . . will comprehend all the sports of 1904. M. de Coubertin seemed desirous also that a subsidy of $200. should be given by the Exposition to the Olympic Review, which is the official paper of the Committee, so as to establish the relation which unites the Olympian Committee with St. Louis.[5]

The Executive Committee of the St. Louis Exposition during their March meeting of 1903 approved the payment of the two hundred dollars to the IOC and on a separate motion approved the payment of $6,954.47 to the Chicago Olympic Committee. At least Chicago was partially compensated for its one and a half years of Olympic efforts, but it could be said that St. Louis bought the 1904 Olympics. The March minutes of the St. Louis Executive Committee read, "In the presence of the Committee Mr. Shapleigh, Chairman of the Special Committee on Olympian Games, approved the voucher providing for payment of $6,954.47 to E. A. Potter, Treasurer of the Olympian Games Association of Chicago."[6]

The second request—"The Committee, (read Coubertin), has asked only that this title, (Olympic games), will comprehend all the sports of 1904"—seems reasonable if the experience of the Paris Olympics of 1900 are kept in mind, where the word "Olympics" was deliberately omitted in any reference to sports competition of any kind.[7] Obviously, Coubertin's desire was to ensure that the mistakes of 1900 were not repeated in 1904. The Olympics, while associated with the exposition, had to be recognized as an international entity in their own right. Coubertin's request was also made before the organizational structure of the exposition was implemented. Coubertin was unaware that an entire department, Physical Culture, would, for the first time in the history of international expositions, be organized and devoted to conducting sports competition throughout the seven-month period of the exposition. While the universal use of the term "Olympics" for all sports competition at St. Louis did cause some confusion as to which events constituted the Olympic games, a close inspection reveals that even though all events were conducted under the Olympic umbrella, the designation of the events of the Olympic games are discernible. At Paris it was unclear which sports were Olympic because the term was never used. At St. Louis, it was unclear which sports were parts of the Olympics because the term was always used. Coubertin's request swung the pendulum from one extreme to another, but the competition, while at times confusing in regards to Olympic status at St. Louis, was nevertheless well promoted.

David Francis departed New York on February 12, 1903, for a nineteen-day tour of Europe to promote the St. Louis Louisiana Purchase Exposition. He received a telegram aboard ship just prior to departure informing him that the IOC had sanctioned the transfer of the Olympic games to St. Louis. Francis made two brief visits to Paris on March 2 and March 7. On both occasions his itinerary was fully scheduled by the French commissioner, Lagrave. A meeting was arranged for Francis with the president of France, Laubet, and other French dignitaries were invited to receptions and dinners to hear Francis speak. There was a lavish banquet organized by Lagrave in honor of the American, David Francis, on March 7, and yet while Lagrave and Coubertin obviously knew one another, it is evident that Coubertin did not attend any of the functions where he could have met Francis.

On March 7, as he was leaving Paris for Berlin, Francis composed a letter to Coubertin. While Francis did not meet Coubertin in Paris, he must have received a letter from him, perhaps delivered by Commissioner Lagrave, because Francis refers to two separate letters of Coubertin in his letter of March 7.

> Dear Sir:
>
> I regret exceedingly not being able to see you today in Paris. I have just read your letter while en route from Paris to Berlin, and hasten to make reply.
>
> I cleared from New York for Europe on February 12, and found in my stateroom on the steamer a telegram from Saint Louis stating the Olympian Games had been transferred from Chicago to Saint Louis. Of course I was very much gratified at the decision, as was no doubt the Director of Exhibits, in whose Division the Olympian Games are classed. I shall read with interest on my arrival in Saint Louis your letter addressed to me there. This is written on the Nord Express while I am en route to Berlin. If

you receive this missive in time to send me to Bremen or Southampton care the KRONPRINZ WILHELM a copy of your letter addressed to me at Saint Louis, I shall be able to give some thought to the matter while en route to America.

My inability to remain longer in Paris was not only a loss to myself personally but I fear to the Exposition also. Rest assured that nothing short of very positive engagements which could not be delayed, could have prevented me from seeing you in Paris, where I arrived at 11 o'clock last evening and left at 1:50 this afternoon, after being the recipient of a most complimentary function at the Hotel Continental at 11 o'clock today.

With assurances of personal esteem, I am,
Your obedient servant,
(signed) David R. Francis
President.[8]

In stark contrast to the open hostility of the president of the Paris Exposition to the Olympic games, this letter from Francis was a cordial and sincere effort to express his gratitude for the games and his disappointment in being unable to meet with Coubertin. If the two men could have met, perhaps developed a mutual regard for one another, maybe Francis would have extended a personal invitation to Coubertin to visit St. Louis for the Exposition and Olympic games. Coubertin's presence in St. Louis almost certainly would have resulted in a more formal Olympic program and pageantry. Members of the American press assumed Coubertin's attendance. His photograph and an article appeared in the Topeka, Kansas *Journal* on April 7, 1903, with the headline: "A Sporting Baron" and read, "Baron Pierre de Coubertin is one of the leading sporting authorities of Europe, and he will come to this country to view the great international games at the St. Louis exposition of 1904."[9] The attendance of the president of the International Olympic Committee at the St. Louis Olympics would certainly have enhanced the international prominence of the Olympic games.

Frederick Skiff, director of exhibits, almost immediately took action to develop the organizational plans for the Olympics. Only three weeks after St. Louis was awarded the games, on March 2, Skiff wrote a letter to Francis requesting permission to form the Physical Culture Department. The Executive Committee of the exposition, acting on behalf of Francis during his absence in Europe, directed Skiff to proceed.[10] Baron

Coubertin remained active and by mid-March had written to the Amateur Athletic Union of the United States, in care of James Sullivan, the organization's influential secretary, requesting the AAU to serve as the representatives of the IOC and take control of organizing the Olympics for 1904.

> Time is unfortunately rather short to organize the games, and therefore we ask from you that the officers of the Amateur Athletic union consent to act as our representatives on this occasion to draw up with the authorities of the exposition the technical programme of the games, which ought to reach Europe no later than the end of May.[11]

Coubertin slightly altered the truth to achieve results when he continued,

> I informed President Francis when he was traveling in Europe of this plan, and I would esteem it a favor if you would call on him after his return and set things aright as soon as possible.
>
> I thank you for this great service which you in so doing will have rendered the cause of international sport.[12]

Coubertin in his letter to David Francis requested that Albert Spalding head the Olympic organizing efforts. He did not repeat this request to Sullivan and the AAU. Sullivan promptly notified Walter Liginger, president of the AAU, of Coubertin's request. Liginger, on March 27, 1903, notified Coubertin that the AAU would accept responsibility for organizing the 1904 Olympics. An Olympic Games Committee was promptly formed by the AAU president and announced on April 4: Walter Liginger, Milwaukee—Chairman; Bartow Weeks, New York Athletic Club; E. E. Babb, Boston Athletic Association; James E. Sullivan, New York; and John J. O'Connors, president of the Western Association of AAU in St. Louis.[13]

Immediately, the American press began to speculate and campaign for the designation of an Olympic games director. On April 9 the *New York Herald* headlines read, "THE OLYMPIAN GAMES; St. Louis Fair to Produce Notable Carnival of Sport; The Directorship Question; James E. Sullivan the Logical Choice For the Position—He is the Dictator of American Athletics—The Story of His Varied Career." The article began by remarking on the efforts of the St. Louis exposition organizers in regards to the Olympic games, ". . . the authorities of the world's fair are extending every effort to make the contests the most notable ever held. The stadium, plans for which are now under way, will be of mammoth size and of imposing design." Coubertin is acknowledged as "the well known French publicist" and the president of the IOC, which transferred the Olympics to St. Louis. The full text of Coubertin's letter to Sullivan requesting the leadership of the AAU for the Olympic games is presented. Brief mention is made of Albert Spalding and his being unavailable for the directorship of the Olympic games: "A. G. Spalding having been unable through other duties to shoulder the work of director of sports for the big fair, sportsmen are wondering who will be chosen in his place." The other duties engaging the attention of Spalding was his formation of a "Special Baseball Commission" to research and determine the origin of American baseball. This was the organization responsible for creating the myth that Abner Doubleday invented baseball at Cooperstown in 1839 and resulted in the publication of Spalding's book *America's National Game* in 1911. The rest of the article discusses the career of Sullivan, but leaves little doubt who should become the director for the Olympic games: "The general opinion is that Secretary Sullivan would be the best man in the country to fill the position."[14]

While the major concern was the appointment of a director for the Olympics, other plans were being made to ensure an international field of athletes for St. Louis. The *Chicago Chronicle* on April 11 reported, "French Athletes Will Come."

> M. Lagrave, the French commissioner to the St. Louis exposition, has appointed Jules Marcadet, who is prominent in athletic circles, to take charge of the French exhibit of physical culture and has designated a committee to assist in securing the participation in the exhibit of the leading athletic societies in France . . . and taking an active part in the Olympian games.[15]

James Sullivan received a telegram from Frederick Skiff requesting a meeting in St. Louis. Sullivan, in New York, boarded a train for St. Louis on the afternoon of April 15. He met with Skiff and Alfred Shapleigh, a member of the executive committee and chairman of the athletic committee for the Louisiana Purchase Exposition. Upon his return to New

York on April 23, Sullivan provided an analysis of St. Louis athletic plans for 1904 to the *New York Evening Sun:* ". . . it is the intention of the World's Fair people to make amateur sports a prominent feature of its exposition in 1904. . . . The Olympian games, of course, will be the principal feature, as the Exposition authorities have been promised exhibits for the department of physical culture, and this will naturally include competing teams from many countries."[16] The expectation, "and this will naturally include competing teams from many countries," did not materialize.

While Sullivan was in St. Louis, AAU President Liginger announced in the *Milwaukee Sentinel* on April 17 that James Sullivan would be in charge of the Olympic games and that officials of the St. Louis exposition would soon make an official announcement. Sullivan and the Olympics were national news for the next several months as newspapers around the country carried stories on the Olympic games and James Sullivan's fabled career. There were no other candidates. Sullivan was the unanimous choice of the national press. Several months later, on July 16, 1903, the *St. Louis Republic* announced the formal selection of James E. Sullivan as chief of the Physical Culture Department and director of the Olympic games. The same article reported on the plans already made for the Olympic games.

> The Olympic games at the St. Louis Exposition will attract to this city the greatest athletes of the entire world. . . . This is the first time in the history of expositions that athletics have been officially recognized. An appropriation of $75,000 has been made for prizes. A stadium, with a seating capacity of 35,000, is being erected on the Exposition grounds. A permanent gymnasium belonging to Washington University will be a part of the display.[17]

The *Republic* continued to report on the "Elaborate Programme" of athletic events planned for the Department of Physical Culture over the entire seven-month period of the Exposition.

> It is the intention of the department to devote two days to championship games of the Amateur Athletic Union of the United States; the Olympic games will occupy a week; a cross-country championship contest will be

given; bicycling will have three days; national interscholastic championships, two days; quoits, one day; national swimming championship of America, several days; lawn tennis, two weeks. Two days have been set aside for cricket, two for association football, two for Gaelic football and two days for an international hurling match. The Roque championship will be a feature, as well as basket-ball championship for schools, young men's Christian associations and college athletic clubs. One day will be devoted to gymnastic championships. Three days will be given to archery for men and women; two days to equestrian polo and two to lacrosse, the idea being to enter all the American teams in one contest and pit the winner against the champions of Canada. There will be a championship meeting for colleges of the Western States and a national inter-collegiate meeting, as well as separate days devoted to the German-American Turner societies. Two days have been set aside for the Y.M.C.A. championships; wrestling matches will occupy two days; automobiling is to receive attention, but the courses have not yet been selected. These races will occupy a week. Negotiations are pending with the North American Association of Amateur Oarsmen to bring to St. Louis the champion rowing teams to compete in the national events. A liberal appropriation has been made for college football and baseball. The handicap college athletic meetings will be held early in the year. There will be schoolboy meetings, for the schools of St. Louis, and meetings for the colleges of St. Louis and the West.[18]

Thirty-two separate sport competitions are listed above, with the Olympic games scheduled for only a one-week period. Other sports involving international competition, such as gymnastics, lacrosse, tennis, and swimming, are mentioned, but not as part of the Olympic games. In 1904, there was no official Olympic program of sports and in the minds of many people, including James Sullivan, the Olympics were viewed simply as an international track and field championship event and are listed as such in the above article.

Sullivan complied with Coubertin's directive, made the previous February at the time of the transfer of the Olympics from Chicago to St. Louis, that the title "Olympics" refer to all sports of the 1904 exposition. He did not contact Coubertin to explain the extensive athletic program, distinct from the Olympics, planned for St. Louis; he merely attached the Olympic title, as directed, to all the sports. Some sports, while appropriate for inclusion on the World's Fair program, blatantly violated the spirit of Olympism. Competitions restricted to the high school students of St. Louis hardly qualified for the title "Olympic," but every sports medal awarded by Sullivan, including the student athletes of

St. Louis winners, bore the Olympic title.[19] The seemingly contradictory use of the term "Olympic" did not create any confusion in 1904.

Coubertin abandoned the St. Louis Olympics after he was notified by AAU President Liginger on March 27 that the AAU accepted Coubertin's request that the AAU organize and conduct the Olympics. Coubertin ceased communicating with anyone involved with the management of the St. Louis exposition or Olympic games, and St. Louis officials made no effort to keep the Baron informed. This lack of communication and Coubertin's decision not to visit St. Louis during the Olympics prevented the establishment of the Olympic games as a recognized international institution in 1904. Four years later, with Coubertin fully engaged, the London Olympics, again a component of a World's Fair, built on the St. Louis experience and achieved international success and recognition. The lack of leadership on the part of Coubertin and the IOC, including American member William Sloane, resulted in a missed opportunity for the Olympic movement in St. Louis.

Three days of dedication ceremonies were held on April 30, May 1, and May 2, 1903, to commemorate the one hundredth anniversary of the purchase of the Louisiana Territory from France and exactly one year before the scheduled opening of the Louisiana Purchase Exposition. On the opening day of festivities President Roosevelt attended and made a stirring patriotic speech on the importance of the Louisiana Purchase to the American nation. May 1 was Diplomatic Day, devoted to recognition of the foreign nations planning to participate in 1904. The final day of celebration was States Day of Dedication, recognizing the participating states within the union. William Harper, the University of Chicago president who had once planned to host the 1904 Olympics, attended, and on the last day of the dedication ceremonies offered an invocation. Nearly one hundred correspondents from the United States and around the world attended the three days of ceremonies. On the evening of May 2 the reporters were guests of the exposition for a performance at the Olympic Theatre by Julia Marlow and afterwards a dinner at Faust's restaurant.[20]

Frederick Skiff officially created the Department of Physical Culture on August 1, 1903. James Sullivan, named chief of the department two weeks earlier, assumed the mantle of leadership for the great sports extravaganza for the World's Fair of 1904 with the Olympic games as the main event. Sullivan and the AAU Olympic Committee met in St. Louis August 10–11. In compliance with the request of Coubertin, the dates for the Olympic games were set for August 29 to September 3, 1904. The *St. Louis Republic* made an announcement of the medals and prizes for the Olympics on September 29. "The prizes for the games, besides the Olympic medals, will be of the highest value allowed by the AAU rules and will be more ornate than any similar prizes ever awarded to amateurs in this country. Silver cups will be presented to the winners in addition to the regular prizes."[21] Preparations continued to ensure all would be ready for opening day of the great Louisiana Purchase Exposition of 1904, but most of the work remaining, while important, even crucial, was uneventful, and an atmosphere of eager but quiet anticipation settled over St. Louis.

The morning of April 30, 1904, brought blue skies and a brilliant sun to St. Louis. It was a perfect spring day for the opening of the Louisiana Purchase Exposition. Officials and dignitaries began assembling on the lower floor of the Hall of Congresses around 8:30. Shortly after nine o'clock the procession, lead by the Jefferson Guards and accompanied by the band of John Philip Sousa, marched to the Plaza of St. Louis, the center of the grounds, and at the base of the Louisiana Monument gathered for the opening ceremonies. After almost ninety minutes, all members of the procession were finally assembled in their proper places and David Francis stepped to the podium, called the vast assemblage to order, paused for sustained and enthusiastic cheers, bowed his head for the invocation, and then began his opening remarks. The final words uttered by Francis were, "Open ye gates! Swing wide ye portals! Enter herein ye sons of men! Learn the lesson here taught and gather from it inspiration for still greater accomplishments."[22] William H. Thompson, treasurer of the exposition, and Isaac Taylor, director of works and the mastermind behind the arrangement and construction of buildings and grounds, spoke after Francis. Taylor concluded his address by presenting the keys to the exhibit palaces to President Francis. A music interlude followed with Sousa's band rendition of the Von der Stucken's march, "Louisiana." Frederick Skiff spoke next and received the exposition keys from Francis. A chorus of four hundred then sang *Hymn of the West,* written by Edmund Clarence Stedman, music by John Knowles.

Speeches were then made in turn by Mr. Rolla Wells, mayor of St. Louis; Thomas Carter, president of the National Commission; Senator Henry E. Burnham of New Hampshire; Representative James A. Tawney; Albino R. Nuncio, commissioner-general from Mexico; Michel Lagrave, commissioner-general from France; E. H. Harriman, railroad magnate; and finally William H. Taft, secretary of war, serving as the official representative of the president of the United States, Theodore Roosevelt. Upon the conclusion of Taft's speech, Francis dispatched a telegram to Roosevelt in the White House.

> President Francis, of the Louisiana Purchase Exposition Company, presents his compliments to the President of the United States and begs to say that the management of the Louisiana Purchase Exposition awaits the pleasure of President Roosevelt who is to transmit the electrical energy which is to unfurl the flags and start the machinery of the great Exposition.[23]

The Francis telegram arrived in the East room of the White House, where President Roosevelt made the following remarks to an assembly of invited guests for the unique ceremony opening the World's Fair and the Olympic games:

> I have received from the exposition grounds the statement that the management of the Louisiana Purchase Exposition awaits the pressing of the button which is to transmit the electrical energy which is to unfurl the flags and start the machinery of the Exposition.
>
> I wish now to greet all present, especially the representatives of the foreign nations here represented, in the name of the American people, and to thank these representatives for the parts their several countries have taken in being represented in this centennial anniversary of the greatest step in the movement which transformed the American republic from a small confederacy of states lying along the Atlantic seaboard to a continental nation.
>
> This Exposition is primarily intended to show the progress in the industry, the science and the art, not only of the American nation, but of all other nations in the great and wonderful century which has just closed. Every department of human activity will be represented there, and perhaps I will be allowed, as honorary president of the athletic association, which, under European management, started to revive the memory of the Olympic Games, to say that I am glad that in addition to paying proper heed to the progress of industry, of science, of art, we have also paid

proper heed to the development of athletic pastimes, which are useful in themselves, which are useful as showing that it is wise for nations to be able to relax as well as work.

I greet you all. I appreciate your having come here on this occasion, and in the presence of you representing the American government and the governments of the foreign nations, I here open the Louisiana Purchase Exposition.[24]

Roosevelt, in a letter to Henry Furber (May 28, 1902), had volunteered to open the Olympic games in Chicago before they were transferred to St. Louis, and earlier in the spring of 1904, largely through the efforts of Casper Whitney,[25] one of the American members of the International Olympic Committee, Roosevelt had agreed to serve as honorary president of the Olympic games. While the games were part of the greater exposition, Roosevelt's remarks indicate the significance of the Olympics to the World's Fair. The opening of the fair included the opening of the Olympic games in St. Louis.

After his brief speech, Roosevelt pressed the golden telegraph key that flashed the signal to set the machinery in motion in St. Louis. President Cleveland had pressed the same golden key to commence the machinery of the Chicago World's Fair in 1893. At the exposition, Francis received the signal from the White House, raised his arms toward the sky, and declared the exposition open. Simultaneously, as Francis describes the scene in his official report, "ten thousand flags fluttered from their masts, the fountains shot their spray into the air and from the caverns under Festival Hall the waters leaped and sent their roaring torrents down the cascades, the whirl of mighty machinery became the song of hundreds of motors and engines, two hundred thousand voices and scores of bands made the wind ring, and the greatest of universal expositions was open."[26]

The magnitude of the World's Fair of 1904, physically and emotionally, was enormous. In terms of sheer size it was the largest exposition the world had ever witnessed. Forest Park, the fairground site, measured 1.75 miles by 1.05 miles, a total of 1,272 acres, dwarfing the 664 acres of the 1893 Chicago exposition. Official attendance tabulations indicated that more than nineteen and a half million people passed through the turnstiles. The city of St. Louis added 450 new cars to the transit system, with trains running to the fairgrounds every fifteen minutes. A railroad network was built within the grounds to transport people among the exhibits. St. Louis rebuilt more than seventy miles of streets and built more than thirty miles of new streets. Commenting on the extensive nature of the contents of the exposition, Francis remarked, "So thoroughly does it represent the world's civilization that if all man's other works were by some unspeakable catastrophe, blotted out, the records here established by the assembled nations would offer all necessary standards for the rebuilding of our entire civilization."[27]

The director of exhibits, Skiff, organized the fair into sixteen separate departments with the intent "to demonstrate man and his works, emphasizing education."[28] The goal was to illustrate the progress of human civilization from barbarism to modern western culture, emphasizing the superiority of the latter. Exhibits featuring "primitive" peoples from around the world—Patagonians from Argentina, the Ainu people of Japan, American Indians, and pygmies from Africa—provided visual opportunities for fairgoers to observe "savage" cultures. Exhibits displaying the latest technological advances offered a sharp contrast to the primitive civilizations and excited expectations for a new era in living standards for the twentieth century. Airships and automobiles, the latter introduced to the American public three years earlier at the Pan-American Fair in Buffalo, represented the latest innovations in transportation and promised to transform human interaction. International congresses brought leading educators, scientists, and scholars from around the world, including Max Weber, Hugo Munsterberg, Henri Poincaré, and William R. Harper, to share and exchange current ideas in disciplines ranging from history and philosophy to the natural sciences and mathematics.

Impressions made on visitor psyches were equally impressive: "so long as I've lived on God's green earth I never looked to see nothin' like this! It's fine!" "We are enjoying every minute," "Beautiful beyond description," were typical exclamations of fair patrons. Joe Mitchell Chapple described the experience of many visitors to the fair when he wrote in the *National Magazine*, "The Fair is a succession of mental shocks, cumulative and educative," and concluded that the most impressive was "the deep, far reaching, ethical, and educative import of the Universal Exposition in St. Louis." At the stroke of midnight, December 1, 1904, after seven months, the World's Fair came to a close. Francis made a brief address concluding with, "Farewell, a long farewell, to all thy splendor." The band played *Auld Lang Syne,* and the chilly evening's festivities concluded with a massive fireworks display, ending with the words "Farewell—Goodnight" blazing across the night sky.[29]

Photographers, using the bulky and heavy equipment of the time, tried to capture and portray the essence of the World's Fair, including the Olympic games. The most enterprising, energetic, and prolific of these photographers was Jessie Tarbox Beals, the first woman news photographer. She achieved this distinction when hired by two newspapers in Buffalo, New York, in 1902, the *Inquirer* and *Courier,* to provide photographs to illustrate news articles. Jessie moved to St. Louis from her home in Buffalo in the spring of 1904 to devote all her time and energy to photographing all aspects of the Louisiana Purchase Exposition. During the six months of the World's Fair, working seven days a week from dawn to dusk and into the night, she produced more than five thousand photographic plates. Many were sold to the *World's Fair Bulletin,* the official publication of the Louisiana Purchase Exposition, and many more to magazines and newspapers across the country.

Beals, just thirty-three years of age, became a celebrity during the exposition. Bespectacled like a reference librarian, attired in puffy sleeved blouses with a knee-length duster flapping behind her and a long flowing skirt brushing the grass just above the ground, always a grand ornate hat on her head and the forty-pound camera and tripod in tow, she made quite a sight scampering back and forth across the extensive acreage of the exposition grounds. Photographs reveal her in action behind the camera at the start of a swimming event and whisking along in the background of a throwing event at the Olympic stadium, in characteristic attire, with camera equipment in hand and a young male assistant trailing behind trying to keep up.

Upon her departure from Buffalo, the local newspapers reported, "Buffalo lost one of its best professional women today when Mrs. Jessie Tarbox Beals, staff camera artist, departed on an early morning train for St. Louis."[30] Mrs. Beals viewed the Louisiana Purchase Exposition as an opportunity to establish her professional reputation and achieve her ultimate goal of opening her own studio in New York City. The first few days in St. Louis were frustrating. Jessie, counting on her reputation in Buffalo, applied for an official press permit that would allow her unrestricted access to the exposition. Apparently unimpressed and doubting the ability of a woman to succeed in what was considered a male occupation, fair officials denied her press permit request. Undaunted, Jessie contacted the local St. Louis newspapers, hoping to be hired as a staff photographer. All claimed to be fully staffed. Brash, single-minded, and gifted with the "ability to hustle," as she put it, Jessie resumed pleading her case for a press permit, ultimately prevailing. This was a significant event and no small accomplishment. St. Louis newspaper headlines reported, "Woman Gets Permit to Take Pictures At the Fair." The article went on to state, "The first permit to be issued to a woman authorizing the taking of photographs on the World's Fair Grounds has been granted to Mrs. T. Beals. Mrs. Beals secured notice through her work in obtaining photographs of the double suicide of Mr. and Mrs. Pennell of Buffalo who rode their automobile over a cliff into a quarry. She also received numerous souvenirs from Sir Thomas Lipton in token of his appreciation of her work. . ."[31]

Sir Thomas Lipton, the Irish yachtsman and tea magnate, visited Buffalo in August of 1903 on his way to view Niagara Falls. He was in America to compete in the America's Cup race with his yacht, *Erin.* Jessie, never one to miss an opportunity, approached him, and as reported in the *Courier,* "Sir Thomas genially gave the *Sunday Courier* photographer a few poses."[32] These "few poses" brought national recognition to the work of Jessie T. Beals.

Once Jessie had her press permit and recognition from the St. Louis newspapers, she became overnight a fully accredited press photographer for *Leslie's Weekly,* the *New York Herald,* the *New York Tribune,* and three newspapers in Buffalo and all the local St. Louis papers. The intrepid photographer was beyond intimidation. When Theodore Roosevelt made a visit to the fair, Jessie devoted a full day of energy to photographing the president, once ordering him to halt and pose for a picture. By the end of the day Jessie had recorded thirty-two images of the president and his family. In her diary Jessie wrote of that day, "I followed his carriage all day running across lots to get ahead of him and make a new picture at every stop. When the day was over and he stopped at the Philippine Village, I was there again to take a last picture. I heard him ask his Secretary, 'Good Lord, Loeb, where in the world does that woman get all her plates?'"[33]

Jessie possessed more than tenacity. Learning of the scheduled balloon races, she became inspired to photograph the grounds from the basket of a balloon. Never lacking courage, only official permission to ascend in a balloon, Jessie ignored the exposition authorities and, as told in a later account, "Just as one of the balloons was being set free, the huge crowd was thunderstruck to see a woman, a camera slung over her shoulder, grip the top of a basket and pull herself aboard. The balloon was off, and with it, the intrepid woman photographer." The bird's-eye photographs, taken from a height of nine hundred feet, produced a magnificent panoramic view of the World's Fair. Published in the *World's Fair Bulletin,* they drew effusive praise from David Francis: "I wish to thank you cordially for the beautiful photographs of the Main Basin and the landscape surrounding same; it is a view which I wish to remember."[34] At the conclusion of the exposition, Francis personally recommended, and the judges for photography awards approved, the awarding of a prestigious gold medal in recognition of Jessie's work.

The popularity of the World's Fair in St. Louis did not end for Americans on December 1, 1904. Forty years later the movie *Meet Me in St. Louis,* starring Judy Garland, portrayed family life centered around the World's Fair in St. Louis and introduced the popular song, *Meet Me in St. Louis, Louis* (lyrics by Andrew B. Sterling and music by Henry Mills). The film won an award as one of the ten best of 1944.

> Meet me in St. Louis, Louis,
> Meet me at the fair,
> Don't tell me the lights are shining
> Any place but there;
> We will dance the Hoochee-Koochee
> I will be your tootsie wootsie
> If you will meet me in St. Louis, Louis
> Meet me at the fair.[35]

In 1986 the 1904 World's Fair Society, headquartered in St. Louis, was organized to study and perpetuate the memory of the Louisiana Purchase Exposition. It is an active organization with more than five hundred members, and maintains a Web site, publishes a monthly newsletter, and conducts monthly meetings and special events to share information and memorabilia of the 1904 World's Fair.

St. Louis Olympian Games

There was no Olympic charter in 1904 to guide the St. Louis Olympic organizers. The Olympic games had been held only twice before and only once successfully. Any rules that existed were only in the mind of Pierre de Coubertin, and after his final letter to James Sullivan in March of 1903 Coubertin abruptly ended his involvement with the St. Louis Olympics. Coubertin had won the power struggle with Sullivan over control of the Olympic games, but he still could not overcome his personal dislike of Sullivan. While Coubertin may have been disappointed with the transfer of the Olympics to St. Louis, it was his personal feud with Sullivan that caused him to disassociate himself from the St. Louis Olympics. Just as he had at the Paris Olympics in 1900, Coubertin, to the detriment of the Olympic movement, withdrew his involvement in 1904.

President Roosevelt welcomed the Olympic games to St. Louis and America in his remarks from the White House opening the World's Fair on April 30, and for the next seven months athletic events were an integral part of the Louisiana Purchase Exposition. On Sunday, May 1,

1904, the *St. Louis Post-Dispatch* ran a special fair edition with the head-lines, "Olympic Games At the World's Fair An Athletic Festival; Stadium Will Be Scene of Some Remarkable Contests; Marathon Road Race Will Be One of the Features; Greatest Athletic Fest Ever Held Will Be Olympian Games; Champions From All Over the World Will Compete For Laurels." The following paragraph read, "The Olympic games, a revival of the contests of ancient Greece, which will be held in the stadium from August 29 to September 3 inclusive, will unquestionably be the most important feature of this remarkable athletic festival." Then on May 12, just two days before the beginning of athletic competition, the *Post-Dispatch* reported, "All is now in readiness for the opening of the Olympic games in the stadium. . . . local athletes will thus have the distinction of competing for the first Olympic medals in America." And later, "Central High School Victorious in Olympic Games." Journalists were not the only ones using the Olympic name indiscriminately. The chief of the Department of Physical Culture and director of the Olympic games, James Sullivan, included the following statements in his official final report: "During the Olympic Games, which extended from May to November . . ." and ". . . Olympic Games held from August 29th to September 3rd brought together in the stadium the most noted athletes."[1] It was acceptable in 1904 to have two definitions for "Olympic games," and all understood the different contexts.

In April the *Post-Dispatch* published a schedule of athletic events for the World's Fair under the title, "Program of the Olympic Games." While the dates for some of the events were later changed, the program clearly indicates that the events from August 29 to September 3 were only part of the "Olympic games" scheduled from May to November.

Program of the Olympic Games

May 14—Interscholastic meet
May 21—Open Handicap athletic meeting
May 28—Interscholastic meet for schools of Louisiana Purchase
    Territory
May 30—Western college championships
June 2—AAU handicap meet
June 3—AAU Jr. championship
June 4—AAU Sr. championship
June 11—Olympic college championships, open to colleges of the
    world

June 13—Central Assoc. AAU championships
June 18—Turner's mass exhibitions
June 20–25—College baseball
June 29,30—Interscholastic championships
July 1,2—Turner's international and individual team contest
July 4—AAU all around champions
July 5,6,7—Lacrosse
July 8,9—Swimming and Water Polo championships
July 11,12—Interscholastic basketball
July 13,14—YMCA basketball championships
July 18,19—College basketball
July 20–23—Irish sports
July 29—Open athletic club handicap meeting of the Western Assoc.
     AAU
Aug. 1–6—Bicycling
Aug. 8–13—Tennis
Aug. 18—YMCA gymnastic championships
Aug. 19—YMCA handicap meeting
Aug. 20—YMCA championship meeting
Aug. 29–Sept. 3—Olympic Games
Sept. 8–10—World's fencing championships
Sept. 12–15—Olympic cricket championships
Sept. 19–24—Golf
Sept. 26–Oct. 1—Military athletic carnival
Oct. 14, 15—AAU wrestling championships
Oct. 27—Turner's mass exhibition
Oct. 28, 29—AAU gymnastic championships
Nov. 10, 11—Relay racing, open to athletic clubs, colleges, schools, and
     YMCA's
Nov. 12—College football
Nov. 15–17—Association football
Nov. 17—X-country championships
Nov. 24—College football and local x-country championships: East vs.
     West[2]

Olympic concepts and principles were only in the embryonic stage of development in 1904 and existed only in vague and imprecise fashion in the minds of only a few individuals, with Pierre de Coubertin and Princeton's William Milligan Sloane being the most prominent; neither of them attended the St. Louis Olympics. In the public mind of 1904 there was no need for precise and exclusive definitions. An argument could be made that the Olympic games of 1904 consisted only of those events occurring from August 29 to September 3, and were mainly track and field events. Another equally valid argument could be that the St. Louis Olympics spanned the entire seven months of all athletic competition from May to November of the World's Fair. Both positions, while plausible, are inadequate. Coubertin and the IOC, from its inception in 1894 through 1903, had discussed Olympic philosophy and principles to guide Olympic competition, and these discussions provided the basis for the eventual Olympic charter published a few years after the St. Louis Olympics. While unpublished in 1904, there were Olympic expectations.

In his meticulously researched statistical analysis of the St. Louis Olympics,[3] Olympic historian and author Bill Mallon provides four Olympic principles to determine which events should be considered as constituting the Olympic games of 1904. First, competition must be open to international participants. Second, competition must not include handicapped events. Third, competition must not have designated restrictions or limitations such as age, religion, national origin, or level of competence (junior, intermediate, or novice events). And fourth, competition is restricted to amateur athletes. Only this last concept is no longer part of the Olympic creed, having fallen victim to the Cold War competition between the corporate- and the state-sponsored athlete.

A review of the athletic events, using the four criteria above, immediately reveals those events which cannot be considered Olympic in status or stature. Events open only to Americans or Irish clearly violate Olympic expectations, as do those events restricted to geographical regions or level of competition such as college or high school competitions. Handicapped events are similarly disqualified.

The St. Louis Olympic games, with opening ceremonies conducted on May 14, were held from July 1 through November 23 and consisted of the following fifteen sports.

Sport	Dates	Facility
1. Archery	September 19–21	Stadium
2. Boxing	September 21–22	Gymnasium
3. Cycling	August 2–5	Stadium
4. Diving	September 7	Exhibition Lake
5. Fencing	September 7–8	Gymnasium
6. Golf	September 19–24	Glen Echo Country Club

7. Gymnastics	July 1, 2, 4	Stadium
8. Lacrosse	July 2, 7	Stadium
9. Rowing and Sculling	July 30	Creve Coeur Lake
10. Soccer	November 16–18, 23	Stadium
11. Swimming	September 5–7	Exhibition Lake
12. Tennis	August 29–September 3	Courts adjacent to Stadium
13. Track and Field	August 29–September 3	Stadium
14. Weight Lifting	September 3	Stadium
15. Wrestling	October 14–15	Stadium

"Olympic Contests This Afternoon," proclaimed the *St. Louis Post-Dispatch* on Saturday May 14. Skies were clear and the temperature "delightfully cool" for the opening ceremonies scheduled to begin at 2:30. The assembled spectators, officials, and athletes waited until 2:50 for the arrival of the distinguished guests while listening to music performed by Weil's Band (John Philip Sousa and Band were performing at the same time at the Grand Band Stand). David Francis led the group of dignitaries as they disembarked from an intramural car just east of the stadium entrance. Immediately, with the band playing "inspiring airs" and leading the way, seventy-five athletes, assembled in line two-by-two on the stadium infield by James Sullivan, began marching toward the east gate of the stadium. During pauses in the music, the boys "roared their school yells enthusiastically." Sullivan informed Francis that all was in readiness to begin the Olympic games. When the marching athletes reached a point in the field opposite the east gate they executed an about-face and marched down the center of the infield. Francis, with Secretary of State John Hay (representing President Roosevelt) at his side, led a double file of silk-hatted officials and commissioners down the field immediately in the rear of the column of bathrobed and bare-legged athletes. Senator Carter and members of the National Commission, with exposition officials Frederick Skiff, Walter Stevens, and Isaac Taylor, were among the party of dignitaries, as was the author, historian, and lifelong friend of Secretary of State Hay, Henry Adams. Foreign dignitaries included Baron Moncheur, the Belgian minister, and Herr Theodore Lewald, the German commissioner, among others.[4]

As the band reached the seats, the crowd began cheering when the double row of athletes divided and Francis, Secretary Hay, and their party turned to the left in the middle of the stadium and proceeded to boxes reserved for them in the grandstand. Just as Hay was seated the band struck up the Star Spangled Banner. Hay arose and removed his hat. The others in the party did likewise, and every man in the stands and on the field followed suit. After the national anthem performance Hay was escorted to the infield to commence the competition.

> Mr. Sullivan handed the Secretary the pistol with which the inaugural shot of the Olympic games was to be fired. With an "after you my dear Alphonse" gesture Mr. Hay gave the pistol to Mr. Francis. He fired it and the first heat of the 100-yard dash was on. The party was then escorted about the stadium and after a brief inspection they returned to their boxes. There Mrs. Hay, Miss Adams, Mrs. Francis and other ladies joined the party. They had been driven to the stadium under the escort of Lt. Haight of the Fourth U.S. cavalry, military aide to the committee on ceremonies."[5]

Back in their seats, Hay, Adams, and party relaxed and prepared to enjoy the competition. The *Post-Dispatch* reported that "Secretary Hay displayed much interest in the high jumping and pole-vaulting contests, which were carried out almost directly in front of his box. 'We used to do that about twenty-five years ago, Henry,' the Secretary remarked to Mr. Adams as a pole vaulter cleared the nine-foot mark. 'Yes,' responded the historian, dryly, 'and it will be a long time before we do it again.' At 4:15, before the games were concluded, Secretary Hay left the stadium."[6]

The competition witnessed by the secretary of state and Henry Adams was the Missouri high school track and field championships. All the athletes in the opening ceremonies were high school athletes from Missouri. Olympic expectations for pageantry and ritual were present. The opening ceremonies contained all the elements: inspiring music, a parade of athletes, a representative of the head of state, and a large contingent of dignitaries including international representatives. President Roosevelt was not present at the opening ceremonies because he steadfastly refused to attend the World's Fair during an election year until the election was over. In an age so different from our own it was regarded as unseemly for presidential contenders to directly solicit votes. The *Post-Dispatch* reported in June, "The President has been urged frequently to visit the Fair, but has steadily refused, as he says it would be impossible to go there and not make speeches, and he has announced that he will make no political speeches until after the election." Further, in early November, "The President . . . often has expressed a desire to see the Exposition, but did not do so for fear his visit would be construed as a campaign tour. As the election is now over, it is believed that he will accept the invitation." President Roosevelt, after winning the election, finally did attend the World's Fair and on November 26 made a brief visit to the stadium, as reported by the *Post-Dispatch:* "The route then led to the Stadium that the President might watch the Carlisle-Haskell Indian football game for a few minutes."[7]

John Hay was the distinguished elder statesman of the Roosevelt administration, having entered government service as the private secretary to President Abraham Lincoln in 1861 and culminating his career as secretary of state in the McKinley and Roosevelt administrations. Hay was the consummate diplomat, and in 1900 opposed the creation of European and American national spheres of influence in China because he believed the national integrity of China should not be sacrificed. His view, not altogether altruistic, stated that American trade interests would be better served by a China open door policy allowing all nations equal trade access to all of China. Hay, universally opposed initially, eventually prevailed. In 1904, only President Roosevelt himself exceeded the acclaim, prestige, and popularity of John Hay within the American public. Unable to attend the opening Olympic ceremonies due to political decorum concerns during an election year, he appointed the prominent and distinguished Hay to be his representative.

Gymnastics (July 1, 2, 4)

The Olympic competition began on July 1 with gymnastics. There were actually two separate gymnastic competitions and a third event called the All-Around Championship, the equivalent of the modern track and field event the decathlon, but in 1904 it was considered a part of the gymnastic competition. Turnverein or German gymnastic competitions were held on July 1 and 2. These were part of the Olympic games. Four months later, on October 28, competitions in Swedish gymnastics were held, but these events were AAU championships and should not be considered part of the Olympic games. It was common for Olympic and AAU championships to be conducted in the same sport at the World's Fair, track and field and tennis being other prominent examples along with gymnastics. At the turn of the century, the German and Swedish schools of gymnastics were vying for supremacy in the gymnastic world. The main difference between the two systems was that German gymnastics consisted of apparatus and track and field events, while Swedish gymnastics consisted only of apparatus events.

The *Post-Dispatch* announced the Olympic gymnastic competition with the following headlines and comments: "Stadium Olympic Competition Will Resolve Itself Into Contest Between Germany and U.S.; Berlin Team Is A Strong One." "The meet will probably resolve itself into a contest between Germany and the U.S. as the team from Berlin, now en route from New York to St. Louis is the largest entered and the strongest. The principal cities of the U.S. are represented and the meet will attract country-wide interest. It will without doubt be the greatest competition ever held by Turner societies. Medals are to be given to the winners in each event, and the team scoring the greatest number of points will be presented with a magnificent silver cup."[8]

The gymnastic athletes performed all events outside on the stadium field. The three apparatus events were the horizontal bar, parallel bars, and the side and long horse. Three routines, two compulsory and one optional, were performed on the horizontal and parallel bars. A compulsory routine for both the long and side horse and an optional routine on the side horse were required of each competitor, bringing the total number of gymnastic events to nine. Each athlete was awarded a score from 0 to 5 for each of the nine events; the maximum apparatus score was therefore 45. The three track and field events were the long jump, shot put, and 100 yard dash. The gymnastic and track and field scores were added together to determine the individual and team winners of the combined competition. Individual winners were also recognized in each of the separate twelve gymnastic events and the three track and field events.

Austria (1), Germany (7), Switzerland (1), and the United States (112) were the nations competing with a total of 121 athletes. Results of the individual competitions were as follows:[9]

Combined Apparatus and Track and Field Event Results

	Total	Gym.	T/F	Parallel	High	Horse	LJ	Shot	100yd.
1. Julius Lenhart Austria	69.80	43.00	26.8	14.40	14.60	14.00	10.0	9.3	7.5
2. Wilhelm Weber Germany	69.10	41.60	27.5	14.17	13.93	13.50	10.0	10.0	7.5
3. Adolph Spinnler Switzerland	67.99	43.49	24.5	14.53	14.53	14.43	8.2	9.8	6.5

Apparatus Event Results

	Total	Parallel	Horizontal	Horses
1. Adolf Spinnler Switzerland	43.49	14.53	14.53	14.43
2. Julius Lenhart Austria	43.00	14.40	14.60	14.00
3. Wilhelm Weber Germany	41.60	14.17	13.93	13.50

Track and Field Event Results

	Total	Long Jump	Shot Put	100 Yd.
1. Max Emmerick USA	35.7	13.6	11.1	11.0
2. John Grieb USA	34.0	12.2	11.8	10.0
3. William Merz USA	32.9	11.9	10.5	10.5

Scoring for the track events was based on 10 points for each event with fractions of points added or subtracted from the score based upon a performance standard. In the long jump, 18 feet earned 10 points, with a tenth of a point added for each tenth of a foot beyond 18 feet and a tenth of a point subtracted for each tenth of a foot under 18 feet. Thirty feet earned 10 points in the shot put, with a tenth of a point added or subtracted for each tenth of a foot beyond or short of the standard. The standard for the 100 yard dash was 11.0 seconds, with half a point added to or subtracted from the standard score of 10 for each fifth of a second faster or slower than 11.0 seconds.[10]

The *Post-Dispatch* reported that the German gymnastic team would provide strong competition for the Americans, but although the Germans tried to enter a team, they were prohibited from doing so. It seems there was an AAU rule requiring all team members to be from the same gymnastic club. The Germans represented various clubs, and thus were denied the opportunity to compete in the team gymnastic competition.[11] As a result the team competition was an all-American affair restricted to thirteen teams representing various cities of the United States. This type of eligibility restriction violated Olympic expectations and as such the team gymnastic competition should not be considered part of the Olympic games of 1904.

The most notable gymnast was George Eyser of the United States. He finished tenth in the apparatus competition and dead last, 118 out of 118, in the track and field events, scoring a zero in the 100 yard dash. Later, on October 28, competing in the AAU championships, which consisted solely of apparatus exercises (Swedish gymnastics), Eyser's performance markedly improved. He finished second in the combined exercises, first in the parallel bars, tied for first on the long horse, second on the side horse, third on the horizontal bar, and first in the rope climb. George Eyser was a world-class gymnast, but unfortunately, in 1904, Olympic gymnastics included track and field events, and Eyser had an especially difficult time running the 100 yard dash with his wooden leg.[12]

The All-Around Championship, consisting of ten track and field events, was held in the stadium on Independence Day, July 4. Seven athletes representing two nations, the United States (five athletes) and Ireland (two), took part in the competition. All ten events—100 yard sprint, shot put, high jump, 880 yard walk, hammer throw, pole vault, 120 yard hurdles, 56 pound weight throw, long jump, and the mile run— were held in one day. Performance point tables were used to award scores for each field event with points tabulated for the running events based on the distance each runner finished behind the winner. As an example, seven points were deducted from the runner's score for each foot a runner finished behind the winner in the 100 yard run, the distance being estimated at the finish of each running event by race officials. A close contest was expected between Ellery Clark and Adam Gunn, both two-time American champions, and the Irish champion Thomas Kiely. Clark, not feeling well, competed in the first five events before withdrawing from the pole vault competition. He did not compete in the final four events. After three events Adam Gunn was in first place, with Kiely in sixth. Truxtun Hare of the United States, in second place, was the surprise of the competition. Kiely won the next two events, the 880 yard walk and hammer throw, to move into third place. Gunn had slipped to second with the surprising Hare assuming the top spot. Gunn won the pole vault, but Kiely won both the 120 yard hurdles and the 56 pound weight throw to move into first position. Gunn was second and Hare had fallen to third. Truxtun Hare won the final two events, the broad jump and one mile run, closing the gap, but Kiely, second, and Gunn, third, in the broad jump managed to hold their positions. Thomas Kiely, with 6,036 points, was Olympic All-Around Champion. Adam Gunn, 5,907 points, and Truxtun Hare, 5,813 points, were the silver and bronze medal winners respectively.[13]

All-Around Champion Results

1. Thomas Kiely	Ireland	6,036 points
2. Adam Gunn	USA	5,907 points
3. Truxtun Hare	USA	5,813 points
4. John Holloway	Ireland	5,273 points
5. Ellery Clark	USA	2,778 points
6. John Grieb	USA	2,199 points
7. Max Emmerich	USA	DNF

On June 29, just prior to the Olympic gymnastic competition, the Department of Physical Culture received a most distinguished guest from Rome. Cardinal Satolli, the papal representative, was most interested in the Olympic games, with Rome having been selected by the International Committee to host the 1908 Olympics. The *Post-Dispatch* reported that a special athletic program consisting of gymnastics, handicapped track events (100 yard, 400 yard, 800 yard, one mile, and 120 yard high hurdles), a lacrosse contest, and a basketball game was presented by the Department of Physical Culture for the visitor from Rome. "It is the intention of the department [physical culture] to make the papal delegates' visit a memorable one from an athletic standpoint, and to show him what the American athlete can do. The fourth Olympiad will be held in Rome, and, as Cardinal Satolli is interested in that event, he will naturally be much interested in the work of the American athletes."[14] Mt. Vesuvius erupted in April 1906, lasted ten days, caused tremendous social and economic destruction including the loss of two thousand lives, and prevented Rome from hosting the 1908

Olympic games. London, scheduled to host an international exposition in 1908, accepted the honor of hosting the fourth Olympiad. Thus, three consecutive Olympics (Paris 1900, St. Louis 1904, and London 1908) were conducted as part of a World's Fair.

Lacrosse (July 5, 7)

Four teams, the Brooklyn Crescents, St. Louis AAA (Amateur Athletic Association), Winnipeg Shamrocks, and a team of Mohawk Indians from Ontario, entered the lacrosse competition. Representing the origins of lacrosse, since the game began as a sport among the Indian tribes of North America, the Mohawks lined up against the St. Louis squad on July 5. Losing to St. Louis, the Mohawks were eliminated from further Olympic competition while St. Louis earned the right to meet the winner of the Brooklyn-Winnipeg game for the championship. After playing two matches on their way to St. Louis, one in St. Paul, Minnesota (6–6 tie), and another in Chicago (14–5 win), the Winnipeg team arrived in St. Louis the night of July 5. The Brooklyn team never arrived. Winnipeg was therefore awarded the victory. On Thursday afternoon July 7, the two winners clashed. The Canadians demonstrated superior skills, preventing the Americans from scoring in the first half, but only scoring a single goal themselves to take a narrow lead. The two teams battled evenly during the next quarter, with each team scoring twice. After three quarters of play the Canadians led by the slimmest of margins, 3–2. The Americans could not maintain their intensity during the final fifteen-minute quarter, however. They failed to score in the final period while the Canadians scored five times, making the final score 8–2. Referring to the Winnipeg team, the *St. Louis Globe-Democrat* disappointedly proclaimed, ". . . the Canadian champions won the Olympian championship." The victorious Canadians celebrated their victory and spent the next couple of days touring the World's Fair. One of the players, Sandy Cowan, tried his luck with one of the wheels of fortune along the Pike. Eight hundred dollars ahead, Cowan continued until he lost his winnings and then some, lamenting to his hometown newspaper upon their return to Winnipeg on July 11 that while he had immensely enjoyed the trip and the lacrosse victories, he should have walked away from the wheel of fortune when he was eight hundred dollars ahead.[15]

Lacrosse Results

1. Canada; Winnipeg Shamrocks

George Cloutier (G), George Cattanach (P), Benjamin Jamieson (CP), Jack Flett (D), George Bretz (D), Eli Blanchard (D), Hilliard Laidlaw (C), H. Lyle (H), W. Brennaugh (H), L. H. Pentland (H), Sandy Cowan (IH), William Burns (OH).

2. USA; St. Louis Amateur Athletic Association

Hunter (G), Patrick Grogan (P), William Passmore (CP), George Passmore (D), Partridge (D), J. W. Dowling (D), A. H. Venn (C), Murphy (H), Gibson (H), Sullivan (H), Ross (IH), Woods (OH).

3. Canada; Mohawk Indians

Black Hawk (G), Black Eagle (P), Almighty Voice (CP), Flat Iron (D), Spotted Tail (D), Half Moon (D), Lightfoot (C), Snake Eater (H), Red Jacket (H), Night Hawk (H), Man Afraid Soap (IH), Rain in Face (OH).

G-goalkeeper, P-point, CP-cover point, D-defense, C-center, H-home, IH-inside home, OH-outside home

Rowing and Sculling (July 30)

Two levels of rowing and sculling events were contested. The Olympic competition occurred on July 30 and consisted of five events—single sculls, double sculls, coxless pairs, coxless fours, and coxed eights. An intermediate competition in the same five events took place the day before on July 29, but does not qualify as Olympic-caliber since participation was restricted based upon ability. The Olympic events also served, for the American participants, as the U.S. Championships of the National Association of Amateur Oarsman. Canada was the only nation to compete against the Americans, entering a team, the Toronto Argonaut Club, in the coxed eights race. There were other entries from Canada as well as Germany, but these athletes competed in the non-Olympic intermediate events.

All events were held at Creve Coeur (French for heartbreak) Lake, a facility located northwest of Forest Park and just outside the St. Louis city limits. The lake, just like the stadium and gymnasium, still exists today. All five events were contested over a course a mile and a half long. Three events, coxless pairs, single sculls, and double sculls, were out and back races, rowing out three-fourths of a mile, turning around, and rowing back to the starting point. The coxless fours and coxed eights races were point-to-point affairs, rowing a straight mile and a half from start to finish. There were a total of forty-four participants, nine Canadians and thirty-five Americans. Results for each of the five races are as follows:[16]

Single Scull Results

1. Frank Greer	USA	East Boston Amateur Athletic Boat Club
2. James Juvenal	USA	Pennsylvania Barge Club, Philadelphia
3. Constance Titus	USA	Atalanta Boat Club, New York

Double Scull Results

1. Atalanta Boat Club-USA
   John Mulcahy (bow), William Varley (stroke
2. Ravenswood Boat Club-USA
   James McLoughlin (bow), John Hoben (stroke)
3. Independent Rowing Club-USA
   Joseph Ravanack (bow), John Wells (stroke)

Coxless Pairs Results

1. Seawanhaka Boat Club—USA
   Robert Farnam (bow), Joseph Ryan (stroke)
2. Atalanta Boat Club—USA
   John Mulcahy (bow), William Varley (stroke)
3. Western Rowing Club—USA
   John Joachim (bow), Joseph Buerger (stroke)

Coxless Fours Results

1. Century Boat Club—USA
   Arthur Stockhoff (bow), August Erker (2), George Dietz (3), Albert Nasse (stroke)
2. Mound City Rowing Club—USA
   Frederick Suerig (bow), Martin Fromanack (2), Charles Aman (3), Michael Begley (stroke)

3. Western Rowing Club—USA

Gustav Voerg (bow), John Freitag (2), Louis Helm (3),
Frank Dummerth (stroke)

Coxed Eights Results

1. Vesper Boat Club—USA
Louis Abell (coxswain), Frederick Cresser (bow), Michael Gleason (2),
Frank Schell (3), James Flanagan (4), Charles Armstrong (5),
Harry Lott (6), Joseph Dempsey (7), John Exley (stroke)

2. Toronto Argonauts—Canada

Thomas Loundon (coxswain), A. B. Bailey (bow), William Rice (2),
George "Pat" Reiffenstein (3), Phil Boyd (4), George Strange (5),
William Wadsworth (6), Donald MacKenzie (7), Joseph Wright
(stroke)

William Jennings Bryan was the Democratic candidate for president
in 1896 and 1900, losing to William McKinley in both elections. The
Democrats wanted a new face to campaign against Roosevelt in 1904.
One of the names prominently suggested by various Democratic leaders
was David R. Francis, who had been successful in his efforts to have
St. Louis host the Democratic National Convention during the summer
of 1904. On May 19 the *Post-Dispatch* ran an article reporting that
Francis was being considered as the Democratic presidential candidate.
Headlines on June 25, just prior to the national convention read, "Fran-
cis Says He Is Not A Candidate—But No Man Could Refuse; Visits of Tam-
many Emissaries Have Revived Presidential Talk About Head of World's
Fair, but He Says He Is Trying Only To Make Fair A Success."[17]

During the national convention the Democrats ultimately selected
Judge Alton Parker of New York as their nominee, but for several months
there seemed a distinct possibility that Francis might aspire to a higher
presidential office.

Cycling (August 2–5)

There were professional and handicap cycling events at the World's
Fair that were not part of the Olympic games. There were seven amateur and Olympic cycling races, including three sprint events of a fourth
of a mile, a third of a mile, and a half mile; middle distance events of 1,

2, and 5 miles; and finally a long distance event of 25 miles. All races were contested on the stadium track, with one lap equaling a third of a mile. The mile race therefore required three laps, 5 miles, fifteen laps, and the 25 mile race required seventy-five laps. *Bicycling World* magazine described the racing surface in the August 2 issue as "a track of cinders, flat as a billiard table, very dry and dusty." Crowds were very sparse for the four days of cycling competition. The first day of racing, August 2, had the largest crowd—125 spectators—but there were only "a few spectators" each day afterwards according to *Bicycling World*.[18]

The Olympic cycling competition was open to the amateur cyclists of the world, and while German competitors did register, they did not compete. Thus the eighteen American participants were the only competitors in the seven Olympic cycling events. Marcus Hurley performed magnificently, winning five medals, four gold and one bronze, in the six events in which he participated.

The first race was the half mile on August 2, with Hurley easily winning his first gold medal. The quarter mile and 2 mile races were held the next day. Hurley again dominated, winning his second gold medal in the quarter mile and his bronze medal in the 2 mile race. He seized the lead at the start and never looked back in the quarter-mile race. In the final lap of the 2 mile race Hurley had the lead, but his bike slipped on the gravel track, allowing two cyclists to pass him. Four events—the one-third mile, mile, 5 mile, and 25 mile races—all took place on the last day of cycling competition, August 5. Hurley won gold medals in the third-mile and mile races. He had to sprint past the leader in the last few yards to capture the one-third mile victory. In the mile race Hurley took the lead in the backstretch of the final lap and won going away. He was a participant in the 5 mile race, but was involved in a spectacular multi-man crash and did not finish. Hurley did not compete in the 25 mile race. The performance of Marcus Hurley is all the more remarkable considering the short periods of rest between events. The performance of Burton Downing was equally impressive. He competed in all seven events, amassing six medals: two gold (2 mile and 25 mile), three silver (quarter mile, one-third mile, and mile), and one bronze (half mile).

J. Nash McCrea of Springfield, Illinois, dominated the 5 mile race, not with his speed, but with his wild riding style. *Bicycling World* stated

that the racer, nicknamed "Crash McCrea," "does not seem to be a vi-
cious rider, but simply rides all over the track and is dangerous for that
reason."[19] Sure enough, on the next-to-last lap McCrea swerved into the
cyclist beside him, who collided with the two riders next to him. All four
cyclists went down. Four more racers following close behind were unable to avoid the fallen pile of racers, and in an instant their machines
and they too went down. Marcus Hurley was among the second group
of fallen riders, as was Burton Downing.

The long-distance cycling event, 25 miles, was an endurance contest
with ten starters but only four finishers. The absence of Hurley and four
competitors dropping out due to flat tires left the field wide open for
Burton Downing. In the next to last lap, lap 74, A. F. Andrews had the
lead, but on the backstretch of the last lap he was passed by Downing,
who won going away. George Wiley finished third. There was a special
prize for the rider who had led the race for the most laps in this 75 lap
race. George Wiley won that prize, having led for 35 laps.

Cycling Results

Quarter Mile Race
1. Marcus Hurley USA
2. Burton Downing USA
3. Teddy Billington USA

One-Third Mile Race
1. Marcus Hurley USA
2. Burton Downing USA
3. Teddy Billington USA

Half Mile Race
1. Marcus Hurley USA
2. Teddy Billington USA
3. Burton Downing USA

Mile Race
1. Marcus Hurley USA
2. Burton Downing USA
3. Teddy Billington USA

2 Mile Race
1. Burton Downing USA
2. Oscar Goerke USA
3. Marcus Hurley USA

5 Mile Race
1. Charles Schlee USA
2. George Wiley USA
3. A. F. Andrews USA

25 Mile Race
1. Burton Downing USA
2. A. F. Andrews USA
3. George Wiley USA

Track and Field (August 29–September 3)

The premier international sport in 1904 was track and field. This was the competition everyone considered the most prestigious, and unlike some of the other sports, there was no question in anyone's mind that the track and field events from August 29 to September 3 were the main event of the Olympic games. Headlines in the *Post-Dispatch* proclaimed, "Now for the Olympic Games, with the World's Greatest Athletes in Competition." The accompanying article stated, "The famous Olympic games this coming week may be designated as by far the most important feature of a remarkable athletic festival that is continuing throughout the summer in the World's Fair stadium. . . The Olympic games proper, lasting an entire week, will be not only greater than those of Athens and Paris, but doubtless the greatest to be held for years to come."[20]

The Amateur Athletic Union of the United States, at the request of Pierre de Coubertin, was responsible for the administration of the St. Louis Olympics. The AAU had been formed in 1888 to provide uniform standards and rules for the numerous athletic clubs that were organized in most of the major cities of the United States as track and field, then called athletics, became popular during the second half of the nineteenth century. After the AAU was founded, annual national championships were conducted. Originally confined to the population centers of the East Coast, by 1904 athletic clubs existed in the growing cities of the Midwest, in St. Louis, Milwaukee, and Chicago in particular, creating a rivalry between East and West for athletic supremacy honors.

The annual AAU Athletic Championships were held in a different location each year with the host city generating a great deal of civic pride for the honor of hosting the prestigious event. The officials of the Louisiana Purchase Exposition from the very beginning recognized the significance of sports in American society, creating the Department of Physical Culture to organize an athletic festival throughout the entire seven months of the World's Fair. The 1904 AAU championships were one of the very first athletic events coveted by World's Fair officials. In June, the championships were held in St. Louis. The Olympic track and field competition did not serve, simultaneously, as the AAU championships. There was, however, an Olympic team championship for track and field events. American athletes, wearing the team colors of their respective athletic clubs, garnered team points based upon their individual performances, points being given for the top four finishers in each event. Points were simply not awarded for a particular placing if the athlete was not affiliated with an athletic club. The Spalding Cup, emblematic of athletic supremacy and donated by Albert G. Spalding of Chicago, was awarded to the winning athletic club.

On July 10 newspaper accounts reported, "World is Invited to August Games; Official entry blanks for the world's Olympian games have been issued by the Department of Physical Culture of the Fair. Many hundreds of the blanks have been sent to European countries, out of which many candidates for championship honors will come to America."[21] The Olympic invitation read as follows:

The honor of your presence is requested at the third
celebration of the revival of the
Olympic Games,
at the Stadium, Louisiana Purchase Exposition,
Saint Louis, Missouri
August twenty-ninth to September third,
Nineteen hundred and four.
J. E. Sullivan,
Chief, Department Physical Culture.

David R. Francis, President.
A. L. Shapleigh, Physical Culture Committee.
F. J. V. Skiff, Chairman, Director of Exhibits.

One hundred forty-two athletes, representing ten nations, competed in twenty-six track and field events, which in 1904 included the tug of war competition and two weight lifting events. The officials of the Department of Physical Culture scheduled the twenty-six events over a six-day period, from August 29 to September 3, in the following order:

August 29—Monday	August 30—Tuesday	August 31—Wednesday
1. 60 Meter Run	1. Marathon Run	1. Shot Put (16 pounds)
2. 400 Meter Run		2. 200 Meter Run
3. Steeplechase Run		3. 400 Meter Hurdles
4. Running High Jump		4. Standing High Jump
5. Standing Broad Jump		5. Tug-of-War Heats
		6. Hammer Throw (16 pounds)

September 1—Thursday	September 2—Friday	September 3—Saturday
1. 200 Meter Hurdles	No Events Scheduled	1. 100 Meter Run
2. Running Broad Jump		2. 1500 Meter Run
3. Running Hop, Step, and Jump		3. 110 Meter Hurdles
4. Weight Throw (56 pounds)		4. 4 Mile Team Race
5. Tug-of-War Finals		5. Pole Vault
6. 800 Meter Run		6. Discus
7. All-Around Weight Lifting (first 5 sections)		7. All-Around Weight Lifting (last 5 sections)
		8. Standing Hop, Step, Jump
		9. Two-Hand Weight Lift

Large, dark clouds gathered Monday afternoon, August 29, and threatened to wash out the first day of competition, but the storm never materialized. Inside the stadium, bands were "playing inspiring airs,"[22] and the stands were filled to near capacity with more than nine thousand exuberant spectators cheering the athletic performers.

Championships were decided for six events on the first day of competition. The first event was the 60 meter race, won by Archie Hahn of the Milwaukee Athletic Club. George Poage, a teammate of Hahn, from the University of Wisconsin, became the first black American to participate in the Olympic games, running in a heat of the 60 meter competition (he failed to qualify for the finals). A sportsmanship gesture generated a great deal of excitement and comment in another heat of the 60 meter event. Bela de Mezo, the sprinter representing Hungary, unfamiliar with the American starting method, made two false starts and was going to be disqualified by the officials. But the other American runners in the heat, Archie Hahn and Lawson Robertson, along with Robert Kerr of Canada, would not allow Mezo to be penalized. Franz Kemeny, leader of the Hungarian delegation and member of the International Olympic Committee, commended the display of sportsmanship. Mezo finished fourth in the four-man heat, failing to qualify for the finals.[23]

60 Meter Results

1. Archie Hahn	USA	Milwaukee Athletic Club	7.0 seconds
2. William Hogensen	USA	Chicago Athletic Association	7.2 seconds

3. Fay Moulton	USA	Kansas City Athletic Club	7.2 seconds
4. Clyde Blair	USA	Chicago Athletic Association	7.2 seconds
5. Meyer Prinstein	USA	Greater New York Irish Association	
6. Frank Castleman	USA	Greater New York Irish Association	

The 400 meter race, closely contested, produced an unexpected surprise. Percival Molson had won the Canadian championship in 1903 with the fast time of 49 seconds and was favored to win. American Harry Hillman had lost to Molson the year before and had never run close to 49 seconds. In St. Louis, thirteen runners toed the starting line together—there were no preliminary heats. Herman Groman of the Chicago Athletic Club immediately seized the lead. George Poage ran comfortably on the outside in second place. At the halfway point, Hillman, who had been running third, sprinted from an inside position to take the lead. Two other runners, Joseph Fleming of the Missouri Athletic Club and Frank Waller of the Milwaukee Athletic Club, moved into contention past Poage. As the leaders rounded the last turn, Poage made a move on the inside, but was blocked by Waller and Fleming. Meanwhile, Molson had been content to follow the lead group. Seventy-five yards from the finish, Molson made his great effort, and the race became a five-man struggle among Molson, Hillman, Waller, Groman, and Fleming. Molson had misjudged his fellow runners and started his effort too late. Hillman crossed the finish line one yard ahead of Waller. Groman trailed Waller by less than a yard, and Fleming finished fourth after holding off a late charge of Meyer Prinstein of New York. Molson barely managed to finish in the middle of the pack. The American crowd was ecstatic. Harry Hillman, victorious in a hard-fought race, had exerted his personal best effort, but the spectators were anxious for record-setting efforts. Quiet fell over the crowd as the announcer moved into position to proclaim the winning time, "Time: 49 1/5, a new Olympic record." Immediately, a chorus of cheers erupted from the stands "that could be heard for miles around, and the name of Hillman was on everybody's lips."[24]

Percival Molson, paying the ultimate sacrifice, later achieved fame during World War I serving in Princess Patricia's Canadian Light Infantry. He was wounded at the battle of Mount Sorrel in 1916 and awarded the Military Cross. Upon his recovery Molson insisted upon rejoining his unit and while attempting to retrieve a fallen comrade during fighting on the outskirts of Avignon, France, he was struck by mortar fire and killed. McGill University, from which Molson had graduated as president of his class in 1900, and where he had been an outstanding athlete earning numerous athletic honors, immortalized him: the main athletic stadium at McGill University was named the Percival Molson Memorial Stadium.[25]

400 Meter Results

1. Harry Hillman	USA	New York Athletic Club	49.2 seconds
2. Frank Waller	USA	Chicago Athletic Association	49.9 seconds
3. Herman Groman	USA	Chicago Athletic Association	50.0 seconds
4. Joseph Fleming	USA	Missouri Athletic Club	
5. Meyer Prinstein	USA	Greater New York Irish Athletic Club	
6. George Poage	USA	Milwaukee Athletic Club	

Also competing in the 400 meters, order of finish unknown, were Clyde Blair, Chicago Athletic Association; Percival Molson, Canada; Paul Pilgrim, New York Athletic Club; Johannes Runge, Germany; George Underwood, New York Athletic Club; and Howard Valentine, New York Athletic Club.

The steeplechase was the final running event on the first day of Olympic track and field competition. The race, consisting of five laps (2,590 meters), required runners to navigate a 14-foot water jump and two brush hurdles three feet in height during each lap. Ten athletes, nine of them Americans, competed in the steeplechase. John J. Daly of Ireland, the only non-American, was the race favorite. He was the Irish champion and was regarded by the experts as the man to beat. The field was closely bunched at the first and second brush hurdles. At the water jump, completing the first lap of about 500 yards, Daly had a lead of only 10 yards over Harvey Cohn of the Greater New York Irish Athletic Club. James Lightbody of the Chicago Athletic Club was running easily in third place, 20 yards off the pace. Daly increased his lead to 40 yards during the second lap and by the fourth was leading by 60 yards, but began to fade quickly at this point. Cohn also faltered. James Lightbody glided into the lead during the final lap and won going away, unchallenged. Daly hung on to finish second with Arthur Newton of the New York Athletic Club finishing third, 30 yards behind Daly.[26]

Steeplechase Results

1. James Lightbody	USA	Chicago Athletic Association	7:39.6
2. John Daly	Ireland		7:40.6
3. Arthur Newton	USA	New York Athletic Club	
4. William Verner	USA	Chicago Athletic Association	

Also competing, order of finish unknown, were Harvey Cohn, Greater New York Irish Athletic Association; David Munson, New York Athletic Club; and Richard Sandford, Brooklyn YMCA.

Three field events were contested on the first day: running high jump, standing broad jump, and the hammer throw. There were two categories, running and standing, for the three jumping events (high jump, broad jump, and hop, step, and jump) in 1904. The broad jump is now called the long jump, while the hop, step, and jump is known as the triple jump.

Six athletes representing three nations competed in the running high jump. Sam Jones, of the New York Athletic Club, was the overwhelming favorite in the competition, having won the AAU championships in 1901, 1903, and 1904. He did not disappoint, winning the competition with a jump of 5 feet, 11 inches. Garrett Serviss of Cornell University and Paul Weinstein of Germany tied at 5 feet, 9¾ inches. Serviss captured the silver medal in a jump-off with Weinstein, clearing the same height a second time while Weinstein failed at the same height.[27]

High Jump Results

1. Sam Jones	USA	New York Athletic Club	5 Feet, 11 inches
2. Garrett Serviss	USA	Cornell University	5 feet, 9¾ inches
3. Paul Weinstein	Germany		5 feet, 9¾ inches
4. Lajos Gonczy	Hungary		5 feet, 9 inches
5. Emil Freymark	USA	Missouri Athletic Club	
6. Ervin Barker	USA	University of Iowa	

Ray Ewry of the New York Athletic Club dominated the standing broad jump competition, easily winning the gold medal. Ewry was one of the outstanding athletes not only in the St. Louis games but also in Olympic history. He began his Olympic career in Paris in 1900, winning all three of the standing jumping events. He repeated that performance in St. Louis, then won both Olympic jumping events at London in 1908 (the standing triple jump was not an event in London). Ewry won every event he entered during the course of his Olympic career—eight gold medals in all. He was also victorious at the unofficial Interim Olympic games held at Athens in 1906, winning two more gold medals in the two standing jumping events. Ray Ewry, imitating Theodore Roosevelt (asthma) and personifying the national cult of the strenuous life promoted by Roosevelt, overcame a childhood affliction, paralysis in both legs, through a dedication to exercise.

Standing Broad Jump Results[28]

1. Ray Ewry	USA	New York Athletic Club	11 feet, 4 inches
2. Charles King	USA	Affiliation Unknown	10 feet, 9 inches
3. John Biller	USA	National Turnverein Newark, New Jersey	10 Feet, 8¼ inches
4. Henry Field	USA	Affiliation Unknown	10 feet, 5½ inches

Of the six events contested on the first day, the hammer throw was, according to the *Post-Dispatch*, "the all-star event and seemed to arouse more interest than any other event of the day." John Flanagan of the Greater New York Irish Athletic Club, the defending Olympic champion and winner of more than ten national titles in America, England, and Ireland, was the heavy favorite to retain his Olympic title. John Dewitt of Princeton University and Ralph Rose of the Chicago Athletic Club were expected to provide the main competition. There were no surprises in the hammer throw. Each athlete was allowed three throws. On his first attempt Flanagan threw the 16-pound weight 168 feet, 1 inch. This proved to be his best effort and could not be matched by any other competitor. Dewitt finished second and Ralph Rose, third.[29]

Hammer Throw Results

1. John Flanagan	USA	Greater New York Irish Atletic Club	168 feet, 1 inch
2. John DeWitt	USA	Princeton University	164 feet, 11 inches
3. Ralph Rose	USA	Chicago Athletic Club	150 feet, ½ inch
4. Charles Chadwick	USA	New York Athletic Club	140 feet, 4½ inches
5. James Mitchel	USA	New York Athletic Club	
6. Albert Johnson	USA	St. Louis YMCA	

After the busy first day of Olympic competition only one event, the marathon race, was held on Tuesday, August 30. The marathon, a modern event conceived to honor the classical heritage of Greece and symbolize the historical connection between the Olympics of antiquity and the modern games, had, since inception at the first Olympiad in Athens, achieved premier status in the track and field community as the most prestigious event on the Olympic program. Event prestige was not the sole reason that the marathon race was the signal event of the St. Louis Olympic games, however. Heroic efforts, fraudulent escapades, colorful personalities, and unique sports medicine practices all combined to make the marathon race the most memorable event of the 1904 Olympics.

Thirty-two runners, representing four nations, assembled at the starting line before ten thousand stadium spectators. It was hot, 90 degrees, at 3 p.m. when David R. Francis fired the starting pistol.[30] The runners completed five laps around the one-third mile track, giving the stadium crowd ample opportunity to observe and comment upon the running styles and attire of the participants before they exited by the east gate. The top American runners were Arthur Newton, veteran of the Paris Olympic marathon four years earlier; Sam Mellor, winner of the Boston marathon in 1902; John Lorden, Boston winner in 1903; Michael Spring, Boston champion only four months earlier in April; and four-time Boston competitor and second-place Boston finisher Thomas Hicks. Albert Coray, a Frenchman, was a participant in the marathon, but it can not be fairly claimed that he was a representative of France. He had arrived in Chicago and the United States in 1903. A year later, while remaining a French citizen, Coray competed in the St. Louis Olympics as a member of the Chicago Athletic Club, contributing to the team point totals for Chicago.

Len Tau and Jan Mashiani, two black men of the Tsuana tribe of South Africa, were in St. Louis as part of the South African World's Fair exhibit, which staged reenacted battles of the recent Boer War. Tau and Mashiani, messenger runners during the war, competed in only one Olympic event, the marathon. Both men ran the course barefoot and finished ninth and twelfth respectively. Tau, had he not been chased about a mile off course by a dog, would have been even more successful.[31]

Greece was one of the few European nations, along with Germany and Hungary, that sent a team of officials and athletes to the St. Louis Olympic games, and it was Comte Alex Mercati, a Greek official who, in a letter to James Sullivan, best exemplified Olympic ideals, stating, "The Grecian athletes do not go to America with the expectation of winning all the trophies, but that they may meet their American colleagues, and those of other nations, and become better acquainted; that they may carry back to Athens and to Greece the good fruits of this meeting, and in this manner benefit their native land." Ten athletes represented Greece in the marathon, one of whom, John Furla (sometimes spelled Thula), was a Greek-American with American citizenship, but Furla ran as a Greek.[32]

Cuba, freed from Spanish rule in 1898 in the Spanish-American War, had achieved national independence only two years prior to the St. Louis Olympic games. Felix Carbajal, a Cuban national and former mailman, decided to travel to St. Louis to compete in the Olympic marathon. Needing funds to finance his trip, Carbajal demonstrated his running talents throughout Cuba, once running the entire length of his native island. His journey to the United States was not uneventful. Upon arriving in New Orleans, Carbajal threw caution to the wind and gambled on dice.[33] He lost the remainder of his funds and was forced to walk and hitchhike to St. Louis. Slight of build and only five feet tall, Carbajal nevertheless presented a striking if nonathletic appearance as he toed the starting line. Attired in a white long-sleeve shirt, long, dark pants, a beret worn slanted on his head, and a pair of heavy street shoes, Carbajal seemed ill prepared for the heat and distance to be endured to finish the marathon. A fellow Olympian, American athlete Martin Sheridan, produced some scissors and cut off his trousers at the knee, providing some benefit. Clothes aside, Carbajal may have been the best runner in the field. Charles J. P. Lucas, a marathon race official in 1904, wrote, "Of the first four men to finish, Carbajal was the best physically . . . Wherever a crowd had assembled along the road to see the runners pass, Carbajal would stop to chat in broken English, and must have lost almost 60 minutes in time. On one occasion he stopped at the author's automobile, where a party were eating peaches, and begged for some. Being refused, he playfully snatched two, and ran along the road, eating them as he ran. Had Carbajal had anyone with him—he was totally unattended—he would not only have won the race, but would have low-ered the Olympic record."[34]

Conditions were less than the best for the marathon competitors. In addition to the midafternoon start time with the thermometer reaching 90 degrees, the entire course, except the stadium track, was along dirt roads that at the end of August in St. Louis meant clouds of dust. Not only the runners themselves but also the fleet of automobiles used by race officials to accompany the runners stirred up the dusty roads, ob-scuring vision and "choking the life out of all the runners."[35]

Five stadium laps completed, the runners, led by Michael Spring of New York, made their way out the east gate, turned right, ran up a short incline, and making another right ran down Olympian Way, now named Forsyth Boulevard. The first casualty of the race occurred less than half a mile out on Olympian Way when John Lorden, one of the top Amer-ican runners, had a bout of vomiting and gave up his efforts. Spring maintained his lead as the runners passed the courthouse in Clayton, a suburb of St. Louis, but the oppressive automobile dust was having a negative effect on many of the runners. Two miles later, Mellor, Carr, and Newton ran together in the lead. Spring developed cramps and was running with Fred Lorz a quarter of a mile behind the leaders. At the nine-mile mark Lorz also developed cramps and gave up the race, being assisted into an automobile for the ride back to the stadium. At this point in the race Mellor and Newton maintained their lead. Hicks picked up his pace and closed the distance between himself and the leaders, but he remained two miles behind. Thirteen miles from the sta-dium Mellor was first, Newton second, and Hicks moved into third po-sition. Albert Coray of Chicago and William Garcia of San Francisco ran side by side in fourth, followed by the Cuban, Carbajal, and Kneeland, of Boston. The rest of the runners followed, strung out over a distance of three miles. As the runners turned the corner onto the Ballas Road, many more runners began to feel the effects of the searing heat and suf-focating dust. Henry Brawley of Boston slowed to a walk, but continued on. Sam Mellor, still leading the race, experienced severe cramps, slowed to a walk, and eventually was unable to continue. Hicks, expending a great deal of energy to reach the leaders, was paying the price. His sta-mina eroded and he began to struggle. Garcia collapsed into a heap along the side of the road. Race officials removed him to the emergency hospital where it was determined that he was suffering a severe hemorrhage of the stomach; had he remained on the course much longer he surely would have bled to death. Two runners, Newton and Carbajal, were the exceptions, continuing their pace without any concessions to the heat and dust. Fred Lorz reappeared at this point. After riding several miles, Lorz, recovered from his cramps, decided to disembark and again began to run. Race official Charles J. P. Lucas, having earlier seen Lorz in the automobile, ordered him off the course. Lorz claimed the automobile broke down and he was just running to get back to the stadium.[36]

The rules of the Olympic marathon in 1904 allowed runners to be coached and assisted by race officials. Thomas Hicks received an inordinate amount of coaching and some extraordinary assistance during the marathon. From the ten-mile mark to the finish of the race, Hicks was "under the personal care of Hugh C. McGrath, of Charlesbank Gymnasium, Boston, Mass., and the author,"[37] Charles J. P. Lucas. Leaving the Denny Road (now Lindbergh Boulevard), Hicks, while laboring, had gained the lead. The last ten miles of the marathon were an ordeal for Hicks. First he requested water to drink; instead a sponge was used to moisten his mouth. Seven miles from the stadium Hicks was in a state of exhaustion and was given strychnine, one-sixtieth grain, and the white of one egg as stimulants by Lucas. Three miles later Hicks appealed to his handlers to allow him to lie down to rest. He was refused, but since he had a lead of about a mile and a half, he was allowed to cease his feeble jog and slow to a walk.

Suddenly, a runner appeared and flashed by Hicks, looking as if he had just begun the race. Hicks, demoralized, momentarily seemed on the verge of total physical collapse, but took heart and began his slow jog again when informed that the runner, Fred Lorz, was no longer a qualified participant and was out of the race. Officials returned their attention to Hicks, ignored Lorz, and allowed him to continue on his way. Spectators, unaware of his automobile ride and disqualification, began to cheer Lorz upon his arrival at the stadium. On a whim, Lorz decided to run into the stadium and finish the final stadium lap. Unfortunately, the crowd initially hailed Lorz as the marathon winner. The Lorz hoax was quickly exposed and the spectators renewed their vigilance for the true marathon champion. James Sullivan, unamused by the antics of Lorz, banned him from amateur competition for life. Lorz proclaimed his innocence, denied intentional deception, and claimed he never intended to accept the championship trophy. There must have been some merit to his contentions, for within a few months the AAU rescinded the ban and reinstated his amateur status. In April 1905, Fred Lorz won the Boston Marathon.

Meanwhile, the marathon leader, Thomas Hicks, suffering from fatigue and dehydration, plodded on. His face began losing color and turned a pale gray, whereupon he received another dosage of strychnine, the white of two more eggs, and a swallow of brandy to further stimulate his efforts. Warm water, heated on the boiler of a steam automobile, was used to give Hicks a full-body sponge bath. Lucas provides a vivid portrayal of Hicks over the last two miles on the road and his entrance into the World's Fair Stadium:

> Hicks was running mechanically—like a well-oiled piece of machinery. His eyes were dull, lusterless; the ashen color of his face and skin had deepened; his arms appeared as weights well tied down; he could scarcely lift his legs, while his knees were stiff. The brain was fairly normal, but there was more or less hallucination, the most natural being that the finish was twenty miles from where he was running. His mind continually roved towards something to eat, and in the last mile Hicks continually harped on the subject.
>
> Near the finish of the race, at the last mile and a half, were encountered two bad hills. As the brandy carried by the party had been exhausted, Ernie Hjberg, of New York, kindly replenished Hick's canteen, and, though the Cambridge man had beef tea with him, he was refused this liquid, as no chance of upsetting his stomach was to be taken. After he had partaken of two more eggs, again bathed, and given some brandy, Hicks walked up the first of the last two hills, and then jogged down on the incline. This was repeated on the last hill, and as he swung into the Stadium, Hicks bravely tried to increase his speed, but could not, for, as it was, he scarcely had strength enough left to run the last 440 yards of the distance.[18]

The St. Louis Olympic marathon, so eagerly anticipated, provided all the heroic drama associated with the event. Correspondent J. W. McConaughy of the *Post-Dispatch*, a witness at the finish of the classical marathon race, wrote,

> The big stone gymnasium was throwing a long, faint shadow up the back stretch and darkness was slowly closing down the Stadium and its 10,000 watchers when the first of the big dusty autos, the Post-Dispatch car, dashed

up Olympia Way with the word that the leading runner of the Marathon race had passed Clayton and was well on the last leg of the great run. Who is he? Who is he?, yelled the crowd. Number 20, Hicks of Cambridge. He's about a mile back on the road. 'An American! An American!' was the roar that shamed every other sound heard at the Stadium this summer. And again the thousands lined the Stadium fence, the intra-mural station, the side of Olympia Way and every other point where a first glimpse of the runner might be had. Another few minutes of straining eyes and then far down Forsyth Road there was a little cloud of dust moving slowly on and then a procession of autos. Nearer and nearer it came until the great throng saw that it was the first of the marathon runners. Then his begrimed number, a distorted 20, was visible and the next minute the winner of the Marathon race staggered into the grounds along the Stadium fence, while wave upon wave of applause followed him through the lane of packed spectators until he entered the stadium at the head of the chute in full view of the benches. Then pandemonium broke loose. Slowly, weakly he moved around the last quarter-mile and, with barely enough strength to break the tape, fell into the dozen arms waiting to catch him.[39]

Hicks was taken to the box of David R. Francis to receive the silver victory cup donated by Francis for the marathon, but was too weak to accept his award. After resting briefly in a chair, Hicks was next taken to the gymnasium for a physical examination. A team of prominent doctors and physical educators, including Dr. Luther Gulick of New York, Dr. R. Tait McKenzie of Montreal, and Dr. Clark Hetherington of the University of Missouri, ". . . found that Hicks' vitality was very low." Hicks, five feet, six inches tall, normally weighing 133 pounds, had lost eight pounds during the race, and having achieved his goal of a marathon championship, retired from running.[40]

Incredible as it may seem, not only was Hicks given drugs to aid his performance, but photographs reveal he received physical assistance as well, literally jogging between two officials, McGrath and Lucas, who both supported Hicks by his arms to prevent him from collapsing. The Chicago Athletic Association did enter a protest, not concerned with stimulants or physical assistance, but with the complaint that Hicks was paced by two automobiles, one in front and one behind. The lead auto was the referee vehicle containing Dr. Luther Gulick, Mr. Charles Senter, the judge of the course, and the irrepressible female photographer, Jessie Tarbox Beals. Any question of the legitimacy of the Hicks victory was forever put aside by the official pronouncement of Dr. Gulick: "Hicks won his race in a clear, honest manner, and was the best runner at the distance."[41] The winning time of 3 hours, 28 minutes, and 53 seconds, while slow, was, under the circumstances of extreme heat and oppressive dust, understandable.

William Garcia had almost died, eighteen of the initial thirty-two starters were unable to finish, and Thomas Hicks, the marathon champion, who finished only with the aid of stimulants and physical assistance, was in poor health. Sullivan, expressing the view of many, thought the marathon a dangerous health ordeal for participants and wished to abolish the race as an Olympic event. Commenting on the future of the Olympic marathon, Sullivan stated, "When the games are held at Rome in 1908 . . . , I do not think that the Marathon run will be included in the program. I, personally, am opposed to it and it is indefensible on any ground, but historic."[42]

Marathon Results

1. Thomas Hicks	USA	Cambridge YMCA, Mass.
2. Albert Coray	USA	Chicago Athletic Club
3. Arthur Newton	USA	New York Athletic Club
4. Felix Carbajal	Cuba	
5. Dimitrios Veloulis	Greece	
6. David Kneeland	USA	St. Philips Athletic Association, Boston
7. Henry Brawley	USA	St. Alphonsus Athletic Association, Boston
8. Sidney Hatch	USA	Chicago Athletic Club
9. Len Tau	S. Africa	
10. Christos Zekhouritis	Greece	
11. F. P. Devlin	USA	Mott Haven Athletic Club, New York
12. Jan Mashiani	S. Africa	
13. John Furla	Greece	
14. Andrew Oikonomou	Greece	

Eighteen runners—eleven Americans, six Greeks, and one South African—failed to finish the race. Edward Carr, Robert Fowler, John Foy, William Garcia, Thomas Kennedy, John Lordon, Fred Lorz, Sam Mellor, Frank Pierce, Guy Porter, and Michael Spring were the Americans. Georgios Drosos, Charilaos Giannakas, Ioannis Loungitsas, Georgios

Louridas, Petros Pipiles, and Georgios Vamkaitis represented Greece. The South African was Robert W. "Bertie" Harris.[43]

The Olympic program scheduled five events for Wednesday, August 31: the shot put, 200 meter run, 400 meter hurdles, standing high jump, and the preliminary heats for the tug-of-war competition. Eight athletes, seven Americans and Nikolaos Georgantas of Greece, took part in the first event, the shot put. Each athlete was allowed three throws, with the top three performers receiving an additional three attempts. The Greek, Georgantas, made two attempts, each time being disqualified for improperly "throwing" the shot. Miffed, and frustrated by the rules, Georgantas "left the ring in disgust, refusing to take his third trial."[44]

Ralph Rose, a giant standing 6 feet, 6 inches and weighing 265 pounds, held the world's record and was the odds-on favorite to win Olympic gold. Wesley Coe of Yale University, with a throw of 47 feet, 3 inches, took the early lead, but Rose, on his fifth attempt, heaved a new world's record, 48 feet, 7 inches, to win. An eyewitness described the world record effort as follows:

> As Rose stepped into the ring . . . his face bore an anxious determined expression. Carefully poising the weight in the palm of his high-lifted hand, where it fitted like a marble in the hand of a small boy, leaning back as far as he could without losing his balance, and lifting his leg up to his waist, Rose made one mighty move, throwing his body forward, and the shot flew from his hand, alighting beyond the board marked 48 feet. Cheer after cheer arose from the stand, when the shot alighted on the ground. "World's record! World's record!" yelled 10,000 happy, cheering spectators. As announcer Harvey stepped to the stand after receiving the official figures from the measurer, a hush fell upon the stand. Not a sound could be heard in the stadium. Mr. Harvey stepped to the front of the stadium amid silence. Turning to the center of the stand, he proclaimed: "In putting the 16-pound shot, Ralph Rose, of the Chicago Athletic Association, Chicago, Ill., put the shot 48 feet 7 inches, breaking the American, Olympic, and world's records." Then the cheering broke loose again, followed by the yells of the collegians present.[45]

Shot Put Results

1. Ralph Rose	USA	Chicago Athletic Association	48 feet, 7 inches
2. Wesley Coe	USA	Yale University	47 feet, 3 inches
3. Lawrence Feuerbach	USA	New York Athletic Club	43 feet, 10½ inches
4. Martin Sheridan	USA	New York Irish Athletic Club	40 feet, 8 inches

5. Charles Chadwick	USA	New York Athletic Club
6. Albert Johnson	USA	St. Louis YMCA
7. John Guiney	USA	Missouri Athletic Club
8. Nikolaos Georgantas	Greece	Disqualified

Archie Hahn, winner of the 60 meter sprint on Monday, was the favorite to win the 200 meter race on Wednesday. The finals consisted of four runners: Hahn; Nate Cartmell, Louisville, Kentucky YMCA; William Hogensen, Chicago Athletic Association; and Fay Moulton, representing the Kansas City Athletic Club. The rules of the competition provided for a two-yard penalty if a runner made a false start. Hahn's three competitors all made a false start, but were only penalized one yard because the clerk of the course claimed there was not room to move the runners back farther. Hahn, with his one-yard advantage, got off to a great start, while Cartmell hesitated coming off the line. Only twenty yards into the race, Cartmell was last, a full seven yards behind the leader Hahn, but at the seventy-five-yard mark Cartmell began to accelerate and just past the hundred-meter mark, with the stadium crowd cheering him on, Cartmell put on a burst of speed and passed Hogensen and Moulton. Cartmell closed to within two yards of Hahn at the finish line, but Hahn broke the tape, winning his second gold medal.[46]

200 Meter Results

1. Archie Hahn	USA	Milwaukee Athletic Club	21.6 seconds
2. Nate Cartmell	USA	Louisville YMCA	21.9 seconds
3. William Hogensen	USA	Chicago Athletic Association	
4. Fay Moulton	USA	Kansas City Athletic Club	

In contrast to the 200 meter race, the 400 meter hurdles event generated little excitement. The contest was never in doubt, with Harry Hillman leading throughout the race, but the finish was made closer when Hillman clipped the last hurdle, knocking it over and momentarily losing his balance. He recovered and was still able to win by two yards. Although awarded the gold medal, Hillman, in accordance with the rules of the time, was denied a world's record for knocking over a hurdle. George Poage, an African American, won the bronze medal.

400 Meter Hurdles Results

1. Harry Hillman	USA	New York Athletic Club	53.0 seconds
2. Frank Waller	USA	Chicago Athletic Association	53.2 seconds
3. George Poage	USA	Milwaukee Athletic Club	
4. George Varnell	USA	Chicago Athletic Association	

Ray Ewry easily won the standing high jump. The battle for second place and the silver medal was a much closer contest between Lawson Robertson of the Greater New York Irish Athletic Club and Joseph Stadler of the Franklin Athletic Club of Cleveland, Ohio. Both men cleared 4 feet, 9 inches during the regular competition, half a foot lower than the winning height cleared by Ewry at 5 feet, 3 inches. A jump-off was held to determine second place. Stadler again cleared 4 feet, 9 inches and won the silver when Robertson was unable to reach the same height a second time.

Charles J. P. Lucas, the aforementioned Olympic track official, in *The Olympic Games: 1904,* states in his account of the 400 meter hurdles race that ". . . opposed to Hillman . . . was Poage, the colored sprinter from Milwaukee Athletic Club, the only colored man to compete in the games. . ." On the very next page, describing the standing high jump competition, Lucas writes, ". . . but the contest for second honor was an interesting one. Stadler, of Cleveland, Ohio, and Robertson . . . fought hard and long for second place, Stadler finally cleared the bar at 4 feet 9 inches, while Robertson failed."[47] Scholars, researching Cleveland newspapers, discovered many years later that Joseph Stadler was an African American. The reason for the absence of his racial identity in 1904 remains a mystery. Poage, running the 60 meter race on Monday, can correctly be considered the first African American to participate in the Olympic games. But since both the 400 meter hurdles and the standing high jump concluded on Wednesday, August 31, George Poage and Joseph Stadler deserve dual recognition as the first African-American Olympic medal winners.

Standing High Jump Results

1. Ray Ewry	USA	New York Athletic Club	5 feet, 3 inches
2. Joseph Stadler	USA	Franklin Athletic Club, Cleveland, Ohio	4 feet, 9 inches

3. Lawson Robertson	USA	Greater New York Irish Cleveland, Ohio	4 feet, 9 inches
4. John Biller	USA	National Turnverein, Newark, New Jersey	4 feet, 8 inches
5. Lajos Gonczy	Hungary		4 feet, 5 inches

The finals of the tug-of-war competition were one of seven events on the Olympic program for Thursday, September 1. Six teams—Greece, South Africa, and four American teams, St. Louis Southwest Turnverein #1, St. Louis Southwest Turnverein #2, Milwaukee Athletic Club, and New York Athletic Club—entered the competition. Preliminary and semifinal bouts were held the previous day, with Greece losing to the St. Louis #1 team and the South Africans losing to Milwaukee. In the all-American semifinals, Milwaukee defeated St. Louis #1 and New York emerged victorious against St. Louis #2, leaving New York to face Milwaukee for the championship.

The tug-of-war competition took place on the stadium infield with the ground being dug up to allow for better footing since the athletes were not allowed to wear cleats. There was a five-minute time limit for each match and victory was achieved when one team, consisting of five members, pulled the other team six feet from their starting line. If neither team managed to pull the other six feet in five minutes then the loser was determined as the team that had been pulled over their starting line as the time limit expired. The Greek team, after five minutes of Herculean struggle against the first St. Louis team on Wednesday, was pulled a mere two inches over their starting line as time elapsed to lose their match. On Thursday, Milwaukee defeated New York in the championship match and St. Louis #1 was the victor against St. Louis #2. The New York team, after losing to Milwaukee, was scheduled to pull against St. Louis #1 but withdrew instead. The St. Louis #1 and #2 teams were awarded second and third places respectively while New York, assigned fourth, received one point. The Chicago Athletic Association did not enter a team in the tug-of-war competition, but knowing that every point was crucial for the team championship, Chicago entered a protest claiming the New York squad should be disqualified for withdrawing and subsequently forfeit the one point awarded for their assigned fourth-place finish. It was all to no avail—the protest was dismissed. Another

protest, by a St. Louis team, was based on the rather bizarre fact that all
five athletes of the champion Milwaukee squad were from Chicago. They
were not members of the Chicago Athletic Association, but were members of another Chicago athletic club, either the Columbian Knights
Athletic Association or the Sleipner Athletic Club. In either case, con-
flicting newspaper accounts of Chicago associations notwithstanding,
the five athletes were definitely not members of the Milwaukee Athletic
Club. How this happened and why is simply unknown and remains a
mystery. The St. Louis protest, however, was dismissed.[48]

Tug-of-War Results

August 31	August 31	September 1	September 1
Milwaukee	Milwaukee	Milwaukee	Milwaukee = Champion
vs.	vs.	vs.	
South Africa	St. Louis #1	New York	

Second Place Match

St. Louis #1	New York	St. Louis #1	St. Louis #1
vs.	vs.	vs.	vs.
Greece	St. Louis #2	St. Louis #2	New York (withdrew)

Team Standings

1. Milwaukee Athletic Club
   (Oscar Olson, Sidney Johnson, Henry Seiling, Conrad, Magnusson, Patrick Flanagan)
2. St. Louis Southwest Turnverein #1
   (Max Braun, William Seiling, Orrin Upshaw, Charles Rose, August Rodenberg)
3. St. Louis Southwest Turnverein #2
   (Charles Haberkorn, Frank Kungler, Charles Thias, Harry Jacobs, Oscar Friede)
4. New York Athletic Club
   (Charles Dieges, Samuel Jones, Lawrence Feuerbach, Charles Chadwick, James Mitchel)
5. Tie: South Africa
   (C. Walker, P. Hillense, J. Schutte, B. Lombard, P. Visser)
6. Tie: Greece
   (Nikolaos Georgantas, Perikles Kakousis, Dimitrios Dimitrakopoulos, Anastasios Georgopoulos, Vasilios Metalos)

Another weight event, the 56 pound weight throw, was also conducted
on Thursday. The lead ball with a metal ring through which a strap was
inserted was thrown from a seven-foot circle by grabbing the strap with

both hands, swinging the lead ball slowly from side to side a few times at
the back of the circle, gathering momentum, raising the swing into a
circular motion about the head for several swings, and finally rotating
the body in a full circle once or twice across the circle, letting go with
both hands simultaneously hurling the lead ball into space.

John Flanagan, winner of the hammer throw on the first day of competition, was one of the favorites to win the weight throw. Canadian Etienne
Desmarteau was the other top contender. Desmarteau had defeated Flanagan two years before at the AAU championships. Flanagan and Desmarteau were both policemen, Flanagan in New York and Desmarteau in
Montreal. Both were outranked by another competitor, thirty-eight-year-
old Charles Hennemann, chief of police in Keokuk, Iowa. Elder statesman
Hennemann had won the AAU championship fifteen years previously in
1889. Ralph Rose, winner of the shot put contest the day before and the
bronze medalist in the hammer throw, hoped to upset the co-favorites.[49]

Rose opened the competition, but fouled. Desmarteau entered the ring
next and flung the lead ball 34 feet, 4 inches. Flanagan, committing five
fouls out of six attempts, managed one fair throw of 33 feet, 4 inches, a full
foot behind the winning distance of Desmarteau and a mere inch ahead
of James Mitchel to finish second. Rose was unable to challenge. His best
throw barely exceeded 28 feet. The fates were not kind to Olympic champion Etienne Desmarteau for within a year typhoid fever claimed his life.[50]

Weight Throw Results

1. Etienne Desmarteau	Canada	Montreal Athletic Club	34 feet 4 inches
2. John Flanagan	USA	Greater New York Irish Athletic Club	33 feet 4 inches
3. James Mitchel	USA	New York Athletic Club	33 feet 3 inches
4. Charles Hennemann	USA	unattached	30 feet 1½ inches
5. Charles Chadwick	USA	New York Athletic Club	
6. Ralph Rose	USA	Chicago Athletic Association	

The 800 meter race was the highlight event on this fourth day of track
and field competition. Thirteen runners—one German, two Canadians,
and ten Americans—toed the starting line. Spectators witnessed contrasting starting positions when the German, Johannes Runge, and the
two Canadians, Peter Deer and John Peck, assumed a standing position
while the Americans crouched into the sprinter's position, called the

kangaroo start in 1904. The starter's pistol fired and the American Harvey Cohn immediately took the lead, setting a torrid pace trying to run away from the field. With only eighty yards remaining Cohn seemed on his way to victory, but he could not sustain his efforts. At this point, Cohn, fading quickly, was passed by several runners and was no longer a factor in the race. James Lightbody of the Chicago Athletic Association, the winner of the steeplechase race three days previous on the opening day of Olympic track competition, began his surge to the outside of the other runners. Lightbody had been content to lag well behind for most of the race, allowing the other runners to exhaust themselves trying to stay with the furious early pace set by Cohn. His strategy worked to perfection. Lightbody, running erect, his long quick stride covering large tracts of real estate, moved to the outside as the runners entered the final stretch and majestically passed the laboring leaders to win by two yards and capture his second gold medal. Emil Breitkreutz of the Milwaukee Athletic Club, who led the field until passed by Lightbody, made a valiant effort for the silver medal, but his strength was spent. Howard Valentine of the New York Athletic Club with one last exertion surged passed Breitkreutz to finish second by one tenth of a second. Several of the runners in the 800 meter race, having exerted themselves to a state of near exhaustion, had to be carried from the field.[51]

800 Meter Results

1. James Lightbody	USA	Chicago Athletic Association	1:56.0
2. Howard Valentine	USA	New York Athletic Club	1:56.3
3. Emil Breitkreutz	USA	Milwaukee Athletic Club	1:56.4
4. George Underwood	USA	New York Athletic Club	
5. Johannes Runge	Germany		
6. William Verner	USA	Chicago Athletic Association	

Order of finish is unknown for the seven other participants: George Bonhag, Greater New York Irish Athletic Association; Harvey Cohn, Greater New York Irish Athletic Association; Peter Deer, Montreal Athletic Club, Canada; Lacey Hearn, Chicago Athletic Association; John Joyce, unattached; John Peck, Montreal Athletic Club, Canada; and Paul Pilgrim, New York Athletic Club.

There being no preliminary heats, five men stood at the starting line for the finals of the 200 meter hurdles race. Harry Hillman won his third gold medal, having won both the 400 meter sprint and 400 meter hurdles races earlier in the week. Charles Lucas describes the race as a two-man contest between Hillman and George Poage until Hillman pulled away at the finish to win by two yards in record time. Inexplicably, official records show Frank Castleman of the Greater New York Irish Athletic Club finished second while Poage placed third. Harry Hillman continued his Olympic career after 1904, competing at Athens in 1906 and winning a silver medal in the 400 meter hurdles at the London games of 1908. Two years later Hillman became a coach at Dartmouth, a post he held for the next thirty-five years until his death in 1945. He was also a member of the U.S. Olympic coaching staff for the games of 1924 (Paris), 1928 (Amsterdam), and 1932 (Los Angeles).[52]

200 Meter Hurdles Results

1. Harry Hillman	USA	New York Athletic Club	24.6 seconds
2. Frank Castleman	USA	Greater New York Irish Athletic Club	24.9 seconds
3. George Poage	USA	Milwaukee Athletic Club	
4. George Varnell	USA	Chicago Athletic Club	
5. Frederick Schule	USA	Milwaukee Athletic Club	

Two jumping events—the broad jump and the hop, step, and jump, now called the long and triple jump respectively—rounded out the events for Thursday, September 1. Each participant received three attempts. The gifted athlete Myer Prinstein (Greater New York Irish Athletic Club) dominated both events. Prinstein had competed at the 1900 Paris Olympics, winning the silver medal in the broad jump and gold medal in the hop, step, and jump. He won the gold for both events in St. Louis, the only person in Olympic history to do so.[53]

Broad (Long) Jump Results

1. Myer Prinstein	USA	Greater New York Irish Athletic Club	24 feet 1 inch
2. Daniel Frank	USA	New Westside Athletic Club, New York	22 feet 7¼ inches
3. Robert Stangland	USA	New York Athletic Club	22 feet 7 inches
4. Fred Englehardt	USA	Mohawk Athletic Club, New York	21 feet 9 inches
5. George Van Cleaf	USA	New York Athletic Club	
6. John Hagerman	USA	Pacific Athletic Association, San Francisco	

American John Oxley, Chicago Athletic Association, and three foreign athletes, Bela de Mezo from Hungary and Corrie Gardner and Leslie McPherson, both from Australia, Melbournian Hare and Hounds Athletic Club, also competed in the broad jump competition, but their order of finish is not known.

Hop, Step, and Jump (Triple Jump) Results

1. Myer Prinstein	USA	Greater New York Irish Athletic Club	47 feet 1 inch
2. Fred Englehardt	USA	Mohawk Athletic Club, New York	45 feet 7¼ inches
3. Robert Stangland	USA	New York Athletic Club	43 feet 10 inches
4. John Fuhler	USA	Milwaukee Athletic Club	42 feet 4½ inches
5. George Van Cleaf	USA	New York Athletic Club	
6. John Hagerman	USA	Pacific Athletic Association, San Francisco	
7. Samuel Jones	USA	New York Athletic Club	

Friday was an open day with no track and field events scheduled. The final day of track and field competition took place on Saturday, September 3, and was the busiest day of the week. Nine events plus the closing ceremonies were scheduled. The running events contested were the 100 and 1500 meters, 110 meter hurdles, and the last event of the competition, the 4 mile team race. The standing hop-step-jump and pole vault were the remaining jumping events, with the discus throw and two weight-lifting events rounding out a full last day of competition. Closing ceremony festivities were planned to celebrate the entire week of track and field competition.

Three heats and the final for the 100 meter sprint were all run on this day. The first two finishers in each heat qualified for the final. Archie Hahn got off to his usual great start and while Nate Cartmell of the Louisville YMCA finished with a flourish, he was unable to overtake Hahn. Hahn, the Milwaukee Meteor, won the race by almost two yards in 11 seconds flat. Hahn joined Harry Hillman as triple gold medal winners. Also dubbed the Wisconsin Wonder, Hahn, standing only 5 feet, 6 inches tall, owed his sprinting success to his efficient starting technique and attention to the mechanics of sprinting. Later, during his track and field coaching career, Hahn published *How to Sprint*, still an acclaimed work.[54]

100 Meter Results

1. Archie Hahn	USA	Milwaukee Athletic Club	11.0 seconds
2. Nate Cartmell	USA	Louisville YMCA	11.2 seconds
3. William Hogensen	USA	Chicago Athletic Association	
4. Fay Moulton	USA	Kansas City Athletic Club	
5. Fred Heckwolf	USA	Missouri Athletic Club	
6. Lawson Robertson	USA	Greater New York Irish Athletic Club	

The 1500 meter run was the most anticipated race of the day. James Lightbody was the favorite, previously winning the steeplechase and 800 meter races, and was expected to join Hillman and Hahn in the prestigious triple gold medalist circle. Expectations were fulfilled. At the halfway mark Lightbody ran easily in third place and down the final stretch he coasted past his rivals, winning by six yards. His time of 4:05.4 established a new world's record.

1500 Meter Results

1. James Lightbody	USA	Chicago Athletic Association	4:05.4
2. William Verner	USA	Chicago Athletic Association	4:06.8
3. Lacey Hearn	USA	Chicago Athletic Association	
4. David Munson	USA	New York Athletic Club	
5. Johannes Runge	Germany		
6. Peter Deer	Canada		
7. Howard Valentine	USA	New York Athletic Club	
8. Harvey Cohn	USA	Greater New York Irish Athletic Association	
9. Charles Bacon	USA	Greater New York Irish Athletic Association	

Two Australians, Corrie Gardner and Leslie McPherson of the Melbournian Hare and Hounds Athletic Club, competed in the two heats preceding the finals of the 110 meter hurdles event, but failed to qualify for the finals. The top two finishers in each of the heats advanced to the finals. Past and current AAU champions Fred Schule (1903) and Frank Castleman (1904) won their heats to advance. Chicago sprinter Thad Shideler, equaling the world record of 15.0 seconds for this event only three months earlier, finished second to Castleman in their heat. The championship race promised an exciting and close contest. As it turned out Schule led the field over the course of ten hurdles and won the race by two yards with a time of 16 seconds flat. Shideler finished second while Castleman disappointed, finishing last in the four-man field.[55]

110 Meter Hurdles Results

1. Fred Schule	USA	Milwaukee Athletic Club	16.0 seconds
2. Thaddeus Shideler	USA	Chicago Athletic Association	16.3 seconds
3. Lesley Ashburner	USA	Cornell University	
4. Frank Castleman	USA	Greater New York Irish Athletic Association	

Charles Dvorak was the class of the field in the pole vault competition. Five athletes cleared the bar at 11 feet, but only Dvorak cleared first 11 feet, 3 inches and then 11 feet, 6 inches, winning the gold medal. A series of jump-offs were held to break the tie of the four jumpers at 11 feet.[56]

Pole Vault Results

1. Charles Dvorak	USA	Chicago Athletic Association	11 feet 6 inches
2. Leroy Samse	USA	Indiana University	
3. Louis Wilkins	USA	Chicago Athletic Association	
4. Ward McLanahan	USA	New York Athletic Club	
5. Claude Allen	USA	Greater New York Irish Athletic Association	
6. Walter Dray	USA	Yale University	
7. Paul Weinstein	Germany		

The discus competition was expected to be tightly contested. Nikolaos Georgantas, the Greek champion, along with Ralph Rose, winner of the shot put earlier in the week, and Martin Sheridan, the 1904 AAU champion, were all considered possible victors. All participants were allowed three throws. The top three athletes were then given another three throws. Georgantas, Rose, and Sheridan, as expected, advanced after the three preliminary throws and after six attempts Rose and Sheridan were tied with a distance of 128 feet, 10 inches. Georgantas won the bronze medal for Greece with a toss of 123 feet, 7½ inches. Rose and Sheridan were given an additional three throws. Neither man equaled his previous best, but Sheridan won the gold medal with a distance of 127 feet, 10¼ inches while Rose managed only 120 feet, 6¾ inches. Rose, winning the silver, became a triple medal winner, having previously won the bronze in the hammer throw and gold in the shot put.

Discus Results

1. Martin Sheridan	USA	Greater New York Irish Athletic Association	128 feet 10½ inches
2. Ralph Rose	USA	Chicago Athletic Association	128 feet 10½ inches
3. Nikolaos Georgantas	Greece		123 feet 7½ inches
4. John Flanagan	USA	Greater New York Irish Athletic Association	
5. John Biller	USA	National Turnverein, Newark, New Jersey	
6. James Mitchel	USA	New York Athletic Club	

Ray Ewry, labeled the "human frog" by the French at the Paris games in 1900, completed his domination of the standing jumping events at St. Louis by winning his third gold medal in the standing hop, step, and jump. Ewry outdistanced Charles King, silver medal winner, by almost a foot and a half. African American Joe Stadler won his second medal, finishing third.

Standing Hop, Step, and Jump Results

1. Ray Ewry	USA	New York Athletic Club	34 feet 7¼ inches
2. Charles King	USA	Unknown Affiliation	33 feet 4 inches
3. Joseph Stadler	USA	Franklin Athletic Club, Cleveland	31 feet 6 inches

The Olympic weight-lifting events were conducted as part of the track and field competition in St. Louis as was customary during this time period. There were only two events: the two-hand lift and an all-around championship consisting of ten separate events. The first five events of the all-around contests occurred on Thursday, September 1. The two-hand lift and the concluding five events of the all-around took place on Saturday, September 3. Greek strongman Perikles Kakousis easily defeated his American opponents in the two-hand lift, the only weight-lifting event he entered, by hoisting just over 246 pounds. The weight-lifting decathlon-style event consisted of nine dumbbell exercises and an athlete option for the tenth and final exercise. New Yorker Fred Winters won six of the nine dumb-bell events and with only the optional event remaining held a five-point edge in the scoring, 38 to 33 over Oscar Osthoff of the Milwaukee Athletic Club. Five points were awarded for first, three for second, and one for third in the nine dumb-bell contests. The final event, however, allowed the judges to award any number of points up to twenty-five. Winters chose to perform one-arm push-ups while Osthoff selected handstand push-ups for his final exercise. The judges awarded Winters only seven points for his efforts, while Osthoff received fifteen points to score a come-from-behind 48 to 45 victory, garnering the gold medal to go along with his previously earned silver medal in the two-hand lift. Results for the two weight-lifting events are as follows:

Two Hand Lift Results

1. Perikles Kakousis	Greece		246¼ pounds
2. Oscar Osthoff	USA	Milwaukee Athletic Club	186 pounds
3. Frank Kungler	USA	St. Louis Southwest Turnverein	175½ pounds
4. Oscar Olson	USA	Milwaukee Athletic Club	149½ pounds

All Around Championship Results

1. Oscar Osthoff	USA	Milwaukee Athletic Club	48 points
2. Frederick Winters	USA	Affiliation Unknown	45 points
3. Frank Kungler	USA	St. Louis Southwest Turnverein	10 points

The 4 mile team race was the last event on the Olympic track and field program. The Chicago Athletic Association held a slim lead in team points over the New York Athletic Club, but the winner of the last event would win the coveted Spalding Victory Cup, symbol of Olympic track and field supremacy. Albert G. Spalding, sporting goods magnate of Chicago, donated the handsome trophy. Only the two rival athletic clubs entered teams of five runners each. Two Chicago runners had competed in the marathon earlier in the week, silver medalist Albert Coray and eighth-place finisher Sidney Hatch. One New York runner, Arthur Newton, was a marathon veteran, having placed third to win the bronze medal. James Lightbody of Chicago, winner of the 800, 1500, and steeple-chase events, was the clear favorite to win at this shorter distance and lead the Chicago team to Olympic victory. It was not to be. Newton, who had finished third in the steeplechase behind Lightbody, took an immediate lead, ran away from the field, including Lightbody, and won by several hundred yards. Lightbody finished second. Teammates William Verner and Lacey Hearn followed Lightbody to the finish line to capture third and fourth respectively, but it was not enough. Coray and Hatch brought up the rear in ninth and tenth place respectively. Chicago placed 2, 3, 4, 9, and 10, for a team total of 28 points. New York placed 1, 5, 6, 7, 8, for a team total of 27 points. New York won the race by one point and the overall Olympic team championship.[57]

Four Mile Team Race Results

1. New York Athletic Club	USA	27 points
Arthur Newton	1	21 minutes, 17.8 seconds
George Underwood	5	
Paul Pilgrim	6	
Howard Valentine	7	
David Munson	8	
2. Chicago Athletic Association	USA	28 points
James Lightbody	2	
William Verner	3	
Lacey Hearn	4	
Albert Coray	9	
Sidney Hatch	10	

The track and field competition completed, ten thousand spectators took to their feet and erupted in applause and cheers for "the greatest athletic meet ever held in the United States," as proclaimed by the *St. Louis Post-Dispatch*.[58] President Francis joined the crowd, rising in his box in preparation to present the Spalding Cup, symbol of the Olympic team championship, to representatives of the victorious New York Athletic Club. The celebration abruptly ceased when it was announced that the Chicago Athletic Association had filed a protest against the New York Athletic Club and that the final awards ceremony was canceled. Everett C. Brown, chairman of the Chicago Athletic Association, disputed the points awarded to New York in the hammer throw and the tug-of-war events. John DeWitt placed second in the hammer throw, winning the silver medal. Prior to his arrival in St. Louis, DeWitt, a student at Princeton University, had written a letter to Olympic AAU officials stating that he did not care whether he represented the New York Athletic Club or Princeton University. Apparently officials assigned him to New York. Chicago failed to file a protest at the time of the hammer throw competition on the first day of competition. Chicago also claimed the one point awarded to the New York tug-of-war team for fourth place was invalid because the New Yorkers withdrew from competition after losing to Milwaukee in the championship bout. Scheduled to face the St. Louis Turners #1 team to decide second and third places, New York defaulted and was assigned fourth place. Although they spoiled the grand finale presentation in St. Louis at the stadium, Chicago's protests were ultimately disallowed, and the New York Athletic Club belatedly received the coveted Spalding Trophy and the title of Olympic team champions.[59]

Tennis (August 29–September 3)

Olympic tennis was played on dirt courts constructed just outside the stadium and in front of the physical culture gymnasium. Competition for singles and doubles was held the same week as the track and field contests, August 29 to September 3. There were twenty-seven participants in the singles event, all Americans but one.[60] Dr. Hugo Hardy of Germany won his first match but then lost in straight sets to Beals C. Wright of Boston (6–2, 6–1), the eventual champion. Shunzo Tokaki, reported as the tennis champion of Japan, was a member of the Tokyo Tennis Club and won the championship of that club in 1903. He arrived in St. Louis in late June. During an interview Tokaki stated, "I was sent to America by the Twiiku Kwai Physical Culture Association, which is the leading organization of its kind in our country, to make a study of physical culture and in order to detect the deficiencies of the Japanese in athletics. Our people are very fond of athletics and if there is any American game that might prove beneficial to them they desire to adopt it. . . . Of course you will be surprised to learn that baseball is played in Japan. It has been played throughout the land of Mikado for the past ten years, and many Japanese youngsters can be seen every afternoon playing baseball on vacant lots. The rules are the same as in the U.S. There are, however, no professional baseball players in Japan."[61] Tokaki agreed to compete in the Olympic singles tennis tournament, but after losing to Ralph McKittrick in the Missouri State Tennis Championships in early July, the twenty-one-year-old Japanese star failed to appear almost two months later for the Olympic tennis tournament. Perhaps it was the loss or more likely the seven-week wait between events that caused Tokaki to miss the Olympic games.

Four men dominated Olympic tennis. Alphonzo Bell of Los Angeles, Robert LeRoy of Columbia University, Edgar Leonard of Boston, and Beals Wright of Boston were the finalists in the singles tourney, and in the doubles event Bell and LeRoy met Leonard and Wright for the championship.

There was one other notable tennis participant, Dwight Davis, a wealthy and prominent resident of St. Louis. The previous year at the age of twenty-four Davis "retired" from tennis, but the following year decided to compete in the Olympics. He finished ninth in singles and, teaming with fellow St. Louisan Ralph McKittrick, who had defeated Shunzo Tokaki in June, finished fifth in doubles. Davis was a self-confident Harvard senior in 1899 when he originated the international tennis trophy bearing his name, the Davis Cup. He went on to a distinguished career in public service. He volunteered for service in World War I, achieved the rank of lieutenant colonel, and was awarded the Distinguished Service Cross for extraordinary heroism. One of the founders of the American Legion, Davis was secretary of war in the Coolidge administration, governor general of the Philippines under Hoover, and was briefly considered for the Republican presidential nomination in 1928.[62]

In the semifinals singles competition Robert LeRoy defeated Edgar Leonard (6–3, 6–3) and Beals Wright emerged victorious against Alphonzo Bell (6–3, 6–4). The *St. Louis Globe-Democrat* provided the following account of the exciting championship match: "Wright showed himself to be worthy of the reputation with which he is accredited. His play was steadily brilliant and he drew the applause of the highly interested spectators, of whom there were a goodly number, notwithstanding the counter attraction offered by the final events of the Olympic games. Leroy's playing bordered on the sensational throughout the game, and the execution of difficult strokes was frequent. He made such a showing as to make him a logical candidate for championship honors when he has gained the strength which comes with maturity."[63] The nineteen-year-old Robert Leroy had to settle for the silver medal, losing to Wright (6–4, 6–4). The straight single elimination tournament provided no opportunity for a playoff to decide third position, so Bell and Leonard shared the honors.

Beals Wright came from a distinguished athletic family. The twenty-four-year-old Olympic tennis star was the son of George Wright, an exceptional professional baseball player and the nephew of Harry Wright, an innovator in professional baseball organizations who achieved national acclaim as "the father of the professional game." Beals Wright garnered his second gold medal by teaming with fellow Bostonian Edgar Leonard to win the doubles championship against LeRoy and Bell. The Boston teammates won the best-of-five sets 6–4, 6–4, 6–2. "The teamwork of the winners was superb, while LeRoy and Bell were not far behind the champions in skill. Wright and Leonard have played together before and know each other's style well enough to be able to anticipate just where the ball would next be sent. Their victory was a well-earned one," read the newspaper description of the hard-fought match.[64]

Tennis Results: Singles

1.	Beals Wright	USA
2.	Robert LeRoy	USA
3.	Edgar Leonard	USA
	Alphonzo Bell	USA
5.	Charles Cresson	USA
	W. E. Blatherwick	USA
	John Neely	USA
	Semp Russ	USA
9.	Fred Sanderson	USA
10.	Ralph McKittrick	USA
	J. Cunningham	USA
	Hugo Hardy	Germany
	F. R. Feltshans	USA
	Dwight Davis	USA
	Hugh Jones	USA
16.	Frank Wheaton	USA
	Chris Forney	USA
	William Easton	USA
19.	Nathaniel Semple	USA
	Forest Montgomery	USA
	Joseph Charles	USA
	Malcolm Macdonald	USA

	Orien Vernon	USA
	J. Stewart Tritle	USA
	Douglas Turner	USA
	Andrew Drew	USA
27.	George Stadel	USA

Doubles

1.	Beals Wright/Edgar Leonard	USA
2.	Robert LeRoy/Alphonzo Bell	USA
3.	Joseph Wear/Allen West	USA
	Clarence Gamble/Arthur Wear	USA
5.	Frank Weaton/—Hunter	USA
	Charles Cresson/Semp Russ	USA
	Ralph McKittrick/Dwight Davis	USA
	Hugh Jones/Harold Kauffman	USA
9.	N. M. Smith/Joseph Charles	USA
	W. E. Blatherwick/Orien Vernon	USA
	Forest Montgomery/J. Stewart Tritle	USA
	Nathaniel Semple/Malcomb Macdonald	USA
	Paul Gleason/Hugo Hardy	USA/Germany
	George Stadel/Frederick Semple	USA
	Andrew Drew/Douglas Turner	USA

Swimming (September 5–7)

Life Saving Exhibition Lake was the scene of the Olympic swimming and diving events. It was a man-made lake created for daily exhibits by the U.S. Coast Guard to demonstrate rescue operations at sea. The Coast Guard used the east end of the lake. The aquatic events were conducted from a pier and floating rafts on the lake's west end. The swimming events consisted of nine events over a three-day period, September 5, 6, and 7. There were twenty-three participants representing four nations. Besides the United States, athletes came from Austria, Germany, and Hungary.[65] The United States did not dominate the swimming competition. Germany won four gold medals to three for the USA, while Hungary earned two golds.

Swimming events began on Monday, September 5, two days after the conclusion of the tennis and track and field competitions, with two contests: the 100 yard freestyle and an event considered strange today, but common at the time, the plunge for distance. Six swimmers arrived at the starting line for the finals of the 100 yard freestyle having advanced from two semifinal heats with the six fastest times. The course was swum from the wooden floating platform buoyed by barrels to a finish line marked by a horizontal bamboo pole supported by a barrel float in the middle and attached to two flagged upright poles on either side. Spectators observed from the shore as judges watched from a rowboat at the finish line to record the results. Zoltan von Halmay of Hungary easily outdistanced his five American rivals to win the gold medal with a time of 1:02.8.

In the plunge for distance event, swimmers dove from a raised starting block into the water and without propelling themselves with arms, legs, or upper body, glided as far as possible under water. Distance was measured to where a swimmer's face emerged, or to his position at the end of sixty seconds. Each competitor was given three attempts.[66] Five swimmers, all Americans, participated. William P. Dickey of the New York Athletic Club, competing in the only event he entered, captured the gold with a distance of 62 feet, 6 inches, a full 5 feet farther than Edgar Adams, the second-place finisher.

Four events were scheduled for Tuesday: 50 yard freestyle, 220 yard freestyle, one mile freestyle, and 100 yard backstroke. There was some controversy in the 50 yard race. In the finals, American J. Scott Leary lodged an immediate protest at the finish line, claiming that he had been interfered with by Zoltan von Halmay. The protest was just as immediately disallowed, but the judges could not agree on which swimmer had actually finished first. The Hungarian judge gave the edge to his countryman while American judges claimed Leary had won. Without agreement, a swim-off was ordered. After two false starts, one by each man, a fair start was made with Halmay taking an early lead. Leary was unable to close the distance, resulting in a second gold medal for Halmay.[67]

In the 220 yard freestyle race swimmers were required to complete two laps of a 110 yard course. There were four participants, three from the United States and one from Germany. Charles Daniels, New York Athletic

Club, won his first gold medal in a close finish with Francis Gailey of the San Francisco Olympic Club. Seven swimmers representing four countries participated in the one-mile freestyle race. Sixteen laps of the 110 yard course were required for the event. After the midway mark Emil Rausch, Germany, and Geza Kiss, Hungary, took a commanding lead over the rest of the field. Toward the end, Rausch swam away from Kiss to win easily. Kiss finished in second, a full minute and ten seconds behind Rausch. Three swimmers did not finish the course. Six swimmers competed in the 100 yard backstroke, three Germans and three Americans. The Americans were no match for the Germans. Led by Walter Brack, Germany dominated the race, sweeping the first three places.[68]

Three events were scheduled for the last day of Olympic swimming competition, Wednesday, September 7: 440 yard freestyle, 880 yard freestyle, and 440 yard breaststroke. Only four participants competed in the 440 yard race. Charles Daniels easily outdistanced his rivals to win his second gold medal in this event. Germany's Emil Rausch collected his second gold medal with a comfortable win against five other contestants in the 880 yard contest. Francis Gailey finished second to Rausch to win his third silver medal. In the 440 yard breaststroke Germany, as in the backstroke event, again, with the same three swimmers, dominated. This time Georg Zacharias bested fellow countryman Walter Brack, but the Germans were denied a sweep when American Jamison Handy, a student at the University of Michigan and a member of the Chicago Central YMCA team, barely finished ahead of Georg Hoffman to win the bronze medal. Handy, eighteen years old in 1904, died in 1983 at the age of ninety-seven and was the last surviving medalist of the St. Louis Olympics.[69]

Swimming Results

50 Yard Freestyle

1. Zoltan von Halmay	Hungary		28.0 seconds
2. J. Scott Leary	USA	San Francisco Olympic Club	28.6 seconds
3. Charles Daniels	USA	New York Athletic Club	
4. David Gaul	USA	Philadelphia Swimming Club	
5. Leo "Budd" Goodwin	USA	New York Athletic Club	
6. Raymond Thorne	USA	Chicago Athletic Association	

100 Yard Freestyle

1. Zoltan von Halmay	Hungary		1:02.8
2. Charles Daniels	USA	New York Athletic Club	
3. J. Scott Leary	USA	San Francisco Olympic Club	
4. David Gaul	USA	Philadelphia Swimming Club	
5. David Hammond	USA	Chicago Athletic Association	
6. Leo "Budd" Goodwin	USA	New York Athletic Club	

220 Yard Freestyle

1. Charles Daniels	USA	New York Athletic Club	2:44.2
2. Francis Gailey	USA	San Francisco Olympic Club	2:46.0
3. Emil Rausch	Germany		2:56.0
4. Edgar Adams	USA	New York Athletic Club	

440 Yard Freestyle

1. Charles Daniels	USA	New York Athletic Club	6:16.2
2. Francis Gailey	USA	San Francisco Olympic Club	6:22.0
3. Otto Wahle	Austria		6:39.0
4. Leo "Budd" Goodwin	USA	New York Athletic Club	

880 Yard Freestyle

1. Emil Rausch	Germany		13:11.4
2. Francis Gailey	USA	San Francisco Olympic Club	13:23.4
3. Geza Kiss	Hungary		
4. Edgar Adams	USA	New York Athletic Club	
5. Otto Wahle	Austria		
6. Jamison Handy	USA	Chicago Central YMCA	

One Mile Freestyle

1. Emil Rausch	Germany		27:18.2
2. Geza Kiss	Hungary		28:28.2
3. Francis Gailey	USA	San Francisco Olympic Club	28:54.0
4. Otto Wahle	Austria		

John Meyers, Missouri Athletic Club; Louis Handley, New York Athletic Club; and Edgar Adams, New York Athletic Club also participated, but did not finish the race.

100 Yard Backstroke

1. Walter Brack	Germany		1:16.8
2. Georg Hoffmann	Germany		
3. Georg Zacharias	Germany		
4. William Orthwein	USA	Missouri Athletic Club	

Edwin Swatek and David Hammond, both of the Chicago Athletic Association, were participants, but it is unclear who finished fifth and sixth.

440 Yard Breaststroke

1. Georg Zacharias	Germany		7:23.6
2. Walter Brack	Germany		
3. Jamison Handy	USA	Chicago Central YMCA	
4. Georg Hoffmann	Germany		

Plunge for Distance

1. William Dickey	USA	New York Athletic Club	62 feet 6 inches
2. Edgar Adams	USA	New York Athletic Club	57 feet 6 inches
3. Leo "Budd" Goodwin	USA	New York Athletic Club	57 feet 0 inches
4. Newman Samuels	USA	Missouri Athletic Club	55 feet 0 inches
5. Charles Pyrah	USA	New York Athletic Club	46 feet 0 inches

Diving (September 7)

The diving competition consisted of only one event, the fancy dive. On September 7 two nations, the United States and Germany, took part. Judges and competitors were on their own as there were no rules instructing how to evaluate the performance of each athlete and award points. The Germans concentrated on performing complex aerial maneuvers without any concern for their technique on entering the water. Their emphasis was on the "fancy" part of the dive, claiming water entry techniques were irrelevant. American technique was less athletic in the air, but emphasized a smooth water entry. The Germans performed much more difficult dives, but often entered the water on their chests, knees, or even their faces. The American judges rewarded American techniques and declared George Sheldon of St. Louis the winner. The judges also declared a tie for third and ordered a dive-off to determine the bronze medalist. The Germans were incensed. The trophy to be presented the diving champion was donated by Dr. Theodore Lewald, the German commissioner to the World's Fair. He refused to award the trophy to Sheldon, instead lodging a protest with the director of the Olympic games, James Sullivan. The protest was disallowed on September 15 and Sheldon received the trophy and his gold medal. Frank Kehoe of the Chicago Athletic Association was awarded the bronze medal when Alfred Braunschweiger of Germany refused to participate in the ordered dive-off to decide third place.[70]

Diving Results

1. George Sheldon	USA	St. Louis	12.66 points
2. Georg Hoffmann	Germany		11.66 points
3. Frank Kehoe	USA	Chicago Athletic Association	11.33 points
4. Alfred Braunschweiger	Germany		11.33 points
5. Otto Hooff	Germany		

Fencing (September 7–8)

The Physical Culture Gymnasium was the site for the five events of the Olympic fencing competition held September 7 and 8. Three nations, the United States, Germany, and Cuba, were represented, with a total of eleven participants. Two events, the individual foil and the individual dueling swords, were contested on Wednesday, the first day. Nine individuals entered the individual foil competition. Split into two groups, one of five, the other of four, a round-robin tournament format was followed with each fencer facing every other fencer in his group. The top two athletes from each group advanced to the finals. Two men were undefeated in their respective groups. Ramon Segundo of Cuba, grouped with four Americans, became a favorite with the spectators and was loudly applauded for each of his four victories. In the second group Gustav Casmir of Germany faced three Americans and was victorious each time. Losing only to Segundo, Albertson Van Zo Post of the New York Fencers Club and Charles Tatham, a teammate of Post, with a single loss to Casmir, advanced to the finals. Segundo continued his artistry with the foil, besting each of his three challengers and winning the championship. Gustav Casmir was not only unable to match the mastery of Segundo but also lost to Post and the man he had previously beaten, Tatham. Losing all three bouts in the finals, Casmir failed to medal.[71]

The individual dueling swords event is now called épée. Five men, the four finalists in the individual foils and Fitzhugh Townsend of the New York Fencers Club, competed. Again, each of the fencers dueled with every opponent. The winner of each bout was the athlete to score the first touch. Ramon Segundo continued to dominate and won his second gold medal.[72]

Two individual contests and a team event were scheduled on the second day. Segundo did not compete in the individual saber, but his countryman, Manuel Diaz Martinez, won another gold for Cuba. In this event the winner of each bout was the first fencer to score seven touches, and again each fencer faced every other fencer. The other individual event was called the individual single sticks. The format for this event is unknown; only the results have survived. The Cubans did not compete, leaving the field to three Americans. Albertson Van Zo Post scored the most touches and won the gold medal. The final event was the team foil competition with two teams, Cuba and the United States, entered. There were three members of each team, and since Cuba had only two fencers, Albertson Van Zo Post joined the Cubans to compete against the American team of Charles Tatham, Fitzhugh Townsend, and Arthur Fox. The format for this event required each fencer to face each of the three fencers from the opposing team. Thus, there were nine bouts. The Americans scored only two victories, giving the team championship to Cuba by a score of 7 to 2. Ramon Segundo was a triple gold medalist, winning all three events in which he entered. Albertson Post was the most successful American, winning a medal in all five events of the competition: two bronzes, one silver, and two gold.[73]

Fencing Results

Individual Foil

1. Ramon Segundo	Cuba		3–0
2. Albertson Van Zo Post	USA	New York Fencer's Club	2–1
3. Charles Tatham	USA	New York Fencer's Club	1–2
4. Gustav Casmir	Germany		0–3

Individual Dueling Swords (Épée)

1. Ramon Segundo	Cuba	
2. Charles Tatham	USA	New York Fencer's Club
3. Albertson Van Zo Post	USA	New York Fencer's Club
4. Gustav Casmir	Germany	
5. Fitzhugh Townsend	USA	New York Fencer's Club

Individual Saber

1. Manuel Diaz Martinez	Cuba		3–0 21 touches
2. William Grebe	USA	Affiliation Unknown	2–1 20 touches
3. Albertson Van Zo Post	USA	New York Fencer's Club	2–1 18 touches
4. Theodore Carstens	USA	Affiliation Unknown	
5. Arthur Fox	USA	Affiliation Unknown	

Individual Single Sticks

1. Albertson Van Zo Post	USA	New York Fencer's Club	11 touches
2. William Scott O'Connor	USA	New York Fencer's Club	8 touches
3. William Grebe	USA	Affiliation Unknown	2 touches

Team Foil

1. Cuba: Ramon Segundo, Albertson Post, Manuel Martinez	7–2
2. United States: Charles Tatham, Fitzhugh Townsend, Arthur Fox	2–7

Archery (September 19–21)

"Olympic Archery Today; Another Olympic championship tournament opened at the World's Fair stadium this morning when about 30 of the best archers of the U.S. assembled to match their skill with the bow and arrow,"[74] announced the September 19 edition of the *St. Louis Post-Dispatch.* Among those archers assembled on the stadium infield with their long bows and quivers of arrows were six ladies, the only women to compete in the St. Louis Olympics. Five of the female archers were members of the Cincinnati Archers Club while one was a member of the Potomac Archers Club in Washington, D.C. The women competed in two events: the Double Columbia Round the first day and the Double National Round on the second day. A double round consisted of two sessions, one in the morning and another in the afternoon. The Columbia Round required shooting 24 arrows each at 50, 40, and 30 yards. The archery queen was Lida Howell of the Cincinnati Archers. She easily won the Columbia Round competition with a total score of 867. Her closest rival, twenty-year-old Emma Cooke of the Potomac Archers, twenty-five years junior to Ms. Howell, scored 630 total points. The next day Lida Howell continued her dominance, winning her second gold medal in the Double National Round, again scoring an easy victory over second-place Emma Cooke, with total scores of 620 to 419. The National Round required shooting 48 arrows at 60 yards and 24 arrows at 50 yards. Lida Howell reigned supreme in women's archery at the turn of the twentieth century. She won the American National Championship for women an incredible seventeen times and is ranked as one of the finest female archers in history. Emma Cooke and Jessie Pollock were about as evenly matched as humanly possible in both contests. In the Columbia Round they tied in score, 630 points apiece, but Ms. Cooke tallied a total of 126 target hits to 124 for Ms. Pollock to secure second place. In the National Round the results were even closer. Each archer finished with a score of 419 and an identical 103 total target hits. Ms. Cooke was again awarded second place, although it is unclear on what basis.[75]

The archery competition for men began with the Double American Round, which required shooting 30 arrows each at 60, 50, and 40 yards in a morning session, and again in an afternoon session. George Bryant of the Boston Archers scored a comfortable win with a total of 1,048 points to 991 points for Robert Williams of the Potomac Archers. Bryant, winning his second gold medal, scored 820 points to narrowly prevail over Williams, 819 points, in the Double York Round competition. The York Round, consisting of morning and afternoon sessions, required shooting 72 arrows at 100 yards, 48 arrows at 80 yards, and 24 arrows at 60 yards. Archers used the traditional long bow in 1904 to shoot at these distances, as the compound bow did not yet exist. Robert Williams, second to Bryant twice, finally received a gold medal as a member of the victorious Potomac Archers in the team round. Each team had four archers, each shooting 96 arrows at 60 yards. The day before the team round, September 20, Galen Spencer, a member of the Potomac Archers, celebrated his sixty-fourth birthday, setting a record as the oldest American Olympic gold medalist in history. Samuel Duvall, sixty-eight years of age and a member of the second-place Cincinnati Archers, holds the record for the oldest American Olympic medalist. In contrast, Henry Richardson of the Boston Archers was only fifteen years old in 1904.[76]

Archery Results—Women
Double Columbia Round

			50y	40y	30y	Hits	Score
1. Lida Howell	USA	Cincinnati Archers	45/48	48/48	48/48	141	867
2. Emma Cooke	USA	Potomac Archers	34/48	44/48	48/48	126	630
3. Jessie Pollock	USA	Cincinnati Archers	37/48	44/48	47/48	124	630
4. Laura Woodruff	USA	Cincinnati Archers	27/48	39/48	47/48	113	547
5. Mabel Taylor	USA	Cincinnati Archers	14/48	15/48	30/48	59	243
6. Louise Taylor	USA	Cincinnati Archers	5/48	17/48	31/48	53	229

Double National Round

			60y	50y	Hits	Score
1. Lida Howell	USA	Cincinnati Archers	87/96	43/48	130	620
2. Emma Cooke	USA	Potomac Archers	60/96	43/48	103	419
3. Jessie Pollock	USA	Cincinnati Archers	68/96	35/48	103	419
4. Laura Woodruff	USA	Cincinnati Archers	29/96	37/48	66	234
5. Mabel Taylor	USA	Cincinnati Archers	24/96	22/48	46	160
6. Louise Taylor	USA	Cincinnati Archers	21/96	18/48	39	159

Archery Results—Men

Double American Round

			60y	50y	40y	Hits	Score
1. George Bryant	USA	Boston Archers	56/60	60/60	60/60	176	1,048
2. Robert Williams	USA	Potomac Archers	52/62	59/60	60/60	171	991
3. William Thompson	USA	Potomac Archers	51/60	56/60	60/60	167	949
4. C. S. Woodruff	USA	Cincinnati Archers	50/60	56/60	60/60	167	907
5. William Clark	USA	Cincinnati Archers	50/60	55/60	59/60	164	880
6. Benjamin Keys	USA	Chicago Archers	49/60	51/60	58/60	158	840
7. Wallace Bryant	USA	Boston Archers	46/60	54/60	60/60	160	818
8. Cyrus Dallin	USA	Boston Archers	43/60	55/60	58/60	156	816
9. Henry Richardson	USA	Boston Archers	46/60	59/60	58/60	163	813
10. Homer Taylor	USA	Chicago Archers	49/60	52/60	58/60	159	811
11. Charles Hubbard	USA	Cincinnati Archers	46/60	48/60	57/60	151	779
12. Lewis Maxson	USA	Potomac Archers	42/60	56/60	59/60	157	777
13. Galen Spencer	USA	Potomac Archers	47/60	53/60	53/60	153	701
14. Samuel Duvall	USA	Cincinnati Archers	40/60	43/60	58/60	141	699
15. Edward Frentz	USA	Boston Archers	31/60	50/60	54/60	135	665
16. Amos Casselman	USA	Potomac Archers	36/60	45/60	55/60	136	628
17. Thomas Scott	USA	Cincinnati Archers	36/60	44/60	50/60	135	562
18. Ralph Taylor	USA	Cincinnati Archers	33/60	43/60	45/60	121	533
19. Edward Bruce	USA	Chicago Archers	22/60	35/60	55/60	112	516
20. E. H. Weston	USA	Chicago Archers	30/60	36/60	46/60	112	508
21. Edward Weston	USA	Chicago Archers	26/60	34/60	46/60	106	450
22. W. G. Valentine	USA	Chicago Archers	9/60	27/60	47/60	83	345

Double York Round

			60y	50y	40y	Hits	Score
1. George Bryant	USA	Boston Archers	79/144	67/96	46/48	192	820
2. Robert Williams	USA	Potomac Archers	78/144	73/96	40/48	191	819
3. William Thompson	USA	Potomac Archers	70/144	72/96	48/48	190	816

4. Wallace Bryant	USA	Boston Archers	55/144	54/96	35/48	144	618
5. Benjamin Keys	USA	Chicago Archers	45/144	50/96	37/48	132	532
6. Edward Frentz	USA	Boston Archers	46/144	47/96	37/48	130	528
7. Homer Taylor	USA	Chicago Archers	39/144	50/96	41/48	130	506
8. C. S. Woodruff	USA	Cincinnati Archers	33/144	47/96	43/48	123	487
9. Henry Richardson	USA	Boston Archers	26/144	47/96	36/48	119	439
10. Cyrus Dallin	USA	Boston Archers	38/144	44/96	37/48	119	405
11. D. F. McGowan	USA	Potomac Archers	33/144	40/96	22/48	99	383
12. Lewis Maxson	USA	Potomac Archers	33/144	35/96	34/48	102	382
13. Thomas Scott	USA	Cincinnati Archers	33/144	37/96	29/48	99	375
14. Ralph Taylor	USA	Cincinnati Archers	16/144	45/96	33/48	94	328
15. Edward Weston	USA	Chicago Archers	22/144	23/96	31/48	76	268
16. Edward Bruce	USA	Chicago Archers	11/144	33/96	18/48	62	238

Team Round

		60y	Hits	Score
1. Potomac Archers	USA		300	1,344
William Thompson		83/96		
Robert Williams		82/96		
Lewis Maxson		71/96		
Galen Spencer		64/96		
2. Cincinnati Archers	USA		303	1,341
C. S. Woodruff		85/96		
William Clark		79/96		
Charles Hubbard		71/96		
Samuel Duvall		68/96		
3. Boston Archers	USA		282	1,268
George Bryant		85/96		
Wallace Bryant		68/96		
Cyrus Dallin		65/96		
Henry Richardson		64/96		
4. Chicago Archers	USA		224	942
Benjamin Keys		71/96		
Homer Taylor		71/96		
Edward Weston		45/96		
Edward Bruce		37/96		

Golf (September 19–24)

The Glen Echo Country Club, a three-mile train ride from Union Station in St. Louis, hosted the Olympic golf championships. Colonel George McGrew, president and founder of Glen Echo (1901), was also the father-in-law of Albert Lambert, a wealthy St. Louis businessman. The Lambert Pharmacal Company, Warner-Lambert in later years, was the creator of Listerine. On a business trip to his Paris office during the summer of 1900 Lambert learned of the Olympic golf competition and entered the handicapped event, which he won. Three years later, learning the Olympics were coming to St. Louis, Lambert convinced his father-in-law that Glen Echo Country Club, only three years old in 1904, would gain immediate prestige by hosting the Olympic golf championships. Lambert later developed a passion for aviation and was the major sponsor for Charles Lindbergh's transatlantic solo flight in 1927. The international airport in St. Louis was, and is, named Lambert Field in his honor.[77]

Lambert and McGrew were successful in convincing Olympic officials to include golf on the Olympic program and have Glen Echo serve as host. There were two events: a team championship contested on Saturday, September 17, and a weeklong individual championship from September 19 to 24. Six teams entered, but only two teams, from the Western Golf Association and the Trans-Mississippi Golf Association, arrived at Glen Echo. A third team was formed the morning of the event from among those golfers present who were not previously entered in the competition. Since they were all members of the United States Golf Association, that is the team name they used. Each team consisted of ten golfers, each playing 36 holes of stroke play. The ad hoc USGA team did not do well, finishing third. Henry Chandler Egan, winner of the U.S. Amateur title just the week before, led the Western Golf Association to victory.[78]

Seventy-five men, including three Canadians, competed for the individual Olympic golf championship. A qualifying round of 36 holes was held on Monday September 19. Thirty-two golfers survived the 36-hole cut-off score of 183 to qualify for the match play competition. George Lyon of the Lambton Golf and Country Club in Toronto was the only Canadian to advance to match play, shooting 169. Also shooting 169 was Daniel Sawyer of the Chicago Golf Club. Albert Lambert shot 168 to qualify, while Egan posted a score of 166, as did Mason Phelps of the Midlothian Country Club, Chicago. Arthur Stickney of the St. Louis Country Club and Walter Egan of the Exmoor Country Club, Chicago advanced with 165 scores. Francis Newton of the Seattle Country Club posted the second-best score of 164 in the qualifying round. Ralph McKittrick and Stuart Stickney, both of the St. Louis Country Club, tied for first in the qualifying round with scores of 163. An 18-hole playoff was held on Thursday, September 22, with McKittrick posting an 84 to 86 victory and winning the gold medal awarded to the qualifying round champion. McKittrick was a multisport Olympian, having competed in the Olympic tennis tournament two weeks earlier.

Of the top ten finishers in the qualifying round, only Walter Egan failed to win on the first day of match play, losing to Albert Lambert, but the second round of play on Wednesday provided some surprising results. Both McKittrick and Stickney, qualifying round champions, lost—McKittrick to Lambert and Stickney to the Canadian, Lyon. The final eight included Newton, Phelps, Lambert, Lyon, Chandler Egan, Sawyer, and two surprises: Burt McKinnie of the Normandie Golf Club, St. Louis, and Harry Allen of the Bellerive Country Club, St. Louis. McKinnie shot 170, just off the top-ten pace, in the qualifying round. Allen was a true surprise, having posted a 178 qualifying score, but his streak came to an end in the quarterfinals against the newly crowned U.S. Amateur champion, Chandler Egan. McKinnie defeated Sawyer to advance with Egan to the final four. Lyon bested Lambert and Newton edged Phelps to join McKinnie and Egan.

In the semifinals McKinnie played well, but lost a close match to Egan. Francis Newton, the bronze medalist of the qualifying round and five strokes better than George Lyon (164–169), was expected to meet Egan in the finals, but the Canadian champion scored an upset win over Newton in match play to set up an international finals match against Egan. Rain and wind swept over the course on Saturday, making difficult conditions for both golfers. After five consecutive days of playing 36 holes each day, Egan, twenty years old, was the clear favorite over the forty-six-year-old from Toronto. It was a close match, but in the end, George Lyon prevailed to capture the Olympic gold medal. Lyon was a natural all-around athlete gifted with coordination and strength. During the 1890s he was Canada's best cricket batsman. His golf swing was awkward and flat, but his prodigious strength allowed him to be by far the longest driver in the Olympic tournament. After the match, the youngster Egan, exhausted, skipped the awards dinner and went to bed. The old Lyon, basking in his victory glow, attended the awards dinner and to demonstrate his vitality walked the length of the dining room on his hands.[79] Interviewed after the match, the contrasting statements of Egan and Lyon could not be more vivid. Egan's statement:

> I am very sorry to have lost the match. I had nothing to gain and everything to lose. My opponent was the better player and consequently, he won. Candidly speaking, I would have been surprised very much if I had won. I was stale from overplaying. It was surprising to me that I captured the national championship, as at that time also I was overgolfed. After this year I shall retire from the game and do not expect to play for many years to come. I will participate in the intercollegiate golf tournament October 15, which will wind up this season's playing for me. I graduate from Harvard this June and then enter the commercial world.[80]

Lyon, jubilant in victory, eagerly looked forward to his golfing future:

> I came to St. Louis little expecting that I would gain the title of Olympic golf champion. However, I was successful, and I will say that I was compelled to play my hardest to win. I attribute my success principally to my long drives. I outdrove Egan, and it was mainly through this that I won. This is the first time that I competed in a golf tournament in America, and I feel highly honored to think that I captured the much coveted title. In the future I intend to enter all American golf tournaments in which I am eligible.[81]

Golf Results

Qualifying Round

1. Ralph McKittrick	USA	St. Louis Country Club Trans-Mississippi Golf Association	81–82	163
2. Stuart Stickney	USA	St. Louis Country Club Trans-Mississippi Golf Association	81–82	163
3. Francis Newton	USA	Seattle Country Club Trans-Mississippi Golf Association	80–84	164
4. Walter Egan	USA	Exmoor Country Club, Chicago Western Golf Association	80–85	165
4. W. Arthur Stickney	USA	St. Louis Country Club Trans-Mississippi Golf Association	84–81	165

6. Mason Phelps	USA	Midlothian Country Club, Chicago Western Golf Association	86–80	166
6. H. Chandler Egan	USA	Exmoor Country Club, Chicago Western Golf Association	88–78	166
8. Albert Lambert	USA	Glen Echo Country Club, Trans-Mississippi Golf Association	86–82	168
9. George Lyon	Canada	Lambton Golf and Country Club, Toronto	84–85	169
9. Daniel Sawyer	USA	Chicago Golf Club, Western Golf Association	90–79	169
11. Burt McKinnie	USA	Normandie Park Golf Club, St. Louis Trans-Mississippi Golf	86–84	170
11. Doug Cadwalader	USA	Springfield County Club, Ill., U.S. Golf Association	88–82	170
11. Warren Wood	USA	Flossmoor Country Club, Ill. Western Golf Association	84–86	170
14. Robert Hunter	USA	Midlothian Country Club, Chicago Western Golf Association	87–84	171
15. Henry Potter	USA	St. Louis Country Club, Trans-Mississippi Golf Association	87–86	173
16. Simpson Foulis	USA	Chicago Golf Club No Team Affiliation	89–85	174
16. Harold Weber	USA	Inverness Club, Toledo, Ohio U.S. Golf Association	88–86	174
16. Jesse Carleton	USA	Glen Echo Country Club, U.S. Golf Association	92–82	174
19. Nathaniel Moore	USA	Lake Geneva Country Club, Wisc. Western Golf Association	87–90	177
19. Orus Jones	USA	Inverness Club, Toledo, Ohio, U.S. Golf Association	83–94	177
19. Simeon Price	USA	Glen Echo Country Club, U.S. Golf Association	85–92	177
22. Clement Smoot	USA	Exmoor Country Club, Chicago Western Golf Association	91–87	178
22. Harry Allen	USA	Bellerive Country Club, St. Louis No Team Affiliation	93–85	178
22. Arthur Havemeyer	USA	Seabright Country Club, N.J. No Team Affiliation	88–90	178
25. Edward Cummins	USA	Exmoor Country Club, Chicago Western Golf Association	88–91	179
26. Frederick Semple	USA	Bellerive Country Club, St. Louis Trans-Mississippi Golf Assoc.	89–91	180
27. John Cady	USA	Rock Island Arsenal Club, Ill. Trans-Mississippi Golf Assoc.	93–89	182
27. Abner Vickery	USA	Glen Echo Country Club No Team Affiliation	92–90	182

29. Ray Havemeyer	USA	Seabright Country Club, N.J. No Team Affiliation	94–89	183
29. Allen Lard	USA	Columbia Country Club, Md. U.S. Golf Association	93–90	183
29. Harold Fraser	USA	Inverness Country Club, Toledo, Ohio U.S. Golf Association	90–93	183
29. William Smith	USA	Philadelphia Country Club No Team Affiliation	93–90	183

Individual Championship

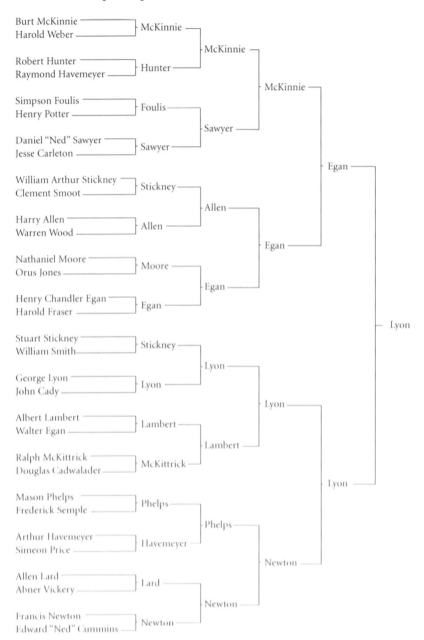

Boxing (September 21–22)

While the golfers were in action at Glen Echo Country Club, Olympic boxing contests were conducted over a two-day period in the Physical Culture Gymnasium. Boxers fought for the Olympic title in seven different weight categories: fly, bantam, feather, light, welter, middle, and heavyweight. Preliminary bouts were fought on Wednesday, September 21, with all championship matches being held the next day. Double gold medalist Oliver Kirk was the most notable pugilist in St. Louis. Kirk, a local twenty-year-old lad, was a member of the Business Men's Gymnasium in St. Louis and made Olympic history by winning the championship in two different classifications. Weighing 114 pounds, Kirk won the bantamweight title for competitors 115 pounds and under and then captured the gold medal in the featherweight division, 125 pounds and under. Boxers from the Olympic Club of San Francisco performed well, winning three championships. George V. Finnegan was victorious in the flyweight division, 105 pounds and under, while teammate Albert Young won the welterweight championship, 145 pounds and under. In the heavyweight division, 159 pounds and over, Samuel Berger captured the third gold medal for the California team. One unfortunate minor episode occurred in the lightweight division. A St. Louis boxer named Bollinger, hoping to win favor with the judges, entered under the name of Carroll Burton, a successful, well-known local boxer. Bollinger did win his first bout in a narrow decision. His hoax, however, was soon discovered; he was disqualified, and the victory awarded to his opponent.[82]

Boxing Results

Flyweight Division (105 lbs. and under)

1. George Finnegan	USA	San Francisco Olympic Club
2. Miles Burke	USA	Affiliation Unknown

Bantamweight Division (115 lbs. and under)

1. Oliver Kirk	USA	Business Men's Gymnasium, St. Louis
2. George Finnegan	USA	San Francisco Olympic Club

Featherweight Division (125 lbs. and under)

1. Oliver Kirk	USA	Business Men's Gymnasium, St. Louis
2. Frank Haller	USA	Cincinnati Athletic Club and Gymnasium
3. Fred Gilmore	USA	Affiliation Unknown

Lightweight Division (135 lbs. and under)

1. Harry Spanger	USA	National Turnverein, Newark, N.J.
2. Jack Eagan	USA	Affiliation Unknown
3. Russell Van Horn	USA	South Broadway Athletic Club, St. Louis

Welterweight Division (145 lbs. and under)

1. Albert Young	USA	San Francisco Olympic Club
2. Harry Spanger	USA	National Turnverein, Newark, N.J.
3. Joseph Lydon	USA	Christian Brothers College, St. Louis
3. Jack Eagan	USA	Affiliation Unknown

There is no record of a match between Lydon and Eagan to determine third place.

Middleweight Division (158 lbs. and under)

1. Charles Mayer	USA	St. George's Athletic Club, New York
2. Benjamin Spradley	USA	Business Men's Gymnasium, St. Louis

Heavyweight Division (159 lbs. and over)

1. Samuel Berger	USA	San Francisco Olympic Club
2. Charles Mayer	USA	St. George's Athletic Club, New York
3. William Michaels	USA	Affiliation Unknown

Wrestling (October 14–15)

October brought cooler temperatures and fall colors to St. Louis. Since July 1 an almost continuous program of Olympic sports had been contested, but October contained only one Olympic competition, wrestling. Unlike boxing, wrestling matches were held outside, on the stadium infield in the same area where the weight-lifting events took place. Like boxing, there were seven weight divisions in the wrestling competition, and all combatants were American. While boxing and wrestling events were open to the amateurs of the world, as a practical matter, most international athletes felt it was difficult, if not impossible, to be away from home during the fall season.

The wrestling competition was a single-elimination tournament, with preliminary matches taking place on October 14. Championship matches occurred the next day. Matches were six minutes long with a three-minute overtime, if necessary. The seven weight divisions were the same as for boxing: 105 pounds and under, 115 pounds and under, 125 pounds and under, 135 pounds and under, 145 pounds and under, 158 pounds and under, and the unlimited class, over 158 pounds. Local strongman Frank Kungler of the St. Louis Southwest Turnverein won the silver medal in the unlimited division to go along with his three bronze medals earned in the tug-of-war competition and the two weight-lifting contests.[83]

Wrestling Results

105 lb. Class

1. Robert Curry	USA	St. George's Athletic Club, New York
2. John Hein	USA	Boys' Club, New York
3. Gustav Thiefenthaler	USA	South Broadway Athletic Club, St. Louis

115 lb. Class

1. George Mehnert	USA	National Turnverein, Newark, N.J.
2. Gustav Bauer	USA	National Turnverein, Newark, N.J.
3. William Nelson	USA	St. George's Athletic Club, New York

125 lb. Class

1. Isidor "Jack" Niflot	USA	Pastime Athletic Club, New York
2. August Wester	USA	National Turnverein, Newark, N.J.
3. Z. B. Strebler	USA	South Broadway Athletic Club, St. Louis

135 lb. Class

1. Benjamin Bradshaw	USA	Boys' Club, New York
2. Theodore McLear	USA	National Turnverein, Newark, N.J.
3. Charles Clapper	USA	Chicago Central YMCA

145 lb. Class

1. Otto Roehm	USA	Buffalo Central YMCA
2. Rudolph Tesing	USA	St. George's Athletic Club
3. Albert Zirkel	USA	National Turnverein, Newark, N.J.

158 lb. Class

1. Charles Erickson	USA	Brooklyn Norwegier Turnverein
2. William Beckman	USA	New Westside Athletic Club, New York
3. Jerry Winholtz	USA	Chicago Central YMCA

Unlimited Class

1. Bernhuff Hansen	USA	Brooklyn Norwegier Turnverein
2. Frank Kungler	USA	St. Louis Southwest Turnverein
3. Fred Warmboldt	USA	North St. Louis Turnverein

Olympic Lecture Series

A series of Olympic lectures discussing the scientific basis of physical training and athletics and the general field of physical culture were organized by the Department of Physical Culture and presented throughout the summer, complementing the Olympic athletic competition. Held in classrooms of the Physical Culture building, lectures were delivered by distinguished leaders of the physical culture movement from around the world. A partial list of presenters and their topics follows:

> C. Stanley Hall, Ph.D., LL.D., president, Clark University, Worcester, Mass. "Health as Related to Civilization."
> R. Tait McKenzie, M.D., McGill University, Montreal, Canada. "Artistic Anatomy in Relation to Physical Training."
> F. A. Schmidt, M.D., Bonn, Germany. "The Physiology of Exercise."
> William G. Anderson, M.D., Yale University. "Gymnastic Dancing and Its Place in Secondary and Collegiate Schools."
> Frederick J. V. Skiff, director of exhibits, Louisiana Purchase Exposition. "The General Advantages of Athletic Exercises to the Individual."
> W. J. McGee, chief, Department of Anthropology, Louisiana Purchase Exposition. "The Influence of Play in Racial Development with Special Reference to Muscular Movement."
> Luther H. Gulick, M.D., Brooklyn, New York, chairman, Physical Training Committee. "Athletics and Social Evolution"; "The Place of the Social and Aesthetic Elements in Physical Training as Exemplified by German Gymnastics."
> James E. Sullivan, chief, Department of Physical Culture, Louisiana Purchase Exposition. "Sketch of the Development of Athletic Implements."[84]

Complementing the Olympic lecture series, numerous conferences and conventions were conducted by organizations connected with the physical culture movement. The Public Schools Physical Training Society, the Physical Directors Society of the Young Men's Christian Associations of North America, the Physical Training Section of the National Education Association, and the American Physical Education Association (now called the American Alliance for Health, Physical Education, Recreation, and Dance—AAHPERD) were the most prominent of the professional organizations conducting meetings in St. Louis. Hundreds of exhibits from schools, colleges, and athletic clubs were displayed in the physical culture gymnasium throughout the exposition. President Francis remarked in his official report on the World's Fair, "From the extensive and representative array of exhibits presented by the department of Physical Culture it was possible for the first time, perhaps, to get a comprehensive idea of the widespread extent, particularly in this country, of the Physical Culture movement."[85]

Soccer (November 16–18, 23)

The World's Fair closed on December 1. Only the week before did Olympic competition conclude with the soccer championships. It was soccer in the United States, but to the rest of the world these were the football championships. The national champions of Canada, the Galt football team from Ontario, dominated the limited competition offered by American teams to win the gold medal. There were only two American teams, both local clubs organized at the last minute at the urging of AAU officials. Joseph Lydon, a prominent St. Louis athlete, was asked to organize amateur soccer teams to compete in the Olympic games. Lydon, of Christian Brothers College in St. Louis, had competed in the welterweight boxing tournament two months earlier, finishing tied for third. Lydon formed a parish soccer league with two of the teams competing in the Olympic games against the Canadians. On November 16 Christian Brothers College with Lydon playing halfback played the Canadian champions, losing convincingly 7–0. The next day the team from Canada almost as effortlessly dispensed with the St. Rose Parish team, 4–0, to claim Olympic victory. On November 18 Christian Brothers College met St. Rose Parish in a playoff to determine second and third place. Both teams continued their scoreless ways, with the game ending in a 0–0 tie. After three overtimes neither team had scored and the game, called due to darkness, was rescheduled for November 23. On that day Lydon's team finally managed to score not one but two goals to defeat St. Rose Parish and capture the silver medal.[86]

Soccer Results

1. Canada—Galt Football Club: Ernest Linton (G), George Ducker (FB), John Gourley (FB), John Fraser (FB), Albert Johnson (HB), Robert Lane (HB), Tom Taylor (F/RW), Frederick Steep (F/RW), Alexander Hall (F/C), Gordon McDonald (F/LW), William Twaits (F/LW).

2. United States—Christian Brothers College: Louis Menges (G), Oscar Brockmeyer (FB/F), Thomas January (FB), John January (HB), Charles January (HB), Peter Ratican (HB), Warren Brittingham (F), Alexander Cudmore (F), Charles Bartliff (F), Joseph Lydon (F/FB), Raymond Lawlor (F).

3. United States—St. Rose Parish: Frank Frost (G), George Cooke (FB), Henry Jameson (FB), Joseph Brady (HB), Dierkes (HB), Martin Dooling HB), Cormic Cosgrove (F/RW), O'Connell (F/RW), Claude Jameson (F/C), Harry Tate (F/LW), Thomas Cooke (F/LW), Johnson (F/LW).

Three days after the last Olympic event, the honorary president of the Olympic games, Theodore Roosevelt, arrived in St. Louis. He completed a whirlwind two-day tour of the World's Fair that included a visit to the stadium to briefly observe a college football game between the two famous Indian schools, Carlisle of Pennsylvania and Haskell of Kansas.[87] But there were no Olympic closing ceremonies. Olympic pageantry, ceremonies, and rituals evolved over the years. The first parade of athletes by nation in the opening ceremonies occurred in 1908 at the London Olympics. The Olympic flag and athlete's oath were not adopted until 1920 at the Antwerp Games, and official closing ceremonies with the raising of the Olympic flag along with the flags of the host nation and the nation to host the Olympics four years hence were not instituted until 1924 at the second Paris Olympics. In St. Louis the absence of closing ceremonies did not diminish the universal euphoric feeling of success shared by spectators, newspaper reporters, Olympic officials, and World's Fair administrators alike. James Sullivan's remarks on the significance and success of the St. Louis Olympics reflected the prevailing sentiment. Sullivan said,

> There always will be a tradition surrounding the stadium and this gymnasium, and the impressions of the Olympic games, the most successful ever held, will never be erased. . . . This beautiful stadium and athletic field . . . will remain, and the memory of the Olympic games of 1904 always will live to spur athletes to further effort and success.[88]

George Philip Bryant
dominated the archery
competition, capturing
two individual gold
medals and a bronze in
the team event. From
Mark Bennitt, ed., *History of the Louisiana
Purchase Exposition.*

Cincinnati Archers team photograph. Archery was the only sport in which women competed. From Mark Bennitt, ed., *History of the Louisiana Purchase Exposition.*

Spectators line the banks of the man-made Life Saving Exhibit Lake to watch as the U.S. Coast Guard demonstrates "life saving techniques at sea." The Olympic diving and swimming events took place in this lake. Courtesy of the St. Louis Public Library, Special Collections.

Hungarian swimmer Zoltan von Halmay, a double gold medalist, won the 50 and 100 yard freestyle events. Courtesy of the St. Louis Public Library, Special Collections.

Wrestling matches were conducted outdoors on the stadium infield. From Mark Bennitt, ed., *History of the Louisiana Purchase Exposition.*

Anton Heida of Philadelphia won the gold medal for his performance on the high bar. From Mark Bennitt, ed., *History of the Louisiana Purchase Exposition.*

Beals C. Wright of Boston was the star of Olympic tennis. Courtesy of the St. Louis Public Library, Special Collections.

Dwight Davis, of Davis Cup fame, demonstrates his serving technique. Courtesy of the St. Louis Public Library, Special Collections.

Members of Shamrock Lacrosse Team

These images of members of the Winnipeg, Manitoba, Shamrocks lacrosse team appeared in the *Chicago Tribune.* The Shamrocks were Olympic lacrosse champions.

Pericles Kakousis of Athens, Greece, lifts 246.25 pounds to win the gold medal in the two-handed weightlifting competition. From Mark Bennitt, ed., *History of the Louisiana Purchase Exposition.*

A view of track and field facilities on the campus of Washington University. From Charles J. P. Lucas, *The Olympic Games of 1904.*

Spectators leaning on the railing and out of the windows of the gymnasium watch the finish of the 200 meter hurdle race. From Mark Bennitt, ed., *History of the Louisiana Purchase Exposition.*

After clearing the bar, gold medalist Charles Dvorak of the Chicago Athletic Association pushes his pole away and falls toward the sand pit. From Mark Bennitt, ed., *History of the Louisiana Purchase Exposition.*

Runners in the team relay race (now called cross country) line up for the last event in the Olympic track and field competition. From Charles J. P. Lucas, *The Olympic Games of 1904.*

Ray Ewry of the New York Athletic Club executes the scissors technique to win the standing high jump. From Charles J. P. Lucas, *The Olympic Games of 1904.*

Marathon runners assemble for the start of the grueling contest. Winner Thomas Hicks, number 20, is on far left side. From Charles J. P. Lucas, *The Olympic Games of 1904*.

Thomas Hicks, marathon winner, gold medal on his chest, poses with marathon trophy and victory cup. From Charles J. P. Lucas, *The Olympic Games of 1904*.

Four marathon officials prepare to follow the runners along the course. From Charles J. P. Lucas, *The Olympic Games of 1904.*

This plaque on a column of the Francis Field gate memorializes the 1904 Olympics. Universal Exposition was another name for the World's Fair. Photo by author.

This handsome gate leading into the Olympic stadium, renamed Francis Field, was erected in 1914 to honor David R. Francis, president of the Louisiana Purchase Exposition and of the Olympic games. Located on the grounds of Washington University, the stadium is still used for athletic events. Photo by author.

The Physical Culture Building built for the 1904 Olympics is now Washington University's Francis Gymnasium. Photo by author.

Place in History

America in 1904 was a nation bristling with energy and confidence. Formerly an isolationist country, the United States had recently become a recognized player on the imperialistic international stage, having flexed her muscles in the Spanish-American War. Inspired by a young, energetic, and athletic president, Theodore Roosevelt, a sports mania rampaged across the country. Eager to celebrate its history, and display its commercial, military, and athletic potential, the United States hosted the world at the 1904 Louisiana Purchase Exposition and welcomed the world's athletes to compete in the international Olympic games.

The Olympic movement was also young and optimistic. Revived in Greece in 1896, the St. Louis Olympics were only the third of the modern period. Originally awarded to Chicago, St. Louis wrested the games from her rival city against the wishes of International Olympic Committee President Pierre de Coubertin and appended them to the Louisiana Purchase Exposition, a World's Fair celebrating the conquest of a continent.

201

Athletes came from eleven countries and four continents to compete. American athletes represented not only their country but also their particular athletic clubs, and their uniforms bore their clubs' insignia. James E. Sullivan, chief of the Physical Culture Department and director of the Olympic Games, had tried in 1901 to organize an international track and field federation in an attempt to steal control of the Olympic movement from Coubertin. The aristocratic French baron and the scrappy Irish-American mutually despised each other, causing Coubertin to withhold his personal involvement from the games.

The elegant new gymnasium and ten-thousand-seat concrete stadium were state-of-the-art for the time, and sporting goods mogul Albert Spalding provided the most up-to-date physical training equipment. Olympic events began on July 1 with gymnastics and continued for nearly five months. There were fifteen Olympic sports in all: gymnastics, lacrosse, rowing and sculling, cycling, track and field, weight lifting, tennis, swimming, diving, fencing, archery, golf, boxing, wrestling, and soccer. Women participated only in archery. African Americans participated for the first time in Olympic competition: George Poage won bronze medals in the 200 and 400 meter hurdles, and Joseph Stadler won silver and bronze medals in the standing high jump and standing hop, step, and jump. The sports-happy American public all across the country followed the events, particularly track and field, in the illustrated newspapers.

The St. Louis Olympics garnered only praise in 1904. Sullivan was not alone in his lavish praise of the games. American journalists were unanimous, saluting the athletes, organizers, and spectators alike. All agreed awareness of the Olympic movement and the prestige of the games had been greatly enhanced, especially in the United States. Even Coubertin lauded the success in St. Louis, going so far as to award Sullivan a special gold medal for his efforts, despite their personal animosity. Sullivan published Coubertin's letter informing him of his award in his report on the Olympic games.

COMITE INTERNATIONAL OLYMPIQUE

Paris, Oct. 19, 1904

Dear Mr. Sullivan:

On behalf of the International Olympic Committee, I beg to send you our warmest congratulations and thanks for the wonderful work you have succeeded in carrying out the organization of the third Olympiad.

As a token of our gratitude, I have the pleasure to state that the medal commemorating the revival of the Olympic games will be awarded to you on the occasion of the International Congress to be held in Brussels in June, 1905, under the presidency of his Majesty the King of the Belgians.

The value of the souvenir comes from the fact that only a very few copies have been given away since ten years, their Majesties the Emperor of Germany and the King of Spain and their Royal Highnesses the Crown Prince of Greece, the Crown Prince of Sweden and Norway and the Prince of Wales being among those who were glad to receive it. President McKinley also received it after the vote making the third Olympiad an American one.

We expect you to present a short but substantial report on the St. Louis games to the Brussels Congress.

Thanking you for the numerous documents and the medals you sent us and congratulating you once more.

I am, dear Mr. Sullivan,

Very truly yours,

BARON PIERRE DeCOUBERTIN
President of the International Olympic Committee[1]

There were no disparaging remarks, only praise in 1904 by the president of the International Olympic Committee.

Two years after the St. Louis games, the Olympics were held again in Athens. The 1906 Olympics were held to fulfill the agreement made by Coubertin and the IOC after the first Olympic games in Athens in 1896. Greece wanted to be the permanent host for the Olympics, but Coubertin would not abandon his vision of rotating the quadrennial games among the major cities of the world. As a compromise Coubertin agreed to have Greece host quadrennial games between each Olympiad. Thus, Athens was scheduled to host Olympics in 1898, 1902, 1906, etc. Political and economic turmoil in Greece prevented games in 1898 and 1902, but Greek society reached a point of sufficient stability by 1906 that the Greek government decided it was again capable of hosting the Olympics. Many years later, after the publication of Coubertin's memoirs, conventional wisdom claimed the 1906 Athens games, called the Interim Games, were organized after the St. Louis games to save the Olympic movement. This is simply untrue.

The Olympics of 1908 (London) and 1912 (Stockholm) did greatly surpass the grandeur, size, and successes of St. Louis. The London games were the third consecutive Olympiad held in conjunction with a World's Fair and as in St. Louis demonstrated the benefit of such an association. Unlike in St. Louis, Coubertin did not request that all sport competition bear the title "Olympic." After three attempts, one too cold—the term "Olympics" was totally absent for Paris games (1900)—and one too hot—the Olympic title was used for all sports in St. Louis (1904)—Coubertin and the IOC got it just right in London: a clearly defined Olympic program of events. At Stockholm the Olympic games reached maturity as a viable, independent, international institution achieving worldwide acceptance and prominence only dreamed of in 1904. The St. Louis Olympics receded in memory. While the 1916 Olympics, scheduled for Berlin, were canceled due to World War I, they continued to flourish after the war, being held in Antwerp in 1920 and returning to Paris in 1924. The Olympics of St. Louis were associated with a bygone era. The world and the Olympics had changed so much in such a short period of time.

Largely forgotten, the 1904 Olympics suffered an even crueler fate with the publication of Coubertin's memoirs in 1931. A selective memory, exaggerated claims, and false statements by Coubertin turned the forgotten Olympics into the failed Olympics. Almost thirty years after the fact, with the Olympics established as an international success and his reputation as Olympic founder secure, but still unhappy over the transfer of the 1904 games from Chicago to St. Louis and unable to put aside his personal resentment toward James Sullivan, who had died in 1914, Coubertin unfairly and inaccurately labeled the St. Louis Olympics a grand failure. Coubertin wrote, "transferring the Games to St. Louis had been a misfortune,"[2] and completely absolved himself of any responsibility for the transfer when he stated, ". . . I wrote unofficially to ask President Roosevelt to decide the matter. As I had expected, he opted in favour of the transfer."[3] Coubertin could make this false statement in 1931. He had outlived his 1904 contemporaries. There was no one alive to refute his allegations; Roosevelt had died in 1919.

Coubertin continued his attack: ". . . the St. Louis Games were completely lacking in attraction. Personally, I had no wish to attend them."[4] Referring to his trip to America in 1893, which included a visit to St. Louis, Coubertin stated, "I harbored great resentment against the town for the disillusionment caused by my first sight of the junction of the Missouri and Mississippi rivers. After reading Fenimore Cooper, what had I not been led to expect of the setting where these rivers with their strange sounding names actually met! But there was no beauty, no originality. I had a sort of presentiment that the Olympiad would match the mediocrity of the town."[5]

Coubertin further charged that the games were completely submerged within the World's Fair and equated the Olympics of St. Louis with the truly failed 1900 Paris games with his statement, "Olympism . . . reduced to the role of humiliated vassal to which it had been subjected in Paris."[6] Even more damning, he accused American Olympic officials of perpetrating a painful racist episode called "Anthropology Days," wherein so-called "primitive peoples" competed against one another in European-style sports for the amusement of Anglo-Saxon spectators: "As far as originality was concerned, the only original feature offered by the programme was a particularly embarrassing one. I mean the 'Anthropology Days' whose events were reserved for Negroes, Indians, Filipinos and Ainus, with the Turks and Syrians thrown in for good measure!"[7]

The facts, conveniently ignored by Coubertin, present a far different reality for the St. Louis Olympics. As an adjunct to the World's Fair, the Olympic games received enthusiastic official support and immense public exposure. An entire Department of Physical Culture was created to organize the Olympic games with the Amateur Athletic Union of the United States serving as the organizing body with the preeminent sports figure in the country, James Sullivan, serving as the Olympic games director. The president of the World's Fair, David Francis, also served as president of the Olympic games and attended the opening ceremonies. The president of the United States, Theodore Roosevelt, served as honorary president for the Olympics and welcomed the world to compete in his opening remarks from the White House to begin the World's Fair. Most of the Olympic events were well attended, especially in the stadium, and newspapers reported Olympic events and victories all across the country to a sports-crazed American public.

Anthropology Days was a two-day affair occurring on August 12 and 13. They were one of three athletic exhibits among primitive peoples in St. Louis, with "Barbarian Games" held on July 17 and "Philippine Tribal Contests" held on September 16. Certainly racist and demeaning and rightly condemned, even in 1904 (Mark Twain refused to attend the World's Fair in his home state of Missouri because of such practices), this event must be viewed within a historical context. In the imperialistic times of 1904, popularly espoused social Darwinism condoned displaying so-called primitive or native peoples in public exhibitions. In fact, the French were the first to display aboriginal peoples at a World's Fair in Paris in 1889. At the time, the young Coubertin supported the concept and praised the French aboriginal exhibit.[8]

Several conversations between Dr. W. J. McGee, chief of the Department of Anthropology, and James Sullivan, chief of the Department of Physical Culture, led to the organizing of Anthropology Days at St. Louis. McGee, the social scientist, sought to collect athletic data to compare results among the natives. Sullivan, the racial purist, saw an opportunity to destroy the popular belief that aboriginal peoples, living close to nature, possessed natural athletic talent, and to confirm the athletic, hence racial, superiority of Anglo-Saxon peoples. Sullivan agreed to host the athletic contests in the stadium. Required to participate against one another in European-style sports completely alien to them, their performances, as might have been expected, were poor when compared to American athletic records. McGee sited lack of training and instruction in sport techniques to explain the dismal results, but Sullivan gloried in the demonstrated inferiority of the aboriginals, stating, "The whole meeting proves conclusively that the savage has been a very much overrated man from an athletic point of view," and, "Lecturers and authors will in the future please omit all reference to the natural athletic ability of the savage. . ."[9] These lamentable comments by the director of the Olympic Games must be understood to be personal views. Anthropology Days were not organized as part of the Olympic program. The word "Olympic" never appears in the newspapers or on the program of events, and this is significant given that the name was almost universally applied in connection with athletic events in St. Louis. The win-

ners in the Anthropology Days contests received American flags, while
Olympic participants received medals.[10]

After the enormously successful and internationally acclaimed London and, especially, Stockholm Olympics, the St. Louis Games were a
remote event which publication of Coubertin's memoirs in 1931 forever
branded as a failure. Still, the tarnished reputation of the St. Louis
Olympics may have been resurrected but for the publication of *An
Approved History of the Olympic Games* by Bill Henry in 1948. After Sullivan and Lucas in 1905, Coubertin's memoirs in 1931 were the first account of the St. Louis games to appear in print. The words "An Approved
History" in the title of Henry's book refer to the fact that Coubertin not
only provided Olympic information to Henry but also reviewed and
approved the accuracy of the manuscript before his death in 1937.
Henry was extremely critical of the St. Louis games and used even
harsher language than Coubertin. Henry perpetuated the exaggerations
and distortions of Coubertin and then added a few of his own. Speaking
of Anthropology Days, Henry wrote, ". . . collection of aboriginal
freaks, rumored to have been drafted from the side shows of the exposition, went through the motions of athletic competition, to the amusement of a handful of spectators."[11] Henry reinforced Coubertin's
assertion that the Olympics were a mere appendage to the World's Fair
with these words: "It was unfortunate indeed that the Olympic games
had to be for the second time staged under the very doubtful circumstances of propinquity to a world's fair. It was inevitable that under such
conditions the Olympic games would be nothing more or less than a
side show for the main exposition."[12] Henry summarily dismissed the
overall Olympic organizational efforts with, "Much of the thrill was
taken out of the events by the whole-sale manner in which they were
staged. The actual Olympic championships—if any of the St. Louis
events are entitled to be dignified by that name—were so hopelessly
tangled up in a welter of handicapped races and other events of a non-
descript nature that it is almost impossible to extricate the events that
might have had Olympic significance from those that had none, the latter being vastly in the majority."[13]

Handicapped events were staged for running, swimming, and field
(throwing and jumping) events. These events were not for the disabled,
but were contests where, based on their recent past performances, athletes

with different levels of talent competed against each other. Those athletes with lesser abilities were given advantages: a runner or swimmer would receive a certain distance head start; throwers and jumpers were assigned additional distances to their performances. The goal was to equalize the competition as much as possible and have close finishes. Handicapped events were a standard practice of the time and everyone recognized the handicapped events as being separate from the Olympic games. In St. Louis, Theodore Bland, the official handicapper for the Western Association of the Amateur Athletic Union, was responsible for determining the various handicaps in track and field. His performance was judged by how close the finish was in each event. Charles Lucas in his 1905 book gives credit for the handicapped events to James Sullivan and explains their purpose as ". . . not only to give the competitors for championship honors a rest between events, but also to bring into action as many new athletes as possible." [14]

In his memoirs Coubertin limited his criticism of the 1904 Olympics to expressing his displeasure with St. Louis as a city, the transfer of the Olympics from Chicago to St. Louis, an association of the Olympics with the World's Fair, and Anthropology Days. Henry, with the approval of Coubertin, continued his ridicule of the St. Louis Olympics, adding the lack of international athletes and finally, in total disregard for the facts, stating that the vast majority of Americans in 1904 were totally unaware of the St. Louis Olympics.

More than thirty years after the St. Louis Olympics Henry writes, ". . . the almost total absence of foreign competition made it impossible to assign to the games the importance that their past history and their colorful future deserve." [15] At first glance this criticism might seem warranted. Exposition and Olympic officials certainly expected larger numbers of foreign athletes. But it was an age of slow, long-distance travel and only a small number of nations were involved in the Olympic movement. The overwhelming numbers of athletes, 523 of 630, were Americans. But comparing the first and third Olympiads, Athens and St. Louis, only eight years apart, provides a more realistic analysis of international representation. Thirteen countries competed at Athens in 1896; in St. Louis there were eleven. Total athletes in Athens, 311; St. Louis, 630. Two hundred thirty Greeks competed in Athens, representing 74 percent of the total number; in St. Louis, the 523 Americans constituted 83 percent of the total. In 1896, America sent 14 athletes to Athens. In 1904, Greece sent 14 athletes to St. Louis. Germany sent 19 athletes to Athens, 17 to St. Louis. Austria, Australia, Hungary, and Switzerland sent comparable numbers of athletes to Athens and St. Louis. Four nations, Bulgaria, Chile, Denmark, and Sweden, were represented in Athens but not St. Louis. Three new nations, South Africa, Canada, and Cuba, were represented in St. Louis. Interestingly, nineteen French athletes competed in Athens, none in St. Louis. James Sullivan dismissed the international athlete issue, concentrating instead on the high caliber of athletic competition. "World's records were made, Olympic records were equaled and surpassed and the competitions were keen and interesting. When one reads over the list of Olympic winners and then over the list of eligible men in the world, there are perhaps two men living to-day who were not in the stadium who could have won Olympic honors."[16]

The American public in 1904 was very much aware that the Olympic games were taking place in America. Henry's criticism that "without any question the great bulk of the American people saw the year 1904 with its St. Louis exposition come and go without knowing that anything in the nature of the Olympic games had been in their country"[17] is totally without merit. Newspaper coverage of Olympic events and personalities saturated the nation, not only in St. Louis but in the major population centers of Chicago, New York, Boston, San Francisco, and Los Angeles as well. Even the lesser cities and towns received reports of Olympic news. The April 7, 1903, edition of the *Topeka Journal* published a photograph of Coubertin with the headline, "A Sporting Baron," and the following: "Baron Pierre de Coubertin is one of the leading sporting authorities of Europe, and he will come to this country to view the great international games at the St. Louis exposition of 1904."[18] While Coubertin's ultimate decision not to attend may have negated the information in this article, clearly Americans were very much aware of the Olympic games in 1904.

Bill Henry is also responsible for creating the myth associating Alice Roosevelt, daughter of Theodore Roosevelt, with the Olympic marathon. Describing the arrival of runner Fred Lorz in the stadium, Henry writes, "After he had been loudly cheered and his picture taken with Alice Roosevelt, daughter of the President of the United States, as she placed a wreath of laurel on his brow, somebody began to check up on him and produced a truck driver who had brought the marathon 'champion' half way to town in his wagon."[19]

While dining at the White House, Secretary of State John Hay and his lifelong friend, author Henry Adams, conveyed their favorable impressions of the St. Louis Exposition, having represented the president at the opening ceremonies for the Olympic games on May 14, and recommended that Roosevelt attend. Citing political protocol during an election year, the president declined until after the election, but his daughter became enamored with the exposition. Alice Roosevelt arrived in St. Louis on May 27. She was the toast of the town and the fair. David Francis, infatuated by her charm, often escorted the vivacious twenty-year-old during her weeklong visit. Scheduled to depart on June 4, she remained one day longer, leaving St. Louis on Sunday, June 5. On Saturday, June 4, Alice Roosevelt, accompanied by Francis, was the guest of honor for the Amateur Athletic Union Track and Field Championships in the World's Fair stadium. The victorious athletes were delighted to receive their medals from the coquettish Alice Roosevelt.[20] Olympic track and field competition took place August 29 through September 3 with the marathon the only event occurring on Tuesday August 30. Alice Roosevelt was not in St. Louis. She did return to the fair with her newly elected father in November, more than a month after the Olympic marathon. Confusing the two track and field championships, AAU and Olympic, while regrettable, is plausible, but there can be no rational explanation for the blatant fabrication of marathoner Fred Lorz having his picture taken with Alice Roosevelt and having a wreath of laurel placed by her on his head. The whole scene is creative fiction, as is Henry's description of another marathoner, the Cuban, Felix Carbajal: ". . . Caravajal, after leading handily for 18 miles felt the pangs of hunger and stopped to eat a couple of apples gathered from a near-by tree. It developed that the apples were green and the pangs of hunger were succeeded by pangs of a far more painful variety—cramps, keeping the Cuban from what seemed like a certain victory."[21] The misspelled name is the least of the inaccuracies. Carbajal ate some peaches, playfully taken from race officials, on the marathon course. He never led in the race, let alone for the first eighteen miles! There were no apples, green or otherwise, and Carbajal never developed cramps. For many years Coubertin's memoirs and Henry's

Approved History sealed the fate of the St. Louis Olympics. Others, simply citing these two sources, perpetuated this deliberately fictionalized
account of the third Olympiad, producing a blurred and tarnished reputation.

The facts reveal a different reality. The first American Olympics, held
in 1904 in St. Louis, were a vigorous spectacle suited to an energetic and
confident nation. The St. Louis Olympics, only the third Olympic games,
captivated the attention of the American press and public. Athletes came
from eleven countries and four continents to compete in state-of-the-
art facilities. They competed in fifteen Olympic sports, and their world-
class performances resulted in many new world and Olympic records
being set. African Americans competed and medaled for the first time
in Olympic history. It is the purpose of this book to refocus the blurred
image and polish the long-tarnished reputation of America's first Olympics. Resurrected from neglect and denigration, the St. Louis Olympics
deserve to be recognized for their significant contribution to enhancing
and promoting the establishment of the infant Olympic games and for
their immensely successful presentation to the American public as part
of the greatest World's Fair of all time.

Notes

1. A Tale of Two Cities

1. Richard D. Mandell, *The First Modern Olympics,* 161, 162; Pierre Coubertin, *Olympic Memoirs,* 15, 50; David C. Young, *The Modern Olympics: A Struggle for Revival,* 90.

2. John J. MacAloon, *This Great Symbol: Pierre de Coubertin and the Origins of the Modern Olympic Games,* 274; Eugene Weber, "Pierre de Coubertin and the Introduction of Organized Sport in France," 12.

3. John E. Findling, "World's Fairs and the Olympic Games," 13; John E. Findling, ed., *Historical Dictionary of World's Fairs and Expositions, 1851–1988,* 5; John E. Findling and Kimberly D. Pelle, eds., *Historical Dictionary of the Modern Olympic Movement,* 13; Bill Henry, *An Approved History of the Olympic Games,* 60; MacAloon, *This Great Symbol,* 274; Sandor Barc, *The Modern Olympic Story,* 37.

4. Robert K. Barney, "Born from Dilemma: America Awakens to the Modern Olympic Games, 1901–1903," 93, 94; *New York Times,* July 28, 1900; John Lucas, "Early Olympic Antagonists: Pierre de Coubertin versus James E. Sullivan," 261.

5. Lucas, "Early Olympic Antagonists," 261, 263.

6. Ibid., 262.

7. James B. Connolly, "The Olympic Games at Buffalo," 567; Lucas, "Early Olympic Antagonists," 261.

8. Lucas, "Early Olympic Antagonists," 262; Coubertin, *Olympic Memoirs,* 39. Barney, "Born from Dilemma," 95.

9. Lucas, "Early Olympic Antagonists," 263, 264.

10. William Sloane letter to Pierre Coubertin, December 12.

11. Barney, "Born from Dilemma," 96, 97.

12. Ibid., 97.

13. Henri Breal letter to Henry Furber, August 29, 1900; Henry Furber letter to William R. Harper, October 30, 1900.

14. MacAloon, *This Great Symbol,* 165.

15. William R. Harper letter to faculty members Vincent, Stagg, Abbott, Mathews, and Thatcher, November 1, 1900.

16. Coubertin, *Olympic Memoirs,* 39; Coubertin letter to Breal, November 4, 1900.

17. Lucas, "Early Olympic Antagonists," 264.

18. Furber letter to Stagg, November 12, 1900; Sloane letter to Coubertin, December 12, 1900, printed in *Revue Olympique,* January 1901, pt. 2.

19. *Chicago Daily Tribune,* February 14, 1901.

20. James Sullivan letter to Coubertin, March 21, 1901.

21. William Sloane letter to Coubertin, April 22, 1901; Casper Whitney letter to Coubertin, April 30, 1901; Theodore Stanton letter to Coubertin, March 15.

22. Chicago Olympian Games Committee to the International Olympic Committee, May 1, 1901; Henry Furber letter to Coubertin, May 2, 1901.

23. Barney, "Born from Dilemma," 101, 102; *Chicago Tribune,* May 22, 1901.

24. William Harper letter to Furber, May 22, 1901.

25. Barney, "Born from Dilemma," 96–97.

26. Harper Barnes, *Standing on a Volcano: The Life and Times of David Rowland Francis,* 63, 110.

27. Barney, "Born from Dilemma," 102; *Revue Olympique,* July 1901, 33.

28. Casper Whitney letter to Coubertin, April 30, 1901; Casper Whitney letter to Harper, April 30, 1901.

29. *New York Times,* May 22, 1901.

30. *Revue Olympique,* July 1901, 40.

31. *Chicago Record-Herald,* January 12, 1902.

32. Pierre Coubertin letter to McKinley, May 28, 1901, IOC Archives; Mark Sullivan, *Our Times: The Turn of the Century,* 47, 51.

33. Pierre Coubertin letter to Roosevelt, November 15, 1901; Theodore Roosevelt letter to Coubertin, December 7, 1901.

34. Pierre Coubertin letter to Roosevelt, December 22, 1901.

35. Barney, "Born from Dilemma," 105; Henry Furber letter to Roosevelt, May 24, 1902; Theodore Roosevelt to Furber, May 28, 1902.

36. Henry Furber letter to Coubertin, May 31, 1902.

37. Casper Whitney letter to Harper, April 30, 1901.

38. Barney, "Born from Dilemma," 106; Henry Furber letter to Coubertin, May 6, 1902.

39. *New York Times,* July 13, 1902.

40. Ibid.

41. *St. Louis Republic,* July 23, 1902.

42. Henry Furber letter to Harper, August 30, 1902.

43. Henry Furber letter to Coubertin, August 17, 1902; Pierre Coubertin letter to Godefroy de Blonay, October 31, 1902; Albert Spalding letter to Frederick Skiff, October 9, 1902.

44. Albert Spalding letter to Frederick Skiff, October 9, 1902.

45. *St. Louis Globe-Democrat,* October 28, 1902; Henry Furber letter to Coubertin, November 26, 1902.

46. Henry Furber letter to Coubertin, November 26, 1902; *World's Fair Bulletin* (February 1903): 27.

47. Henry Furber letter to Coubertin, November 26, 1902.

48. James E. Sullivan, *Spalding's Official Athletic Almanac for 1905: Special Olympic Number, Containing the Official Report of the Olympic Games of 1904,* 163; Henry Furber letter to Coubertin, November 26, 1902.

49. *Chicago Tribune,* November 11, 1902; *Kansas Journal* (Topeka), April 7, 1903.

50. *Daily Maroon* (University of Chicago student newspaper), November 12, 1902; Barney, "Born from Dillemma," 109.

51. *Daily Maroon,* December 12, 1902.

52. Henry Furber official letter to Coubertin, November 26, 1902.

53. Henry Furber personal letter to Coubertin, November 26, 1902.

54. Ibid.

55. Ibid.

56. Ibid.

57. Ibid.

58. Ibid.

59. Ibid.

60. *Chicago Record-Herald,* December 1, 1902.

61. Henri Merou letter to Coubertin, December 2, 1902; George E. Vincent letter to Harper, November 5, 1902; Barney, "Born from Dilemma," 111.

62. Barney, "Born from Dilemma," 112; *St. Louis Republic,* December 12, 1902; Henry Furber letter to Coubertin, December 3, 1902.

63. Barney, "Born from Dilemma," 112; Lamar Middleton letter to Coubertin, December 9, 1902; Henry Furber letter to Coubertin, December 31, 1902.

64. Lamar Middleton letter to Coubertin, December 20, 1902.

65. Ibid.

66. *St. Louis Republic,* December 12, 1902.

67. Barney, "Born from Dilemma," 114; *Chicago Record-Herald,* December 22, 1902; Pierre Coubertin letter to IOC members, December 21, 1902.

68. Coubertin, *Olympic Memoirs,* 41.

69. *Chicago Record-Herald,* December 22, 1902; Coubertin, *Olympic Memoirs,* 41. Barney, "Born from Dilemma," 113.

70. *Bloomington Pantograph* (Illinois), December 23, 1902.

71. Henry Furber letter to Coubertin, December 24, 1902.

72. Coubertin, *Olympic Memoirs,* 43.

73. Pierre Coubertin cablegram to Furber, February 10, 1903; Henry Furber cablegram to Coubertin, February 12, 1903.

74. Pierre Coubertin letter to Chicago Olympic Games Committee, February 11, 1903.

75. Barney, "Born from Dilemma," 116.

2. The Ghost of Plato

1. Henry, *Approved History of the Olympic Games*, 5.
2. Wayne Craven, *American Art: History and Culture*, 111.
3. Ibid.
4. Young, *The Modern Olympics*, 2.
5. Ibid., 2, 3.
6. Ibid., 4.
7. Ibid., 4, 5.
8. Ibid., 5, 6.
9. Ibid., 7.
10. Ibid.
11. Ibid., 14, 15.
12. Ibid., 15.
13. Ibid., 16.
14. Ibid., 17.
15. Ibid., 15, 18.
16. Ibid., 19.
17. Ibid., 8.
18. Ibid., 9.
19. Ibid., 9, 10.
20. Ibid., 19, 20.
21. Ibid., 20, 21, 23.
22. Ibid., 24, 25.
23. Ibid., 26.
24. Ibid.
25. Ibid., 29.
26. Ibid, 30, 31.
27. Ibid., 31.
28. Ibid., 32.
29. Ibid., 33.
30. Ibid., 34.
31. Ibid., 36.
32. Ibid., 37, 38.

33. Ibid., 38.
34. Ibid., 39.
35. Ibid., 41.
36. Ibid., 40.
37. Ibid., 42.
38. Ibid, 43.
39. Ibid., 44, 195, 196.
40. Ibid., 46.
41. Ibid., 48.
42. Ibid., 55.
43. Ibid., 57.
44. Ibid.
45. Ibid., 59, 61.
46. Ibid., 61.
47. Ibid., 75.
48. Ibid., 73, 74.
49. Ibid., 75.
50. Ibid., 76.
51. Ibid., 77.
52. Ibid., 78.
53. Ibid., 78, 80.
54. Ibid., 80.
55. Ibid., 84.
56. Ibid., 85.
57. Ibid.
58. Ibid., 86.
59. Ibid., 87.
60. MacAloon, *This Great Symbol*, 119.
61. Ibid., 167.
62. Young, *The Modern Olympics*, 88, 89.
63. Ibid., 90.
64. Ibid.
65. Ibid., 91.
66. Coubertin, *Olympic Memoirs*, 65.
67. Young, *The Modern Olympics*, 95.
68. Ibid., 98.
69. Ibid.
70. Ibid., 100.
71. Ibid.
72. Ibid., 102.

73. Ibid., 110, 111.

74. Ibid., 112.

75. Ibid., 112, 113, 114, 115.

76. Ibid., 115.

77. Ibid., 116, 120.

78. Ibid., 118.

79. Ibid., 118, 119.

80. Ibid., 120.

81. Ibid., 122.

82. Ibid.

3. Transfer Accepted

1. Findling, ed., *Historical Dictionary of World's Fairs,* 27.

2. Barnes, *Standing on a Volcano,* 91.

3. Pierre Coubertin letter to David Francis, February 10, 1903.

4. Ibid.

5. Michel Lagrave letter to Francis, February 17, 1903.

6. Minutes of the Louisiana Purchase Exposition Committee.

7. Michel Lagrave letter to Francis, February 17, 1903.

8. David Francis letter to Coubertin, March 7, 1903.

9. *Kansas Journal* (Topeka), April 7, 1903.

10. Minutes of Louisiana Purchase Committee.

11. Pierre Coubertin letter to James Sullivan, March 10, 1903.

12. Ibid.

13. *New York Times,* March 27, 1903.

14. *New York Herald,* April 9, 1903.

15. *Chicago Chronicle,* April 11, 1903.

16. *New York Evening Sun,* April 24, 1903.

17. *St. Louis Republic,* July 16, 1903.

18. Ibid.

19. Jim Greensfelder, Jim Lally, Bob Christiansen, and Max Storm, *1904 Olympic Games Official Medals and Badges.*

20. *St. Louis Globe-Democrat,* May 3, 1903.

21. *St. Louis Post-Dispatch,* August 13, 1903; *St. Louis Republic,* September 29, 1903.

22. *New York Times,* May 1, 1904.

23. Ibid.

24. Ibid.

25. James E. Sullivan, *Spalding's Official Athletic Almanac for 1905,* 161.

26. David R. Francis, *The Universal Exposition of 1904*, 174.

27. Ibid.

28. Ibid.

29. Martha Clevenger, *"Indescribably Grand": Diaries and Letters From The 1904 World's Fair*, 32; Timothy Fox and Duane Sneddeker, *From the Palaces to the Pike: Visions of the 1904 World's Fair*, 14.

30. Alexander Alland, Sr., *Jessie Tarbox Beals: First Woman News Photographer*, 32.

31. *St. Louis Post-Dispatch*, April 7, 1904.

32. Alland, *Jessie Tarbox Beals*, 37.

33. Ibid., 37, 41.

34. Ibid., 69, 111.

35. Fox and Sneddeker, *From the Palaces to the Pike*, 17.

4. St. Louis Olympian Games

1. *St. Louis Post-Dispatch*, May 1, 1904; James E. Sullivan, *Spalding's Official Athletic Almanac for 1905*, 162.

2. *St. Louis Post-Dispatch*, April 7, 1904.

3. Bill Mallon, *The 1904 Olympic Games: Results for All Competitors in All Events, with Commentary*.

4. *St. Louis Post-Dispatch*, May 14, 1904.

5. Ibid.

6. Ibid.

7. Ibid., June 17, November 9, and November 26, 1904.

8. Idid., June 29, 1904.

9. Mallon, *The 1904 Olympic Games*, 149–60.

10. Ibid.

11. Ibid.

12. Ibid.

13. Ibid., 63–64.

14. *St. Louis Post-Dispatch*, June 29, 1904.

15. *St. Louis Globe-Democrat*, July 8, 1904; *Manitoba Free Press*, July 11, 1904.

16. Mallon, *The 1904 Olympic Games*, 168–70.

17. *St. Louis Post-Dispatch*, June 25, 1904.

18. Mallon, *The 1904 Olympic Games*, 114.

19. Ibid., 127.

20. *St. Louis Post-Dispatch*, August 28, 1904.

21. Ibid., July 10, 1904.

22. Ibid., August 30, 1904.

23. Ibid.

24. Ibid.

25. Mallon, *The 1904 Olympic Games,* 53.

26. Ibid., 56.

27. Ibid., 59.

28. Ibid.

29. *St. Louis Post-Dispatch,* August 30, 1904; Mallon, *The 1904 Olympic Games,* 62.

30. *St. Louis Post-Dispatch,* August 30, 1904.

31. Ibid.

32. Ibid.; photograph of Greek marathon runners (and for an unknown reason Cuban Felix Carbajal) in the Missouri Historical Society collection.

33. *St. Louis Post-Dispatch,* August 30, 1904.

34. Charles J. P. Lucas, *The Olympic Games of 1904,* 56.

35. Ibid., 62.

36. Ibid., 59, 62, 63–64.

37. Ibid., 59.

38. Ibid., 54.

39. *St. Louis Post-Dispatch,* August 31, 1904.

40. Lucas, *The Olympic Games of 1904,* 54–55, 58.

41. Ibid., 60.

42. *St. Louis Post-Dispatch,* September 1, 1904.

43. Lucas, *The Olympic Games of 1904,* 56–58.

44. Ibid., 73.

45. Ibid., 74.

46. Mallon, *The 1904 Olympic Games,* 52.

47. Lucas, *The Olympic Games of 1904,* 78, 79.

48. Mallon, *The 1904 Olympic Games,* 191, 193.

49. Lucas, *The Olympic Games of 1904,* 86.

50. Mallon, *The 1904 Olympic Games,* 63.

51. Lucas, *The Olympic Games of 1904,* 91, 92–94.

52. Mallon, *The 1904 Olympic Games,* 55.

53. Ibid., 60.

54. Ibid., 51.

55. Ibid., 55.

56. Ibid., 60.

57. Ibid., 58.

58. *St. Louis Post-Dispatch,* September 4, 1904.

59. Lucas, *The Olympic Games of 1904,* 100–101.

60. Mallon, *The 1904 Olympic Games,* 181.

61. *St. Louis Post-Dispatch,* June 26, 1904.

62. Nancy Kriplen, *Dwight Davis: The Man and the Cup,* 21.

63. *St. Louis Globe-Democrat,* September 4, 1904.

64. Ibid.

65. Mallon, *The 1904 Olympic Games,* 173.

66. Ibid., 177.

67. Ibid., 174.

68. Ibid., 175.

69. Ibid., 177.

70. Ibid., 128.

71. Ibid., 130–33.

72. Ibid.

73. Ibid.

74. *St. Louis Post-Dispatch,* September 19, 1904.

75. Mallon, *The 1904 Olympic Games,* 43–44.

76. Ibid.

77. Ibid., 138.

78. Ibid.

79. Ibid., 139.

80. *St. Louis Post-Dispatch,* September 25, 1904.

81. Ibid.

82. Mallon, *The 1904 Olympic Games,* 109.

83. Ibid., 197.

84. Francis, *The Universal Exposition of 1904,* 542–43.

85. Ibid., 543.

86. Mallon, *The 1904 Olympic Games,* 135.

87. *St. Louis Post-Dispatch,* November 26, 1904.

88. Ibid., November 6, 1904.

5. Place in History

1. Pierre de Coubertin letter to James Sullivan, October 19, 1904.

2. Coubertin, "Olympic Memoirs," 43.

3. Ibid., 41.

4. Ibid., 43.

5. Ibid.

6. Ibid., 40.

7. Ibid., 43.

8. John E. Findling, *World's Fairs and the Olympic Games,* 13.

9. Sullivan, *Spalding's Official Athletic Almanac for 1905,* 249.

10. Breitland, *A World On Display—Photographs from the St. Louis World's Fair 1904.* University of New Mexico Press: Albuquerque, Mew Mexico, 1997, 59.

11. Bill Henry, *An Approved History of the Olympic Games,* 77.

12. Ibid., 76.

13. Ibid., 75–76.

14. Lucas, *The Olympic Games of 1904,* 121–22.

15. Henry, *An Approved History of the Olympic Games,* 76–77.

16. Sullivan, *Spalding's Official Athletic Almanac for 1905,* 164.

17. Henry, *An Approved History of the Olympic Games,* 76.

18. *Kansas Journal* (Topeka), April 7, 1903.

19. Henry, *An Approved History of the Olympic Games,* 78–79.

20. *St. Louis Post-Dispatch,* June 5, 1904.

21. Henry, *An Approved History of the Olympic Games,* 79.

Bibliography

Books

Adams, Henry. *The Education of Henry Adams.* New York: Random House Inc., 1931.

Alland, Alexander, Sr. *Jessie Tarbox Beals: First Woman News Photographer.* New York: Camera/Graphic Press Ltd., 1978.

Anonymous. *The Greatest of All Expositions Completely Illustrated.* St. Louis: Official Photographic Co. of the Louisiana Purchase Exposition, 1904.

Baker, William J. *Sports in the Western World.* Totowa, N.J.: Rowman and Littlefield, 1982.

Barc, Sandor. *The Modern Olympic Story.* Budapest, Hungary: University Printing, 1964.

Barnes, Harper. *Standing on a Volcano: The Life and Times of David Rowland Francis.* St. Louis: Missouri Historical Society Press, 2001.

Barnett, Robert. "St. Louis 1904: The Games of the III Olympiad." *Historical Dictionary of the Modern Olympic Movement* (Westport, Conn.: Greenwood Press, 1996), 22–26.

Bartlett, Arthur. *Baseball and Mr. Spalding.* New York: Farrar, Straus, and Young, Inc., 1951.

Benedict, Burton. *The Anthropology of World's Fairs.* Berkeley, Calif.: Scholar Press, 1983.

Bennitt, Mark. ed. *History of the Louisiana Purchase Exposition.* St. Louis: St. Louis Universal Exposition Publishing Company, 1905.

Campbell, A. E. *Great Britain and the United States 1895–1903.* Westport, Conn.: Greenwood Press, 1974.

Clevenger, Martha, ed. *"Indescribably Grand": Diaries and Letters From The 1904 World's Fair.* St. Louis: Missouri Historical Society Press, 1996.

Cockfield, Jamie H., ed. *Dollars and Diplomacy: Ambassador David Rowland Francis and the Fall of Tsarism.* Durham, N.C.: Duke University Press, 1981.

Cohen, Steven D. "More Than Fun and Games." Ph.D. diss., Brandeis University, May 1980.

Corbett, Katherine T. *In Her Place: A Guide to St. Louis Women's History.* St. Louis: Missouri Historical Society Press, 1998.

Coubertin, Pierre. *Olympic Memoirs.* Translation by Geoffrey de Navacelle. Lausanne, Switzerland: International Olympic Committee, 1975.

Craven, Wayne. *American Art: History and Culture.* Boston: McGraw-Hill, 1994.

Daniel, Pete, and Raymond Smock. *A Talent for Detail: The Photographs of Miss Frances Benjamin Johnston 1889–1910.* New York: Harmony Books, 1974.

Davidson, James West, and Mark Hamilton Lytle. *After the Fact: The Art of Historical Detection.* New York: McGraw-Hill Inc., 1992.

Findling, John E., ed. *Historical Dictionary of World's Fairs and Expositions, 1851–1988.* Westport, Conn.: Greenwood Press, 1990.

———, and Kimberly D. Pelle, eds. *Historical Dictionary of the Modern Olympic Movement.* Westport, Conn.: Greenwood Press, 1996.

Fox, Timothy, and Duane R. Sneddeker. *From the Palaces to the Pike: Visions of the 1904 World's Fair.* St. Louis: Missouri Historical Society Press, 2002.

Francis, David R. *The Universal Exposition of 1904.* St. Louis: Louisiana Purchase Exposition Company, 1913.

Greensfelder, Jim, Jim Lally, Bob Christianson, and Max Storm. *1904 Olympic Games Official Medals and Badges.* Saratoga, Calif.: GVL Enterprises, 2001.

Hanson, John W. *The Official History of the St. Louis World's Fair.* St. Louis: The Louisiana Purchase Exposition Company, 1905.

Henry, Bill. *An Approved History of the Olympic Games.* New York: G. P. Putnam's Sons, 1948.

Hilton, Suzanne. *Here Today and Gone Tomorrow: The Story of World's Fairs and Expositions.* Philadelphia: Westminster Press, 1978.

Killanin, Lord, and John Rodda. *The Olympic Games.* New York: MacMillan Publishing Company, 1976.

Kriplen, Nancy. *Dwight Davis: The Man and the Cup.* New York: Random House, 1999.

Korsgaard, Robert. "A History of the Amateur Athletic Union of the United States." Ph.D. diss., Columbia University, 1952.

Lehr, Robert E. "The American Olympic Committee, 1896–1940: From Chaos to Order." Ph.D. diss., Pennsylvania State University, 1986.

Leonard, John W., ed. *The Book of Chicagoans.* Chicago: A. N. Marquis and Company, 1905.

———. *The Book of St. Louisans: A Biographical Dictionary of Leading Men of the City of St. Louis and Vicinity.* St. Louis, 1904.

Lucas, Charles J. P. *The Olympic Games of 1904.* St. Louis: Woodward and Tiernan Printing Company, 1905.

Lucas, John. *The Modern Olympic Games.* New York: A. S. Barnes and Company, 1980.

Lucia, Ellis. *Mr. Football: Amos Alonzo Stagg.* New York: A. S. Barnes and Company, 1970.

MacAloon, John J. *This Great Symbol: Pierre de Coubertin and the Origins of the Modern Olympic Games.* Chicago: University of Chicago Press, 1981.

Mallon, Bill. *The 1904 Olympic Games: Results for All Competitors in All Events, with Commentary.* Jefferson, N.C.: McFarland and Company Inc., 1999.

Mandell, Richard D. *The First Modern Olympics.* Berkeley: University of California Press, 1976.

———. *Paris 1900: The Great World's Fair.* Toronto: University of Toronto Press, 1967.

Mechikoff, Robert, and Steven Estes. *A History and Philosophy of Sport and Physical Education.* Boston: McGraw-Hill, 1998.

Potter, Edward C. *The Davis Cup.* Cranberry, N.J.: A. S. Barnes and Company, 1969.

Rydell, Robert W. *All The World's a Fair.* Chicago: University of Chicago Press, 1984.

Sullivan, James E. *Spalding's Official Athletic Almanac for 1905: Special Olympic Number, Containing the Official Report of the Olympic Games of 1904.* New York: American Sports Publishing, 1905.

Sullivan, Mark. *Our Times: The Turn of the Century.* New York: Charles Scribners, 1934.

Swanson, Richard, and Betty Spears. *History of Sport and Physical Education in the United States.* Boston: McGraw-Hill, 1995.

Wallechinsky, David. *The Complete Book of the Olympics.* 1992 ed. Boston: Little, Brown and Company, 1991.

———. *The Complete Book of the Summer Olympics.* Woodstock, N.Y.: The Overlook Press, Peter Mayer Publishers, Inc., 2000.

Whitney, Casper W. *A Sporting Pilgrimage.* New York: Harper and Brothers, 1894.

Wiggins, David K. *Sport in America.* Champaign, Ill.: Human Kinetics, 1995.

Young, David C. *The Modern Olympics: A Struggle for Revival.* Baltimore: Johns Hopkins University Press, 1996.

Articles

Andrews, Peter. "The First American Olympics." *American Heritage* 41 (May/June 1988).

Barney, Robert K. "Born From Dilemma: America Awakens to the Modern Olympic Games, 1901–1903." *Olympika* (1992): 92–135.

———. "A Myth Arrested: Theodore Roosevelt and the 1904 Games." In Andreas Luh and Edgar Luh, *Umbruch und Koninuitat im Sport,* Bochiem, Germany, 1991.

Becht, June West. "The Forgotten Legacy of George Poage: A Running Start." *St. Louis Post-Dispatch Magazine,* December 6, 1987.

Cassell, Frank A. "Missouri and the Columbian Exposition of 1893." *Missouri Historical Review* 80, no. 4 (July 1986).

Connolly, James B. "The Olympic Games at Buffalo." *Public Opinion* 29 (November 1, 1900): 567.

Cooper, J. Ashley. "An Anglo-Saxon Olympiad." *Nineteenth Century Magazine* 32 (September 1892).

Coubertin, Pierre. "The Mystery of the Olympian Games." *North American Review* (June 1900).

Dyreson, Mark. "The Playing Fields of Progress: American Nationalism and the 1904 St. Louis Olympics." *Gateway Heritage* 14, no. 2 (Fall 1993): 5–8.

Findling, John E. "World's Fairs and the Olympic Games." *World's Fair* 10 (December 1990): 13–15.

Furber, Henry J. "Modern Olympian Games Movement." *The Independent* 54 (February 14, 1902): 384.

Girard, Mary. "Pierre de Coubertin—An Appreciation." *Fortnightly Review* 74. (August 1903): 336–46.

Howell, Maxwell L., and Reet N. Howell. "The 1900 and 1904 Olympic Games: The Farcical Games." Paper presented to the VI International Association of the History of Sport and Physical Education Seminar, Trois-Rivieres, Quebec, July 1976.

Laurens, Henry. "Henry Laurens on the Olympic Games." *South Carolina Historical Magazine* 61 (July 1960).

Lucas, John. "Early Olympic Antagonists: Pierre de Coubertin versus James E. Sullivan." *Stadion* 3, no. 2 (1977): 258–72.

———. "Professor William Milligan Sloan: Father of the United States Olympic Committee." In Andreas and Edgar Luh, *Umbruch und Koninuitat im Sport,* Bochiem, Germany, 1991.

Weber, Eugene. "Pierre de Coubertin and the Introduction of Organized Sport in France." *Journal of Contemporary History* 5 (1970): 3–26.

Whitney, Casper. "International Athletic Organization." *Outing* 37 (January 1901): 473–74.

———. "Olympian Games at Chicago." *Outing* 38 (August 1901): 587.

Newspapers

Albany Argus (N.Y.)
Chicago Record-Herald
Chicago Tribune
Concord Daily Monitor (N.H.)
Daily Maroon (University of Chicago student newspaper)
Deseret Evening News (Utah)
Manitoba Free Press
New York Times
St. Louis Chronicle
St. Louis Globe-Democrat
St. Louis Republic
St. Louis Post-Dispatch

Newspaper Articles in Louisiana Purchase Exposition Scrapbooks. Vols. 31 and 32. Missouri Historical Society Library, St. Louis, Missouri.

Chicago Chronicle, April 11, 1903.
Chicago Herald, December 1, 1902.
Evening Sun (New York), April 24, 1903.
Milwaukee Sentinel, April 17, 1903.
Minneapolis Times, March 6, 1903.
New York Herald, March 8, 1903; April 9, 1903.
St. Louis Globe-Democrat, August 25, 1902; October 28, 1902.
St. Louis Post-Dispatch, April 4, 1903.
St. Louis Republic, July 23, 1902; June 24, 1903; July 16, 1903; September 29, 1903.
St. Louis Star, July 20, 1902.
Topeka Journal (Kansas), April 7, 1903.
World's Fair Bulletin. Missouri Historical Society Library, St. Louis. February 1903, p. 10; May 1904, p. 16.

Letters

Breal to Furber. August 29, 1900. University of Chicago Archives. Stagg Papers, Box 80, Folder 3.
Breal to Furber. October 19, 1900. University of Chicago Archives. Harper Papers, Box 50, Folder 13.
Furber to Harper. October 30, 1900. University of Chicago Archives. Harper Papers, Box 50, Folder 13.

Harper to Professors Vincent, Stagg, Abbott, Mathews, and Thatcher. November 1, 1900. University of Chicago Archives. Stagg Papers, Box 50, Folder 4.

Coubertin to Breal. November 4, 1900. University of Chicago Archives. Stagg Papers, Box 80, Folder 4.

Furber to Stagg. November 12, 1900. University of Chicago Archives. Stagg Papers, Box 50, Folder 4.

Sloane to Coubertin December 12, 1900. International Olympic Committee Archives. Lausanne, Switzerland.

Sloane to Coubertin. February 26, 1901. International Olympic Committee Archives. Lausanne, Switzerland.

Stanton to Coubertin. March 15, 1901. I.O.C. Archives. Lausanne, Switzerland.

Sullivan to Coubertin. March 21, 1901. I.O.C. Archives. Lausanne, Switzerland.

Sloane to Coubertin. March 31, 1901. I.O.C. Archives. Lausanne, Switzerland.

Furber to Coubertin. April 4, 1901. I.O.C. Archives. Lausanne, Switzerland.

Sloane to Coubertin. April 22, 1901. I.O.C. Archives. Lausanne, Switzerland.

Whitney to Coubertin. April 30, 1901. I.O.C. Archives. Lausanne, Switzerland.

Whitney to Harper. April 30, 1901. I.O.C. Archives. Lausanne, Switzerland.

Harper to Olympian Games Committee of Chicago. May 1, 1901. University of Chicago Archives. Harper Papers, Box 50, Folder 13.

Furber to Coubertin. May 2, 1901. I.O.C. Archives. Lausanne, Switzerland.

Harper to Whitney. May 2, 1901. I.O.C. Archives. Lausanne, Switzerland.

Harper to Furber. May 22, 1901. University of Chicago Archives. Harper Papers, Box 50, Folder 13.

Furber to Coubertin. May 24, 1901. I.O.C. Archives. Lausanne, Switzerland.

Coubertin to McKinley. May 28, 1901. I.O.C. Archives. Lausanne, Switzerland.

Merou to Coubertin. May 28, 1901. I.O.C. Archives. Lausanne, Switzerland.

Furber to Coubertin. May 29, 1901. I.O.C. Archives. Lausanne, Switzerland.

Penaloza to Coubertin. Letter printed in *Revue Olympique,* July 1901, 33.

Coubertin to Roosevelt. November 15, 1901. I.O.C. Archives. Lausanne, Switzerland.

Roosevelt to Coubertin. December 7, 1901. Harvard University, Lamont Library. Presidential Papers, Microfilm Series, Reel 327.

Coubertin to Roosevelt. December 22, 1901. I.O.C. Archives. Lausanne, Switzerland.

Furber to Coubertin. May 6, 1902. I.O.C. Archives. Lausanne, Switzerland.

Furber to Roosevelt. May 24, 1902. I.O.C. Archives. Lausanne, Switzerland.

Roosevelt to Furber. May 28, 1902. I.O.C. Archives. Lausanne, Switzerland.

Furber to Coubertin. May 31, 1902. I.O.C. Archives. Lausanne, Switzerland.

Furber to Coubertin. June 21, 1902 I.O.C. Archives. Lausanne, Switzerland.

Furber to Coubertin. August 17, 1902. I.O.C. Archives. Lausanne, Switzerland.

Furber to Harper. August 30, 1902. University of Chicago Archives. Harper Papers, Box 50, Folder 13.

Furber to Coubertin. October 1, 1902. I.O.C. Archives. Lausanne, Switzerland.

Spalding to Skiff. October 9, 1902. Louisiana Purchase Exposition Committee Minutes (LPECM) #961–62.

Coubertin to Godefroy de Blonay. October 31, 1902. I.O.C. Archives. Lausanne, Switzerland.

Furber to Coubertin. November 26, 1902. I.O.C. Archives. Lausanne, Switzerland.

Merou to Coubertin. December 2, 1902. I.O.C. Archives. Lausanne, Switzerland.

Lamar Middleton to Coubertin. December 9, 1902. I.O.C. Archives. Lausanne, Switzerland.

Middleton to Coubertin. December 20, 1902. I.O.C. Archives. Lausanne, Switzerland.

Coubertin to I.O.C. Members. December 21, 1902. I.O.C. Archives. Lausanne, Switzerland.

Furber to Coubertin. December 31, 1902. I.O.C. Archives. Lausanne, Switzerland.

Coubertin to Furber. February 10, 1903. I.O.C. Archives. Lausanne, Switzerland.

Coubertin to Francis. February 10, 1903. LPECM #1268–69.

Coubertin to Chicago Olympian Games Committee. February 11, 1903. I.O.C. Archives. Lausanne, Switzerland.

Furber to Coubertin. February 12, 1903. I.O.C. Archives. Lausanne, Switzerland.

Lagrave to Francis. February 17, 1903. LPECM #1271.

St. Louis Olympic Committee to Chicago Olympic Committee Voucher Payment. March 1903. LPECM #1272.

David R. Francis to Coubertin. March 7, 1903. I.O.C. Archives. Lausanne, Switzerland.

Coubertin to Sullivan. October 19, 1904. Spalding's Almanac.

Index

Spotted Tail, 125
Spradley, Benjamin, 179
Spring, Michael, 137, 139, 143
Stadel, George, 161
Stadler, Joseph, 146, 155
Stagg, Amos Alonzo, 9, 11, 12, 13
Standing broad jump, 131, 135,136
Standing high jump, 131, 144, 146, 196
Standing hop, step, and jump, 132, 152, 155
Stangland, Robert, 151, 152
Stanton, Theodore, 7, 13
Steep, Frederick, 182
Steeplechase run, 131, 134
Stevens, Walter, 117
Stickney, Arthur, 173, 174, 177
Stickney, Stuart, 173, 174, 177
Stockhoff, Arthur, 126
Stockholm, Sweden: as potential Olympic site, 4; and 1912 Olympics, 204, 207
Strange, George, 127
Strebler, Z. B., 180
Stuart, James, 41
Suerig, Frederick, 126
Sullivan, James E., 85, 92, 101, 102, 117, 131, 143, 165, 181, 183, 202, 206, 208; attempt to form rival organization, 6–7, 202; conflict with Coubertin, 7–8, 11, 12, 113; agrees to Chicago, 13; chosen director of 1904 Olympics, 103, 105–6, 205; death, 204
Swatek, Edwin, 164
Swedish gymnastics, 120, 122
Swimming, 117, 161–65, 187–88

Taft, William Howard, 107
Tate, Harry, 183
Tatham, Charles, 166, 167, 168
Tau, Len, 137, 143
Taylor, Homer, 170, 171
Taylor, Isaac, 106, 117
Taylor, Louise, 169, 170
Taylor, Mabel, 169, 170
Taylor, Ralph, 170, 171
Taylor, Tom, 182
Tennis, 117, 158–61, 190–91
Tesing, Rudolph, 180
Thatcher, O. J., 11
Theodosius, Emperor, 40

Thias, Charles, 148
Thiefenthaler, Gustav, 180
Thompson, William, 170, 171
Thompson, William H., 18, 106
Thorne, Raymond, 163
Titus, Constance, 126
Tokaki, Shunzo, 158–59
Tokyo Tennis Club, 158
Tom Brown's Schooldays, 60; influence on Coubertin, 63
Topeka Journal, 209
Toronto Argonaut Club, 125, 127
Townsend, Fitzhugh, 166, 167, 168
Track and field events, 117, 118, 119, 120–23, 135–58, 194; scoring, 121, 122, 210; All-Around Championship, 122
Trans-Mississippi Golf Association, 172
Trieste, Italy, 61
Trikoupis, Charilaos, 74, 75–77
Triple jump, 135, 151–52
Tripolis, Greece, 43
Tritle, Stewart, 161
Tsuana tribe, athletes from, 137
Tug-of-war, 131, 132, 144, 147, 157–58
Turner, Douglas, 161
Turnverein gymnastics, 119
Twain, Mark, 206
Twaits, William, 182
Twiiku Kwai Physical Culture Association, 158
Two hundred meter hurdles, 132, 151, 194
Two hundred meter run, 131, 144, 145

Underwood, George, 134, 150, 157
United States Golf Association, 172
Upshaw, Orrin, 148

Valentine, Howard, 134, 150, 153, 157
Valentine, W. G., 170
Vamkaitis, Georgios, 144
Van Cleaf, George, 151, 152
Van Horn, Russell, 179
Van Zo Post, Albertson, 166, 167, 168
Varley, William, 126
Varnell, George, 146, 151
Veloulis, Dimitrios, 143
Venn, A. H., 125
Verner, William, 135, 150, 153, 157

About the Author

George R. Matthews is a 2017 recipient of the Charles Redd Center for Western Studies Research Grant, and he has twice been awarded the Historical Society of New Mexico and Office of the State Historian Research Fellowship. He is a former U.S. Delegate to the International Olympic Academy in Olympia, Greece, and served as a National Park Service Volunteer for the Lewis and Clark Bicentennial.